Changing Women,
Changing Nation

SUNY series in Latin American and Iberian Thought and Culture

Jorge J. E. Gracia and Rosemary Geisdorfer Feal, editors

Changing Women, Changing Nation

Female Agency, Nationhood, and Identity in Trans-Salvadoran Narratives

Yajaira M. Padilla

Cover: "Desplazados," block print, part of the "Seeds and Corn" series, an original work of art by Alynn Guerra. Courtesy of The University of Kansas.

Published by State University of New York Press, Albany

For information, contact State University of New York Press, Albany, NY
www.sunypress.edu

Production by Kelli Williams LeRoux
Marketing by Kate McDonnell

Library of Congress Cataloging-in-Publication Data

Padilla, Yajaira M.
    Changing women, changing nation : female agency, nationhood, and identity in trans-Salvadoran narratives / Yajaira M. Padilla.
        p. cm. — (SUNY series in Latin American and Iberian thought and culture)
    Includes bibliographical references and index.
    ISBN 978-1-4384-4277-8 (hardcover : alk. paper)
    1. Salvadoran fiction—History and criticism.   2. Revolutionary literature, Salvadoran—History and criticism.   3. Women in literature.   4. Identity (Psychology) in literature.   5. El Salvador—In literature.   6. American fiction—Hispanic American authors—History and criticism.   I. Title.

PQ7534.P33 2012
863'.64099287097284—dc23   2011031101

10 9 8 7 6 5 4 3 2 1

Contents

Acknowledgements   vii

Introduction: Writing Women into Nation, War, and Migration   1

Chapter 1
Campesina as Nation: Feminine Resistance and Power
in Manlio Argueta's *Un día en la vida* and *Cuzcatlán:
Donde bate la Mar del Sur*   15

Chapter 2
Making Militants and Mothers: Rethinking the Image of the
Guerrillera in Women's Revolutionary Testimonios   43

Chapter 3
Setting *La diabla* Free: Women, Violence, and the Struggle
for Representation in Postwar El Salvador   71

Chapter 4
¿Hermanas lejanas?: Female Immigrant Subjectivities and the
Politics of Voice in the Salvadoran Transnational Imagined
Community   93

Chapter 5
Salvadoran-American Sleuthing in the U.S. South and Beyond:
McPeek Villatoro's Romilia Chacón Mysteries Series   123

Conclusion   153

Notes   159

Works Cited   171

Index   183

Acknowledgments

Books are never an individual enterprise. Without institutional support and the generosity of colleagues, friends, and family, one would be hard-pressed to accomplish such a feat. A New Faculty Research Grant and General Research Fund Grant provided by the University of Kansas allowed me to conduct necessary research in Central America and Los Angeles for two of the book's most pivotal chapters. At KU, I have found an amazing network of colleagues to whom I owe a great debt. I would like to thank, first and foremost, Jorge Pérez, my "unofficial" mentor, whose careful reading of all my work, professional and personal guidance, and friendship have been invaluable to me. I am grateful for the knowledge that Stuart Day and Vicky Unruh have shared with me as scholars as well as the professional support they have provided to me as administrators. Outside of KU, my sincerest gratitude goes to Misha Kokotovic, an early mentor and esteemed friend who helped me cultivate my interest in Central American literature and women's struggles, to Arturo Arias and Ana Patricia Rodríguez for taking me under their wings and paving the way for scholars like me, and to Norma Klahn, who taught me the "nuts and bolts" of research and was a strong Latina role model. My friends both in and outside academia, Holly Goerdel, María Bernath, Alyssa Labrado, Andrea Gracia, Misti Oto, and Stacy Carlock, have been a constant source of understanding and warmth, a welcome refuge from the stresses of the profession. Thank you. Words are not enough to express how thankful I am to my parents, Oscar and Alicia Padilla, two courageous individuals who never stopped crossing borders and gave me all that they never had, and to my three siblings, Georgina, Lisa, and Oscar, for putting up with my "bad moods" and helping me laugh through it all. Finally, I wish to thank my husband, Steven Rosales, for weathering the most difficult of times and for bringing such joy and endearing love into my life.

An earlier version of Chapter 3 appeared in *Latin American Perspectives*, published by SAGE/SOCIETY. Chapter 5 also originally appeared as an article published in *Latino Studies*, a Palgrave Macmillan journal. Alynn Guerra was generous enough to let me use her beautiful artwork for the cover. With regard to the translations that appear in the book, I have used quotations from published translations of primary literary works when available and, in some instances, have made modifications. Spanish quotations are followed by their English translations in brackets. Page numbers are provided in parenthesis and follow this same order, Spanish first, then English. If no secondary page number is given, that means that the translation of the material is my own.

Introduction

Writing Women into
Nation, War, and Migration

During the brief span of the last three decades, El Salvador has been witness to some of its most defining political, social, and economic transformations, including a twelve-year civil war dating from 1980 to 1992, a postwar neoliberal project of national reconstruction and modernization, and the mass emigration of Salvadorans to neighboring and international destinations such as the United States. All of these processes have undoubtedly transformed El Salvador and opened new questions regarding national identity, citizenship, and ethnicity. These changes, however, have also generated a new focus on gender given the instrumentality and the unprecedented numbers of Salvadoran women who have been involved in these developments, participating in what have traditionally been considered male enterprises, such as armed revolution, postwar democratization, and migration.

In this book, I engage this gendered history through the optic of cultural production, specifically what I refer to as "trans-Salvadoran narratives"—Salvadoran and U.S. Salvadoran texts dating from 1980 to 2005. Here I explore how the primarily allegorical representations of women in these narratives bring into focus women's actual roles and agency within the context of these interrelated national and transnational occurrences. Viewing this interplay within literature brings to the fore the implications such depictions hold for rethinking wider-reaching issues. What insight can be gained from these representations regarding the gendered dynamics of a Salvadoran national identity that is continuously being redefined and articulated? How do these portrayals of women speak to the construction of gendered ethnicities in and outside the

1

nation, in particular Salvadoran-American identities? And in broader terms, what can they tell us about the multiple intersections of gender, literature, nation, and identity?

An initiating factor of this recent history of Salvadoran women's participation in public life was the country's civil war, the culmination of a long past of social, political, and economic polarization instituted and perpetuated by a dominant oligarchy and sustained by military repression.[1] In the years leading up to the war, Christian-based and grassroots initiatives aimed at changing the then-current system were deemed "subversive" by the state, making them a prime target of the government's military forces. Human rights violations such as disappearances and political assassinations escalated while economic conditions continued to deteriorate. Given the milieu of Cold War politics and the triumph of the Nicaraguan Revolution in 1979, U.S. intervention in El Salvador also significantly increased. Under President Carter, the U.S. government approved a military aid package totaling 5.7 million dollars, eleven times more than the annual aid the country normally received (Montgomery 131), which kept El Salvador's struggling economy afloat but also continued to fund the country's oppressive military regime. Lacking other alternatives, El Salvador's militant left, the Farabundo Martí National Liberation Front (FMLN), adopted a strategy of popular insurrection and armed struggle. Consequently, by 1980 the stage was set for a civil war that took a greater toll on the country than any other event prior, claiming the lives of more than 75,000 Salvadorans and forcing several tens of thousands to flee from their homes.

Among other effects, the civil conflict led to the weakening of patriarchal social and political structures that governed Salvadoran society, allowing women the possibility of integrating themselves, in different capacities and at various levels, into a public sphere from which they traditionally had been excluded.[2] The unparalleled involvement of Salvadoran women during this moment of national crisis was a significant turning point in the country's history in that it not only marked women as visible and necessary participants in national endeavors but also functioned as an important catalyst for women's mobilization with regard to gender equality and civil rights in the postwar years. Whether because of necessity or deeply rooted political beliefs, women of all ages and from different class and ethnic backgrounds participated in the war. Although many campaigned and rallied on behalf of the right, as Marilyn Thompson's "Las organizaciones de mujeres en El Salvador" details, these were a small minority in comparison to the mass mobilization of women under the left's project of popular and armed insurrection. It is estimated that women comprised sixty percent of the popular front and thirty percent of all armed combatants (Vásquez, Ibáñez, and Murguialday 21). Women adopted dynamic positions in and outside the home as activists, military leaders, and in the case of many rural peasants or *campesinas,* sources of support and protection for insurrectionist troops. They became, in essence, what Vásquez et. al term *mujeres-montañas,* the metaphorical mountains that sheltered and aided El Salvador's guerrilla forces.

In the postwar period, characterized by both a tenuous process of national reconstruction and continued international migration, women's involvement in national and transnational developments has been equally imperative and noteworthy. Following the signing of the Peace Accords in 1992, El Salvador began a new phase of neoliberal reconstruction characterized by free-market enterprise and open "democratic" elections. Rather than national rehabilitation, however, such reforms have led to the exacerbation of existing oppressive economic and political conditions accompanied by an increase in social disparity and violence. For women, the adoption of this neoliberal model has resulted in advances in the form of employment opportunities and the founding of a feminist movement as well as setbacks.[3] Similar to Karen Kampwirth's observations regarding feminism in postwar Nicaragua, the new struggles of women for liberation and rights in El Salvador has provoked a conservative backlash characterized by the staunch reaffirmation of women's expected gender roles and repeated attempts to stifle the limited political presence and influence women acquired through their earlier activism in popular and armed movements ("Resisting the Feminist Threat").

Parallel developments and conflicts mark women's participation in Salvadoran migration and as indispensable members of a growing Salvadoran-American community in the United States. Prompted by the economic instability and the violence of the 1980s, thousands of Salvadorans fled the country, seeking refuge in neighboring Central American regions as well as international destinations such as Mexico, Canada, Australia, and the United States. The migratory flow initiated during this period of mass upheaval has continued into the postwar era and, along with the establishment of transnational enterprises, has become an important component of El Salvador's new neoliberal reality and process of national reconciliation. According to the 2007 United Nations Human Development Report on El Salvador, more than a fifth of El Salvador's population resides outside its borders, the majority in the United States. Salvadoran women have not only predominated in these migratory flows and immigrant communities but, in some cases, have also been pioneers.[4] They have assumed new roles as economic providers for their families and as contributors to transnational financial and cultural developments, leading to a new sense of independence and an uneasy renegotiation of traditional social norms. As with the civil war, migration has also become an avenue for women to ascertain alternate forms of agency and to rethink their subjectivity.

Read together, the narratives that inform this study—broadly defined to include testimonials, novels, and poems that relate stories—elucidate a nuanced portrait of this dynamic history of Salvadoran women's participation in national and transnational endeavors. In all of them, women appear as pivotal characters and are a vital component of both their narrative and ideological frameworks. However, precisely because they constitute vital components of *literary* texts—crucial spaces for cultural representation, national imaginings, and identity construction— these depictions of women also afford a broader understanding of the Salvadoran nation and its transformation due to and following the war. Thus, one of the main arguments of this book is that the portrayals of women in these Salvadoran and U.S. Salvadoran narratives also function as a gendered lens through which we see the continuous redefinition of the Salvadoran nation and its subsequent rearticulation as a transnational space. This is a process characterized by both contradictions and conflicts and by the forging and/or renegotiation of gendered, migrant, and ethnic identities.

My claim regarding this interrelationship between women and nation is premised on the fact that in these literary representations, Salvadoran women are posited as either national allegories or portrayed in nationalistic roles such as that of "republican mothers." These symbolic depictions underscore a key connection between how the nation is imagined and how women are imagined within it. Equally imperative is the fact that I analyze these figurative portrayals of women in both Salvadoran and U.S. Salvadoran texts. Rather than view these as two separate literatures, I consider works produced in and outside El Salvador as part of the same body of dialoguing narratives that I call "trans-Salvadoran," as they bring into focus El Salvador's burgeoning transnational reality. In positing this notion of "trans-Salvadoran," I draw on Nestor García Canclini's noted observation that the process of transnationalism is one in which the mark of the "original" nations is maintained (48).[5] The discursive interchange established between Salvadoran and U.S. Salvadoran works is one that transcends El Salvador's imagined and geographic borders (and to a lesser extent those of the United States). Still, the particularities to which these texts speak regarding women's agency, nationhood, and the elaboration of individual and communal-based cultural identities continue to be "anchored" in El Salvador.

Imagining Women in and beyond El Salvador

As Benedict Anderson has effectively argued, print culture provides a means by which people not only construct the nation but also perceive themselves as part of that same "imagined community." Trans-Salvadoran narratives allow for an understanding of how the Salvadoran (trans) nation has been imagined, contested, and redefined during the civil war and in the subsequent postwar period. Such imaginings, as well as the nationalist discourses that facilitate them and on which they depend, are heteronormative and fundamentally gendered (McClintock 89). As such, men and women come to occupy specific roles in the national imaginary, which may or may not be symptomatic of their actual participation in national enterprises. Following Jean Franco, one of the prevalent ways in which women are "plotted" in the "master narrative" of nationalism is as an allegory of the nation, a conceptualization grounded in other symbolic renderings of women that emphasize their link to nature or territory.[6] Women are similarly often cast as "republican mothers," as is the case within nineteenth-century nation-building projects in Latin America. Relegated to the domestic space and beholden to their husbands, women were responsible for not only reproducing but also educating the future citizens of the nation (Pratt, "Women" 51).

The portrayals of women that characterize the trans-Salvadoran narratives I examine work in tandem with, as well as in response to, these traditional forms of female representation and agency. The perseverance of such figurative uses of women calls attention to the similarly gendered discourses that operate in Salvadoran nationalist and transnationalist enterprises of the twentieth and twenty-first centuries. However, it also is suggestive of the noteworthy use of such symbolic appropriations in communicating a broader national reality. In her well-known examination of Latin American foundational fictions, Doris Sommer posits that nineteenth-century romances constituted allegorical representations of the nation, emphasizing the mutually reinforcing and interchangeable relationship between heterosexual coupling and national consolidation. Although not all of the figurative representations of women in Salvadoran and U.S. Salvadoran narratives function as allegories, they nevertheless attest to a similar reciprocity that exists between the ways Salvadoran women are "plotted" and how the Salvadoran nation is imagined. In other words, by revealing how Salvadoran women have participated in and have had their lives impacted by recent national and transnational developments, these literary depictions also afford insight regarding a changing Salvadoran nation.

In many Salvadoran narratives, women continue to function as national allegories—whether they represent a Salvadoran nation in conflict and in need of liberation or a postwar nation in transition and decline. Within U.S.-Salvadoran texts that discuss migratory movements and identities, women become the nation left behind by male migrant "heroes" or a nation that must redefine itself in light of its new transnational reality and the incorporation of so many of its citizens into U.S. society. An insistence on women's roles as "republican mothers" likewise persists in many of these narratives, though refashioned in alternate ways by the discourse of revolution and that of neoliberal progress. Within the left's project of armed revolution, the notion of individual maternity may have been replaced by a collective or "revolutionary maternity," as Ileana Rodríguez suggests, yet the function of this female role remained the same: to bring into being and to ideologically shape the citizens of a future liberated nation (163). Under neoliberalism, the stressing of women's domestic duties as wives and mothers has remained paramount and is a telling development given the rise in Salvadoran women's participation as "reproducers" in the national and global labor markets.

One can read the recurrent use of women as either national allegories or "republican mothers" in these narratives as exemplary of the problematic way in which women are, once again, symbolically appropriated by nationalist discourses yet "denied any direct relation to national agency" (McClintock 90). In keeping with El Salvador's recent history and women's actual participation in the public sphere, however, another reading is possible and more apt. Civil conflict and migration, as well as neoliberal restructuring, have all, to a certain extent, undermined the public and private divide that has been instrumental in regulating women's roles and restricting their access to male national power. Although perhaps not to the same degree as men and with somewhat serious limitations, Salvadoran women have been and continue to be "public players." Many—though not all—of the depictions of women rendered in these narratives underscore the centrality and agency women have acquired in national and transnational enterprises while also showcasing or affirming their marginality.

Notably, it is the reworking and undermining of the same traditional constructs of women as national allegories or as "republican mothers" by these writers that allow for this inclusionary and likewise diversifying image to emerge. Representing El Salvador by way of its rural and indigenous women in testimonial narratives of the 1980s highlights one of the country's most oppressed yet crucial populations during the national conflict. Female protagonists, be they ex-guerrillas or divorced elite housewives who refute or "pervert" the notion of "republican motherhood" in Salvadoran postwar fictions of the 1990s, bring into focus women who are marginalized for not conforming to expected gendered norms. The portrayals of migrant women laboring in garment factories as well as the quest of second-generation daughters to understand their parents' traumatic past of war reveal the feminization of the Salvadoran migrant nation in U.S. Salvadoran narratives produced in the early 2000s. Far from replicating what Chandra Talpade Mohanty signals as the construct of Third-World women as a homogenous group, the figurative depictions of women elaborated in these trans-Salvadoran narratives invoke the "historically specific material reality of groups of [Salvadoran] women" (259). In so doing, they also constitute "counter-narratives" of nation, as Homi Bhabha suggests, that underscore El Salvador's homogenizing and nationalist "fictions" based on racial, class, and gender differences.

An Emergent Salvadoran (Trans)Nation

An engaging and revelatory view of Salvadoran women's lives is but one aspect of the national "story" elaborated through the symbolic portrayals of women in trans-Salvadoran narratives. As with women's participation in the public sphere, the civil war and the mass migration it spurred also marked a significant turning point in El Salvador's history, giving way to the country's reconfiguration as a "transterritorial nation." The contours of and accessibility to this expanding national space—in effect, a burgeoning transnational community—are still in contention. Cultural and economic ties, including the investments of migrants in local businesses in El Salvador and the familial remittances they send, have made migrants a leading financial resource for their sending country. In spite of this, migrants' rights as Salvadoran citizens, including their ability to vote, remain undecided.[7] Compounding this situation further are the added effects of increased deportations back to El Salvador of undocumented immigrants and gang youth as well as the complexities of women's involvement in migration and transnational enterprises.

At the same time, identities defined within and across national and ethnic lines as both Salvadoran and Salvadoran-American are taking shape within this emergent community. El Salvador's postwar process of national reconstruction not only has yielded critical views of the new neoliberal reality but also has posited anew questions of identity. In the wake of the war, ex-guerrillas and ex-soldiers, whose subjectivities were defined in reference to the left or right's political projects, have become disenfranchised subjects in search of new ways of belonging and surviving. Migrants, women, sexual minorities, gang youth, and children occupy a similarly precarious position within Salvadoran society. The marginal status of these others and the new struggles many of these groups have initiated for political representation and basic civil and human rights (women are among the most vocal of these groups) in the postwar period contest official versions of Salvadoran nationhood and identity premised on exclusionary practices and definitions of citizenry.[8] In the process of broadening what it means to be Salvadoran, these "second-class" citizens are also giving way to alternate communal and individual identities that emphasize the importance of gender difference, sexuality, ethnicity, and migrants' experiences and contributions.

Despite residing outside El Salvador, the politics of identity formation for Salvadoran immigrants and second-generation Salvadoran-Americans is also largely rooted in Salvadoran nationhood and history, recalling Stuart Hall's observation that although cultural identities are always in process, they "come from somewhere" (394). Continuing to perceive oneself as Salvadoran—a notion exemplified by the maintaining of emotional, financial, and nationalistic bonds with El Salvador—is an indispensable aspect of the Salvadoran immigrant reality. It provides many Salvadorans living in the United States with a means of ameliorating their feelings of homesickness as well as sense of displacement and alienation as foreign others. For 1.5 and second-generation Salvadorans whose contact with El Salvador has been limited or is nonexistent, establishing a connection with the country from which their parents migrated, including its indigenous roots, and understanding the past of war that prompted such moves are necessary steps in their process of self-individuation as Salvadoran-Americans, and to a larger extent as Latina/os of Central American descent. As is characteristic of the works by the U.S. Salvadoran writers included here, there is also a strong impetus among this group to delineate a more inclusive notion of Salvadoran community, undermining narrow ideals of nationality in both El Salvador and in the United States.

Raymond Williams argues that any given cultural process contains within it both "residual" and "emergent" elements that "are significant both in themselves and in what they reveal of the characteristics of the 'dominant'" (121–22). In keeping with Williams's theorization, the figurative representations of women and the trans-Salvadoran narratives examined here evince "residual" elements linked to "dominant" discourses of female agency and nationhood. However, they also encompass "emergent" elements that are suggestive of new meanings, values, practices, and relationships. Beginning with Salvadoran testimonial narratives from the 1980s, spanning postwar fictions of the 1990s, and continuing with the stories of migration and ethnic incorporation into the United States told in U.S. Salvadoran works, these trans-Salvadoran narratives delineate the contours of an emergent Salvadoran transnational community or (trans)nation in constant transformation. Within this imagined space, neither national sentiments nor partial practices are completely set aside or eroded: all the while, new notions of female subjectivity, transnational action, and cultural identity are contested and posited.

For many of El Salvador's politically committed writers, the polyphonic qualities of testimonial writing—engaging the popular and giving voice to an otherwise silenced collective subject by way of a narrator and interlocutor—provided them with an effective means of communicating the predicament of El Salvador's people during the civil conflict. Previously silenced groups such as rural peasants and women became central, as did the violence and the economic repression they suffered because of El Salvador's oligarchic government and its military forces. As an important ideological weapon and integral part of the left's revolutionary project, these testimonial works likewise emphasized an alternate view of a "liberated" Salvadoran nation and supported the need for armed insurrection. Hence, revealing the plight of rural and urban women in these testimonial works opened a space for counterhegemonic discourses of Salvadoran nationhood and citizenship. Conflicting portrayals of women in Salvadoran postwar fictions evidence not only the variable tensions that surround women's political endeavors with regard to representation and gender equality but also the many searches for identity and political voice (both at the individual and communal levels) that characterize El Salvador's tenuous process of reconstruction. Far from depicting a peaceful and improved postwar society, these narratives point to the imposition of a dominant social and political order marked by neoliberalism that has given way to a precarious reality plagued by violence, injustice, and growing economic disparity. The Salvadorans who inhabit this disaffected world—ex-soldiers, ex-guerrillas, migrants, and women—continue to exist on the edge of the mainstream, destabilizing the fiction of an all-inclusive Salvadoran nationality.

U.S. Salvadoran narratives produced during the same period (1990s–2005) attest to the ways in which mass international migration has affected women's gendered roles as well as the conceptualization of Salvadoran national identity. By depicting women as the wives left behind, as journey takers, and as financial mainstays for their immigrant communities and families, these texts call attention to the redefinition of El Salvador as an imagined transnational community. Through the portrayals of second-generation Salvadoran-American women, these works underscore the forging of new Latina/o identities of Central American origin in the United States. Although they dialogue with

Salvadoran texts, these U.S. Salvadoran narratives also form part of an existing and growing body of U.S. multiethnic literatures. As such, they introduce a Latina/o identity and voice that has been relatively unheard and that has not been previously explored in the same way. They allow for a rethinking of what it means to be Latina/o within the scope of recent waves of immigration from Latin America as opposed to only in reference to established groups such as Mexican-Americans, Puerto Ricans, and Cuban-Americans.

Representing *salvadoreñas*

The trans-Salvadoran narratives included here and their organization across the five chapters that comprise this book follow the periodization of Salvadoran women's public participation in and outside El Salvador over the last three decades and parallel their movement from the point of origin, El Salvador, upward to the United States, and back again, if only through the search for the past that characterizes U.S. Salvadoran texts. The first two chapters allow for a significant and fundamental exploration of the ways in which the civil war created new opportunities for women and redefined them and society, thereby laying a foundation for what would be the future tensions and struggles confronting women in the postwar period. In parallel with the social and historical processes that influenced them, the testimonial works analyzed posit women as allegories of the nation or as "republican mothers" yet in novel ways also capable of transforming and challenging such depictions of women and their lack of national agency. Manlio Argueta's testimonial novels, *Un día en la vida* [*One Day of Life*] (1980) and *Cuzcatlán: Donde bate la Mar del Sur* [*Cuzcatlán: Where the Southern Sea Beats*] (1986), the focus of Chapter 1, relate the social reality of the civil war as experienced by *campesinas*. Through the use of testimonio, Argueta emphasizes the important ways in which rural women became unexpected protagonists in the history of the war—ultimately transforming the conflict as well as themselves. Crucial to this rendering are its allegorical dimensions, in which women are indicative of a Salvadoran peasant nation that has indigenous roots and is, to a certain extent, feminized and empowered. This view of rural female agency and El Salvador stands in contrast to the traditional and exclusionary model of nationhood upheld by the Salvadoran oligarchy and in many respects the one envisioned by the left.

Chapter 2 examines the testimonial narratives of middle-class women who served as female militants or *guerrilleras* in the armed movement, an apt complement to Argueta's portrayals of *campesinas* in that they underscore the actions and sensibility of women from a different class orientation and urban background whose decision to join the struggle was not motivated by necessity but rather by their political beliefs and orientation. Claribel Alegría and Darwin Flakoll's *No me agarran viva: La mujer salvadoreña en la lucha* [*They Won't Take Me Alive: Salvadorean Women in the Struggle for National Liberation*] (1987), Nidia Díaz's *Nunca estuve sola* [*I Was Never Alone: A Prison Diary from El Salvador*] (1986), and Ana Guadalupe Martínez's *Las cárceles clandestinas de El Salvador: Libertad por el secuestro de un oligarca* [*El Salvador's Clandestine Prisons: Liberty In Exchange for the Kidnapping of an Oligarch*] (1976) are clearly marked by a socialist rhetoric of class-based struggle leading to national liberation and relate the integration and perceived roles of women combatants. Women were expected to carry out their duties as loyal militants to the cause without forgoing their responsibilities as wives and mothers given that the understanding of nationhood promoted by El Salvador's leftist groups still promoted the role of women as physical and symbolic bearers of the nation. In these testimonial narratives, what surfaces alongside the innovative constructions of female subjectivity and militancy constructed by Alegría and Flakoll, Díaz, and Martínez is an alternate project of nation building and "republican motherhood" dictated by socialist ideals. In their attempt to espouse a more egalitarian view of female agency and nationhood, these texts also disclose the limitations of such propositions.

Chapter 3 is both a bridge and a jumping-off point for looking at women's endeavors following the civil conflict and the shifting national context in the postwar period. Contending depictions of women in Horacio Castellanos Moya's novel *La diabla en el espejo* [*The She-Devil in the Mirror*] (2000) and in the short stories "La noche de los escritores asesinos" [The Night of the Murderous Writers] (1997) by Jacinta Escudos and "Vaca" [Cow] (1999) and "Mediodía de frontera" [Midday Border] (2002) by Claudia Hernández are at once a poignant indictment of the failings of the neoliberal project of national reconstruction and a key space for exploring the new battles facing women. Like Argueta's testimonial novels, in Castellanos Moya's text women function as an allegory for the nation—one that is corrupt and steadily in decline. A direct correlation exists between women who refuse to behave properly—that is, assume their roles as faithful wives and dedicated mothers—and a fraudulent social and political neoliberal order. By contrast, the depictions of female subjectivity and agency in Escudos's and Hernández's stories offer a different perspective. Both of these authors challenge Castellanos Moya's limited and figurative use of women by problematizing and, in some instances, rejecting traditional notions of women as national allegories and "republican mothers." The search by these women for cultural and political representation is symptomatic of the broader quests for identity, at both the individual and communal levels, that characterize El Salvador's postwar period.

The last two chapters continue the discussions initiated in the previous three chapters while also showcasing the social reality of women as immigrants and second-generation Salvadoran-Americans in U.S. Salvadoran texts that form part of El Salvador's cultural process and also constitute a new subgroup of U.S. Latino literatures.[9] Chapter 4 centers on texts that portray the Salvadoran migratory experience, namely Mario Bencastro's *Odisea del Norte* [*Odyssey to the North*] (1999) and the spoken-word poetry of Leticia Hernández-Linares. Debated in these texts is the role of women in migration and transnational community building, enterprises influenced not only by the legacy of war but also by current debates in El Salvador on migrants' rights and women's liberation. Bencastro's text exemplifies this transnational reality through the portrayal of a male-dominated migratory process in which women constitute either disempowered migrants or dependent wives (allegories for the Salvadoran nation left behind). While speaking of the difficulties migrants confront as they negotiate their liminal status and ethnic categorization as Latinos in the United States through the gendered idealization of their homeland, this particular emblematic rendering of women is suggestive of the patriarchal underpinnings of Salvadoran migration and, by extension, transnational community building. In her chapbook of poetry, *Razor Edges of my Tongue* (2002), Hernández-Linares affords a more women-centered view of migration, highlighting the cultural and financial contributions of female migrants and the need to rethink Salvadoran identity in light of transnational familial ties, cultural practices, and ethnic-based individuation. Hernández-Linares's poetic renderings evince an inclusionary understanding of female migrant participation and the struggles these women face given their gender and, in many cases, their undocumented status.

Marcos McPeek Villatoro's Romilia Chacón mystery series—*Home Killings* (2001), *Minos* (2003), and *A Venom beneath the Skin* (2005)—is the subject of Chapter 5. By way of his depiction of Romilia Chacón, a Latina with both southern and Salvadoran roots, McPeek Villatoro not only redefines the allegorical representation of "woman as nation" that characterizes other trans-Salvadoran narratives but also, in many ways, moves away from it altogether. The result is a unique portrait of female agency and Salvadoran migration to the United States that addresses the construction of ethnic identities and gendered subjectivities. Romilia may be representative of the Salvadoran nation, but it is one that has been incorporated into the United States, much like an immigrant population and its second generations that have begun to establish themselves as part of a U.S.-based multicultural landscape. Nevertheless, ties to the homeland remain crucial. McPeek Villatoro expounds the complexities of Salvadoran-American and, by extension, Central American-American identities through not only Romilia's performance of Salvadoranness but also her "detection" of El Salvador's hidden past of civil conflict and growing understanding of the diverse indigenous ethnicities that comprise the Central American region. Her pursuit of a Guatemalan-American adversary, although an integral aspect of this unearthing of history, also allows for a way of coming to terms with the traumas and lack of justice associated with such a past.

With its analysis of women in the broader context of an emergent "trans-Salvadoran" sense of nation, this book exemplifies the fact that "[w]omen are both of and not of the nation" as Norma Alarcón, Caren Kaplan, and Minoo Moallem write in the introduction to *Between Woman and Nation* (12). As such, this book seeks to add to debates regarding female agency and the positionalities of women within and beyond the Salvadoran national imaginary—one that is, likewise, in constant transformation. El Salvador's recent history, a complicated cross-section of national and transnational processes, affords a fruitful site of exploration for such questions, giving way to a nuanced and lacking discussion centered on Salvadoran and Salvadoran-American female subjectivities. Similarly, it expands current understandings of the gendered dynamics that mark civil war, neoliberal reconstruction, international migration, transnational community building, and the interrelationships that define these developments.

Engaging these matters by way of Salvadoran and U.S. Salvadoran narratives calls attention to a growing body of literary production that has received scant critical attention, with the exception of Salvadoran literature produced during the war (1990–1992). In so doing, this book also provides a needed intervention with regard to the analysis of Central American cultural production and identity. Women's literary portrayals in trans-Salvadoran narratives engage and contribute to a broader understanding of transnational Central American identities and that of Central American-American ethnicities within the broader scope of a U.S. Latino imaginary. The complex portrait of *salvadoreñas* that follows is thus an introduction, a preliminary point of departure, if you will, for burgeoning debates with regard to Central American and Central American-American notions of womanhood, nation, identity, and cultural representation.

Chapter 1

Campesina as Nation

Feminine Resistance and Power in Manlio Argueta's *Un día en la vida* and *Cuzcatlán: Donde bate la Mar del Sur*

By the time Manlio Argueta published his seminal novel, *Un día en la vida*, in 1980, war had become an unavoidable reality in the country. The Farabundo Martí Liberation Front (FMLN), a unified political block consolidated in 1980 and comprising El Salvador's leading left-wing militant organizations, opted to engage in guerrilla warfare and was preparing to launch its first major offensive against state military forces.[1] In keeping with its socialist political ideology, the FMLN sought to eradicate the oppressive class system and inequality instituted and maintained by El Salvador's oligarchic state. Originally a network of fourteen family groups that came into power at the end of the nineteenth century, by 1974 the Salvadoran oligarchy boasted more than sixty-five family firms that owned the majority of the country's land and controlled its agro-export industry based primarily on coffee (Dunkerley, *The Long War* 7). Many of the country's presidents belonged to one of the "families," helping to expand the oligarchy's dominance into the political arena and protect its economic interests. The use of state-sanctioned military violence and repression against the rural labor force on which the Salvadoran agro-export economy depended was a routine practice, most often carried out by the National Guard, a military organization founded under the auspices of the oligarchy in 1912 and charged with the task of policing the coffee fields and maintaining internal order.

A key player in the FMLN's project of national liberation, which it planned to achieve by way of a strategy of popular armed insurrection,

15

was the Salvadoran rural community. Although a major sector of the country's population and one of its most important economic mainstays, this community had lacked a political voice and presence throughout most of El Salvador's history. Attempts by rural peasants to change their exploitative labor conditions and political disenfranchisement, such as the ill-fated 1932 uprising that culminated in the massacre of thirty thousand peasants, including famed Communist leader Augustín Farabundo Martí, by government forces, ensured the continued subordination of rural populations.[2] The rhetoric of liberation theology, a strong undercurrent of many of the Christian missionary groups that provided aid and services to *campesinos* during the 1970s and 1980s, fostered a radical change in this situation. As Tommie Sue Montgomery notes, when one speaks of the Salvadoran church that surfaced during this period, one is speaking of the "*iglesia popular* (popular church)—that is, the tens of thousands of people, most of them poor, who came to believe that 'liberation' is not only something one achieves at death but also something that, with God's blessing, one can struggle for and possibly achieve during one's lifetime" (84). This new understanding of themselves as an oppressed group with the ability to change their precarious condition, coupled with the FMLN's strategic organizing efforts in the countryside, was one of the main reasons for the mass mobilization of El Salvador's rural sector.

Another was the incessant persecution of their communities by the state's military forces, which deemed peasants part of the growing "communist threat" that needed to be eradicated at all costs. Violent affronts on rural livelihoods, including the imprisonment, killing, or disappearance of one or more members of the same family, were commonplace occurrences that forced a restructuring, to a certain extent, of gender roles and hierarchies. Because the majority of the individuals targeted by government forces were men, women had to occupy the leadership positions in community organizations that their husbands had left vacant while also adopting new roles as the sole providers and protectors of their families. Rural women soon found themselves not only fighting for their lives but also in the midst of a significant transformation concerning what had been, up to that time, their limited public agency and their perceived domestic roles.[3] *Campesinas* emerged as historical protagonists whose participation in their community's battle for survival and social justice altered the contours of the civil conflict as much as it did their individual lives.

The ways and extent to which rural women incorporated themselves into the struggle were varied, influenced by generational divides and differing degrees of politicization. Older generations of grandmothers and mothers provided shelter, food, and laundry services to guerrilla forces to which their children oftentimes belonged. They also functioned as a covert conduit for communal information. Younger generations of daughters participated as human rights and labor activists and, in many instances, also incorporated themselves into the armed revolutionary struggle as *guerrilleras*. Although many women enacted roles dissimilar to the ones they were accustomed to and adopted more public personas, the traditional positions they occupied as wives, mothers, and daughters, as well as their ties to the home, remained imperative and, in fact, constituted a significant source of empowerment. Consistent with Jean Franco's discussion of the personal becoming the political in her critical piece "Killing Priests, Nuns, Women, Children," the "maternal power" of rural women during this tumultuous moment in Salvadoran history turned them as well as the family unit into a "major institution of resistance" (11).

Argueta's *Un día en la vida* renders an incisive portrayal of the ensuing political and gendered changes occasioned by the conflict in the countryside. Central to the plot of *Un día* is Guadalupe Guardado (Lupe), a forty-eight-year-old *campesina* whose son, Jacinto, was violently murdered by the National Guard and whose husband José (Chepe) has gone into hiding in the mountains. Lupe's sequential account of a typical twelve-hour day and the memories and experiences she recalls throughout it are a narrative and temporal anchor for the secondary accounts rendered by other *campesinas*, all of whom are connected or related to Lupe through communal or familial ties, as well as those of anonymous members of the National Guard. These accounts, which appear in italics and do not follow a chronological order, add to Lupe's narrative of the *campesino* reality during this period of national crisis. Lupe's day culminates in a tragic encounter between herself and her granddaughter, Adolfina, and the novel's principal antagonist, a member of the National Guard named Corporal Pedro Martínez. In an effort to save herself and her granddaughter, Lupe must deny knowing her husband, who has been captured and tortured by the authorities, and watch in silence as they take him away to his death.

Although *Un día* is arguably Argueta's best-known novel,[4] it is not the only work by Argueta that effectively engages with the plight of El Salvador's rural population during the years of conflict and that situates women at the center of the struggle.[5] His follow-up novel, *Cuzcatlán: Donde bate la Mar del Sur*, published at the height of the civil war in 1986, is an equally compelling piece. In an interview with Zulema Nelly Martínez, conducted while Argueta was writing *Cuzcatlán*, he explains that this second novel can be understood as a continuation of the first in the sense that it delves deeper into the subject of rural oppression and injustice (46). It examines more closely the experience of those in the National Guard, who as *campesinos* also share in this larger story of struggle and experience their own form of victimization by the *gringo* advisors who train them to be the oppressors of their own people, as well as other diverse aspects of El Salvador's history and culture, particularly those that speak to the country's indigenous roots and past.

In *Cuzcatlán*, Argueta tells the story of Corporal Pedro Martínez and his family as narrated and imagined by his niece, Lucía Martínez, a commanding officer in the guerrilla forces. Lucía first appears riding a bus heading toward San Salvador, where she is to attend a popular hearing against Corporal Martínez, who has been captured by the FMLN. Like Lupe's "one day of life," Lucía's bus ride is a fixed temporal point in the text that links together the personal accounts and recollections of Lucía's family members. Spanning more than four generations, these testimonies provide insight into the family's history, including Corporal Martínez's upbringing and *campesino* background. They also, however, give way to a rural collective memory and a historical consciousness characterized by the legacy of conquest and the reality of colonization, as well as indigenous beliefs and resistance. Reading these two novels in dialogue with each other allows one to grasp more fully the multifaceted vision Argueta elaborates of the Salvadoran peasantry and, more importantly, of the women who came to define it.

Although the crucial position women occupy in *Un día* and *Cuzcatlán* has caught the attention of many literary critics, it has not necessarily been a central thread of their analyses. More often than not, it factors as part of a broader overview of Argueta's literary corpus or specific explorations of Argueta's use of testimonial elements—seen by many as the most defining characteristic of Argueta's writing.[6] In this chapter, I give precedence to Argueta's portrayal of women, to what I note as Argueta's use of *campesinas* as both narrative and ideological tools; narrative in the sense that it is the voices and experiences of peasant women that are privileged in these texts and expose the Salvadoran reality of war in *el campo* [countryside]; and ideological because it is by way of women that Argueta communicates an alternate view of rural female agency and nationhood. Although I maintain the importance of Argueta's incorporation of testimonial forms and, in fact, provide a preliminary exploration of this aspect here, I approach the analysis of female representation in these two novels from another conceptual angle: Argueta's casting of *campesinas* as allegories for a Salvadoran nation also conceived, in its majority, as *campesino*.

The importance of this gendered symbolization is one Argueta himself acknowledges when he suggests that the female characters in his works can be likened to a "macrocosmos"—that is, they comprise the constellatory system or macro-lens through which to view the nation and its changes ("La mujer en mis novelas"). As I contend, it is Argueta's reworking of the allegorical construct of "woman as nation" that most clearly evinces the visibility of *campesinas* during this period of civil conflict, revealing them to be agents of not only communal but also national change. In essence, the refashioning of this traditional literary recourse allows for a more nuanced understanding of how *campesinas*, and the broader rural community they represent, redefined their peripheral positions within the nation, thereby also giving way to an alternate ideal of Salvadoran nationhood that challenged the exclusionary model instituted by the oligarchic state.

Women in Argueta's Testimonial Novels

Argueta's novels are characterized by many of the same narrative strategies that define testimonio, especially those produced by women in Latin America, which has led many critics to focus their attention on these aspects of Argueta's work and categorize his novels in a variety of ways: "novels of testimony," "testimonial novels," and "pseudo-testimonios."[7] In addition to being an inextricable part of the thematic foci and narrative structures of *Un día* and *Cuzcatlán*, Argueta's utilization of testimonial elements is also pivotal, as they contribute significantly to the allegorical depiction of *campesinas* and the rural sector each novel elaborates. For this reason, prior to embarking on a more detailed discussion of female representation, it is necessary to provide a basic understanding of the literary context from which these texts emerge and what specific connections can be drawn between them and testimonial narratives.

The Salvadoran literature produced during the civil conflict, including new expressions of testimonio such as Argueta's novels, was, according to John Beverley and Mark Zimmerman, "less self-consciously literary and less politically sectarian, more diverse in its enunciation of class and party, less male-centered, less urban and secular" (135). It was also "more open to perspectives stemming from liberation theology and from both contemporary and pre-Colombian Indian cultures" (Beverley and Zimmerman 135). *Un día* and *Cuzcatlán* exemplify many of these characteristics. First, by casting *campesinas* as the new protagonists of the struggle, these novels move away from the emphasis given to the male intellectual or revolutionary hero as the bearer of history in earlier testimonial narratives.[8] Second, their plots explore the transformative effect liberation theology had on the peasantry as well as the indigenous past and belief system that marks rural subjectivity. Third, in each of these texts, popular forms of speech proper to the rural community and reminiscent of canonical works such as Salvador Salazar Arrué's (Salarrué) *Cuentos de barro* (1933) are important markers.

This broader literary context aside, Argueta's use of testimonial elements is also largely attributable to the ideological functions of testimonio, to the fact that, as Argueta suggests, whoever writes testimonio is conscious that he or she is transforming reality (Martínez and Argueta 54). According to John Beverley's provisional definition, testimonio is

> [. . .] a novel or novella-length narrative in a book or pamphlet (that is printed as opposed to acoustic) form, told in the first person by a narrator who is also the real protagonist or witness of the events she recounts, and whose unit of narration is usually a "life" or significant life experience. ("The Margin at the Center" 24)

Oftentimes, the narrator communicates his or her story to an interlocutor, an intellectual or journalist who transcribes and edits the oral account. The narrator speaks for or on behalf of a community or group, giving voice to an otherwise silenced collective subject, and communicates a problem of greater urgency such as that of repression, poverty, or the struggle to survive. As such, testimonio can also be understood as a cultural act of resistance against social, political, and economic hegemonic practices.

Referring specifically to Latin American women's testimonios, scholars have noted that one of the more prominent traits of these narratives is their emphasis on collectivity. In her article "'Not Just a Personal Story': Women's *Testimonios* and the Plural Self," Doris Sommer clarifies the ways in which the testimonial "I" achieves this pluralized identity. As she states, "[t]he singular represents the plural not because it replaces or subsumes the group but because the speaker is a distinguishable part of the whole" (108). Being women and assuming this key position as representatives of a collectivity or their communities also has profound gendered implications. In these texts, the life experiences recounted by the female "I" include references to women's specific issues and concerns, including the notion of gendered oppression. More than just constituting narratives of resistance in the face of hegemonic practices, Latin American women's testimonios denounce the patriarchy that marks such practices.

In *Un día* and *Cuzcatlán*, the role of the testimonial "I" is mostly assumed by the female narrators Lupe and Lucía. It is they who are charged with the task of speaking on behalf of their communities and of communicating the repression they suffer at the hands of the National Guard. Consistent with Sommer's observations, neither of these women is represented as a separate individual, but rather as an extension of her *campesino* community, whose presence is marked in each novel by the network of secondary voices and testimonies that complement Lupe and Lucía's accounts. The experiences these women underscore in their testimonies also manifest a keen awareness of the obstacles and oppression rural women face within Salvadoran society because of their gender, class, ethnicity, and race. In this sense, Argueta's novels enact what Margaret Randall terms a new female practice of "telling a story" that gives rise to specific issues affecting women.

Even with their stylistic and ideological affinities to testimonio, however, Argueta's novels are still works of fiction. They are, in effect, testimonial *novels* that, in keeping with Elzbieta Sklodowska's classification of testimonial narratives in Latin America, exhibit a greater degree of development in terms of the text's aesthetic function as opposed to only focusing on its communicative qualities (100). Linda J. Craft's *Novels of Testimony and Resistance from Central* affords a fundamental base for exploring the aesthetic functions of Argueta's novels with regard to women's symbolic representation as signifiers of nation. According to Craft, the testimonial novel in Central America, like nineteenth-century foundational fictions, functions as an allegory for the imagined nation because, in opposition to the oppressive social reality in which it is produced, the testimonial novel "[. . .] envisions a just nation where all sectors participate in all aspects of the national life" (26). The trope of "woman as nation" is crucial to the allegorizing function of Argueta's novels and to the alternate concept of nation or the "national popular" that Craft maintains Argueta's novels also suggest (26). Although the "plotting" of women as national allegories has traditionally marked women's marginalization from national and literary endeavors, I argue that this is not the case in Argueta's novels, given his redefinition of female roles and spaces that have customarily been viewed as inferior and disempowered into those of resistance and change.

In *Un día*, women use their identities as mothers, wives, and daughters to challenge and denounce a patriarchal state that claims to uphold and respect these conventional social roles yet continuously violates and disrupts the family dynamic. The existing relationships and solidarity forged by women in the midst of this violence constitutes both a vital survival strategy and a form of gendered resistance. Ironically, then, the domestic attributes that relegate women to the periphery of the nation in times of peace are what make them central and public players in national endeavors during this time of war. Similarly, in *Cuzcatlán*,

Lucía's involvement in the armed struggle as a *guerrillera* is as important as her role as a mother who remains intrinsically tied to the home, to her family, and to the indigenous consciousness and roots that define her people. The unique connection she shares with her grandmother, Beatriz, also recalls the female relationships and solidarity seen in *Un día*.

This conceptualization of female roles and of the domestic space as sites of defiance and strength is one that also informs Argueta's portrayal of the broader *campesino* community in the novel. *Campesinas* function as allegories for a marginalized *campesino* population that through its politicization has been transformed into a decisive force for change. Viewing the *campesino* experience through this localized and gendered lens constitutes a certain feminization of the struggle and of the rural population that serves as its main base. By engaging with the experiences of *campesinas* and positing them as active participants in the conflict, the text recognizes and validates a feminized rural sector historically subordinate to the oligarchic state. This stands in contrast to the state's ideological and patriarchal discourse with regard to not only women, whom it sees as weak and powerless, but also a rural population it views in the same gendered terms.

Consequently, Argueta's rendering of the feminine or feminized in this manner, along with his use of testimonial elements that privilege women's voices and experiences, gives way to a reformulation of *campesinas* as symbolic of the nation that does not necessarily preclude their exclusion from the very nation they symbolize. Quite the contrary, it stresses their inclusion and that of the rest of the rural majority. Such a resemanticization of this allegorical construct calls into question the traditional and exclusionary model of nationhood premised on bourgeois ideals that marks Latin America's foundational fictions and is fundamental to both the oligarchic state's conceptualization of nation and, to a certain extent, that of the revolutionary project, as we shall see in the following chapter. Notably, the epic of the foundational couple is displaced by that of a rural collectivity coming into its own and helping to forge a more just society. Thus, although Argueta's novels remain national modernizing narratives, to recall Craft, the understanding of nationhood they proffer seeks to underscore, above all else, the *campesino* collectivity that is the backbone of the Salvadoran nation and the women who define it.

Feminizing the Struggle, Empowering the Domestic

In *Un día*, Argueta critically engages with the social, economic, and political matters that divided El Salvador and eventually gave way to armed insurrection and war. A consistent theme of the novel is the opposition between members of the National Guard and the rural community, primarily its women. The physical antagonism between these two disparate groups of individuals is a clear expression and condensation of the national crisis. As part of the government's military apparatus, the National Guard is representative of a long-standing oligarchic state that has maintained its power through the use of military repression, electoral fraud, and the monopolization of the country's agro-export industry. *Campesinas*, alternatively, are indicative of popular attempts, influenced by the left and Christian-based organizations, to mobilize and change the stratified economic and political systems upheld by the state. The pseudo-testimonial narrative framework mirrors this fundamental opposition between the characters by drawing a dichotomy between the voices of *campesinas* and those of the male authorities. Each set of accounts relates different aspects of the struggle, and together they form a vocal collage that manifests the division of the Salvadoran people.

Lupe's account and the testimonies rendered by secondary female characters provide a localized history of the conflict and its effects on their livelihoods. María Pía, Lupe's daughter, recalls the arrest of her husband, Helio, and her brutal beating at the hands of the authorities. Adolfina, Lupe's fifteen-year-old granddaughter, relates her experience of politicization and activism. Likewise, María Romelia, who belongs to the same community as Lupe and whose father has also been arrested, is witness to a violent encounter between troops and demonstrators at a protest in San Salvador. She also provides significant insight regarding the death of Lupe's son, Justino, and Adolfina's character as a person.

In opposition to the testimonies and experiences recounted by Lupe and the other women in the novel are those by anonymous members of the National Guard. Although it is never fully stated, it is possible that more than one of these accounts belongs to Corporal Pedro Martínez, who was once a member of the same community. These accounts reveal the vital role and influence of the United States in Salvadoran politics and as such locate the national conflict within a broader international arena. They also betray the oppression of the guardsmen by U.S. imperialist forces. Despite being *campesinos* themselves, as part of the state's military apparatus, they have internalized a sense of self-hatred and have been indoctrinated to believe that their communities are the enemy.

The intimate and complex relationship between the text's dominant themes and its narrative structure makes necessary a simultaneous discussion of both. In the narratives by *campesinas*, Argueta emphasizes the process of politicization undertaken by the rural population during these years as well as the violent repression endured by these communities. As Lupe reveals, the change in attitude between the old church, with its traditional preaching on the necessary submissiveness of the poor and its indifference to their situation, and a new church in which younger priests formed cooperatives and taught the *campesino*s how to defend themselves was imperative to this transformation. The old priests, according to Lupe, preached conformity, offering hope rather than advocating action (24/20). But after "[. . .] un congreso en no se dónde . . . ya la religión no era igual" [a congress was held I don't know where . . . religion was no longer the same] (29/25). The mention of the Second Episcopal Congress in Medellín, Colombia, held in 1968 and Lupe's observations regarding the transformation of religion contextualize the effects liberation theology had on the rural community. This contact with the new church and its teachings, as Lupe later affirms, made *campesino*s aware of their rights and allowed them to shed the ignorance that kept them subordinate to the old church and the oligarchic state it supported (36/31–32).

Liberation theology and the new priests who espouse this rhetoric thus provide the basis for the social and political mobilization of *campesinos*. In the text, many of the men belong to Christian-based cooperatives aimed at procuring some form of political voice for the rural sector. Younger women such as Adolfina and María Romelia have also incorporated themselves into this type of organization. Their testimonies depict the active protests of these organizations, a vital component of the popular movement. In her account, María Romelia tells of the events that take place when she accompanies a group of organized labor activists and university students to San Salvador, the nation's capital, to protest the high price of fertilizer, seeds, and insecticides set by the privately owned banks, making it difficult for *campesinos* to cultivate their lands. As María Romelia explains to her mother: " '[. . .] no se trata de pedir por pedir, sino de reclamar nuestro derecho, pues el gobierno ha dicho que el Banco es para hacer préstamos y se pueda asi comprar semillas y abonos' " ['It's not a matter of begging, but of claiming our rights, because the government has said that the Bank is supposed to make loans so one can buy seeds and fertilizer'] (45/41). By way of her political consciousness and understanding of oppression, María Romelia provides important insight about the *campesino* reality and the ways in which liberation theology acted as an important catalyst for social and political activism.

In this testament of rural political awakening, *campesinas* also relate the violence and state terror perpetrated against their communities. María Romelia's account of the demonstration highlights this aspect when she describes the brutal retaliation of the treasury police against a group of protestors who seek shelter in a transit bus:

> [. . .] vi que los polecías tiraban bombas por las ventanillas. Eran bombas lacremógenas. Y salía una gran humazón. Y luego pusieron otra bomba y comenzo el bus a arder con la gente adentro, pues a todo esto los hombres seguían tirados en el bus porque si salían les iban a disparar a matar. Entonces, después que pusieron las bombas lacremógenas, volvieron a entrar los polecias a ver dentro del bus. Y entonces si les disparaban pues yo oía los gritos adentro. (43)

> [. . .] I saw the policemen throw bombs into the bus. Tear gas canisters. And a huge cloud of smoke started coming out. And then they threw another bomb in and the bus began to burn with the people still inside, because throughout all this the men had had to lie on the floor of the bus because if they had left, they would have been killed. Then, after they threw the tear gas, the policemen went back to take a look. And then they started shooting at the people. I could hear them screaming. (39)

The gruesome scene depicted by María Romelia is exemplary of the state's severe repression and its refusal to yield any of its power or reform the current system. It calls attention to the lack of alternatives the *campesino* population had in seeking change through peaceful means and the inevitability of armed struggle.

María Pía's testimony, which follows that of María Romelia, expresses the all-encompassing nature of the state's attack on the rural community. She begins her account: "Yo soy también de por acá de esta zona, esposa de Helio Hernández. Fue capturado por la guardia nacional. Cuando lo agarraron recibio torturas, es decir le pegaban culatazos en la espalda, en la cabeza" [I'm also from around these parts, I'm the wife of Helio Hernández. He was captured by the National Guard. They picked him up and tortured him, they hit him with the rifle butts on the back and on the head] (69/66). What follows is María Pía's telling of her search for her husband, who was one of the organizers of the protest, and the abuse she endures because of her inquiries. María Pía's victimization and precarious situation, like that of many women in her community, can be understood as a standard or general experience of the Salvadoran people during this historical period. Attempts by the government's military forces to maintain control were carried out by whatever means necessary, including attacks on "formerly immune territories" such as the family and its private dwelling space (Franco, "Killing Priests" 9). The testimonies of María Romelia and María Pía reveal the intensity of the conflict and the oppression of the rural population on both a national and local level, most drastically through the killing and the disappearance of the men who had chosen to organize and demand basic human rights.

Whereas the fictionalized testimonial accounts of *campesinas* engage with the history of *conscientización* [political consciousness] and oppression of *el campo*, those by the anonymous members of the National Guard, titled "Lautoridad" [The Authorities] and "ellos" [Them], reveal the state's oppressive discourse regarding the growing social unrest of the masses as well as the vital role and influence of the United States in Salvadoran politics. The guardsmen conceive of themselves as a "[. . .] heroic, virile military" in battle against "an unruly other located in the feminine position as chaotic and subversive, in need of subjugation and discipline" (Molyneux 61). This gendered power dynamic is most evident in the National Guard's observations with regard to women and the progressive clergy, both of which constitute a feminine and perverse other that must be eradicated at all cost. Women, for instance, who have out of necessity or knowingly chosen to challenge the state's patriarchal authority are construed as whores. Not even one's own mother or the elderly are to be spared: "Y las mujeres, entre más viejas son, más putas. Es la verdad. Todo está claro, porque algunos lo dudan, especialmente por las nanas" [As for women, the older they get, the more whorish. It's true. Everything's clear, but some have doubts, especially because of their mothers] (137/130). Similarly, the young priests who radicalize the community through the teachings of liberation theology are labeled homosexuals. According to the anonymous voice of a soldier who intervenes in Lupe's narrative, the men who attend mass on Sundays " 'tienen vocación de culeros, a saber qué putas le ha[n] visto al cura, quizás como es chelote y galán se han enamorado de él' " ['are faggots. Who knows what the fuck they see in the priest. Maybe because he's such an exotic and gallant type, they've fallen in love with him'] (Argueta, *Un día* 32). This derogatory insult frames the relationship between the male *campesino* parishioners and the priest in terms of a racialized and deviant sexual attraction. As part of this same extended metaphor, the church that allies itself with the peasantry is negatively cast as an institution that not only promotes but also breeds homosexuality. Nowhere is this discourse more apparent than when one of the parish priests is stripped by the National Guard, impaled with a stick in his rectum, and left for dead on the side of the road (32/30).

The sexually charged rivalry between the male corporals and *campesinas* or effeminate priests posits the national conflict as a struggle between a masculinist state and a subversive *campesino* community that the state designates as feminine, deviant, and racially inferior given its indigenous and rural roots. Such an understanding of the *campesino* community evokes Jasbir K. Puar's illuminating discussion concerning the problematic depiction of terrorist Muslim masculinities within the post-9/11 context. Terrorist masculinities, as Puar explains, are represented as "failed and perverse [. . .] emasculated bodies [that] always have femininity as their reference point of malfunction" (xxiii). They are inherently queer, standing in opposition to and having to be disciplined by normative, patriotic, and white "American" sexualities (hetero and homo) (xxiv). Although Puar is referencing a more recent historical junction, that of the "global war on terror," within the Cold War context of Argueta's novel, the *campesino* community functions, in the eyes of El Salvador's oligarchic state, as a similarly threatening racial and sexualized terrorist force. The gendered rhetoric employed by the National Guardsman ultimately speaks to the anxiety provoked in the state by an organized and politically conscious *campesino* population that has become a decisive force in the struggle for the nation.

Interestingly, within the context of U.S.-Salvadoran relations, it is the oligarchic state that occupies the inferior and feminized position, a notion conveyed via the symbolic emasculation of the Salvadoran trainees at the hands of their North American advisors. In the section titled "Lautoridad," the observations of the narrative voice regarding the mashed potatoes served at the training camps are especially revealing: "Ni siquiera sé por qué le llaman puré. Mire, le voy a decir para serle franco, y perdone la palabra: el puré parece caca solo con olor a semen. Imaginese, pero uno tiene que comérselo a la fuerza" [I don't even know why they call it purée. Look, I'll tell you something to be frank, and pardon my language, purée looks like shit except it smells like semen. Can you imagine being forced to eat it?] (Argueta, *Un día* 96/91). The comparison of the food with excrement and semen contextualizes the coercion of the Salvadoran men at these U.S.-run military facilities. The recruits are literally forced to swallow the ideological excrement and semen that the *gringos* serve them. Thus, in this gendered power dynamic with the *gringos*, it is the Salvadoran soldiers who embody the feminine position. It is they who are in need of proper disciplining. By showcasing the victimization of the guardsmen in this way, Argueta draws attention to the underlying motivations behind the guardsmen's brutalization of their own *campesino* brethren. In order to ameliorate their feelings of inferiority and emasculation as subordinates of the U.S.

trainers—the true "autoridad" in this case—they must, in turn, dominate a lesser foe. By the same token, Argueta unveils the culpatory role of the United States in the Salvadoran conflict and in the persecution and death of countless peasants.

This textual mapping of the civil conflict, reflected in both the novel's base plot as well as its testimonial narrative structure that pits female voices against those of the National Guard, highlights the strong presence and agency of rural women. Both of these are due, in part, to the *concientización* experienced by *campesinas*, which is intrinsically tied to their function as mothers and wives. Lupe's politicization, for example, is first and foremost a product of her maternal function as well as her husband's influence. When Lupe begins to menstruate at the age of twelve, an event she refers to as "el cambio" [the change], she also hears for the first time "la voz de la conciencia" [the voice of conscience] (19/15). By her own account, Lupe begins to see the world in a different light, precisely at the same moment that she also becomes aware of her biological capabilities to have children. Furthermore, as José's (Chepe's) trusting and obedient wife, Lupe is accepting of his political beliefs. Given her limited access to the public sphere, José's politicization and involvement in community organizing are Lupe's primary influences and are fundamental to her own process of enlightenment. Through conversations with her husband and his example, Lupe develops what José refers to as "esa conciencia de ser pobres" [that awareness of being poor], consequently obtaining a new understanding of her pueblo's exploitation and the need to fight for one's rights (60/56).

Adolfina's social and political consciousness, more progressive and radical than that of her grandmother, is similarly marked by maternal characteristics. In her account of the violent repression of the demonstration in the capital, María Romelia describes Adolfina as a mature, protective figure who helps her escape from the government troops. Her telling of the episode is infused with continuous references to Adolfina's maternal qualities, which are conflated with her ability to lead. For María Romela, Adolfina is the "compañera que nos venía apiando por grupos y que yo no me le desprendía" [the girl who had been letting groups off one at a time and to whom I clung] (43/39). Upon leaving the bus in which both had taken refuge, they are captured by the treasury police. Adolfina is raped by the policemen, given that at fifteen, she is the older of the two. Although Adolfina does not offer herself willingly to the policemen, she does not deny her age, and this one act determines her being chosen by the policemen over María Romelia. In this scene, Adolfina is cast as the socially conscious *compañera* of the struggle as well as the maternal figure who protects those younger than herself, for, as María Romelia later affirms about her relationship with Adolfina, "[l]e había tomado una gran confianza como si fuera mi mamá" [I'd come to trust her as if she had been my mother] (44/40).

The novel, then, depicts a reality that forces women to empower themselves and their families by redefining and reimagining their traditional roles in society as wives and mothers. In many instances, the female characters in the text insist on the institution of the family and communal ties to defend themselves from the government authorities. When María Pía is violently assaulted in her home by the National Guard following her husband Helio's arrest, she saves herself by holding onto her son: "Y mi niño de quince meses llorando pero yo no lo soltaba, para que no me mataran, porque con el niño no me iban a disparar" [And my fifteen-month-old baby was crying but I wouldn't let go of him, so that they wouldn't kill me, because they would not shoot me with a child in my arms] (76/73). With her child in her arms, María Pía uses her motherhood as a shield against the blows of the soldiers. Lupe and Adolfina employ a similar tactic in their decisive confrontation with Corporal Martínez, thereby preventing him from arresting Adolfina. Adolfina's insistence that Corporal Martínez is the son of one of the community's women, "la Ticha," is a way of making him recognize his family and peasant origins in order to problematize his new identity as "Lautoridad." By drawing attention to his communal ties and alluding to his mother, Lupe and Adolfina, like María Pía, utilize the patriarchal discourse on the sanctity of motherhood to protect and arm themselves.

Although a relevant aspect of the survival strategies employed by *campesinas*, the concept of motherhood and the family is also instrumental in establishing a vital network of communal solidarity. Given the gruesome nature of the murder of Lupe's son, Justino, and the public display of his dismembered body by the authorities, her loss and suffering are well known. Significantly, although Lupe alludes to her son's death, it is the community that recounts it in more detail. María Romelia's second testimonial entry begins: "Dice mi mamá que la pobre Lupe sufrió mucho" [My mother says that poor Guadalupe suffered a lot] (111/105). From then on, the account becomes a veritable heteroglossia of voices and opinions from different eyewitnesses who, in conjunction with María Romelia, collectively piece together Justino's death and its impact on the Guardado family. By way of summary, María Romelia affirms, "Todo lo que dice la gente es una manera de estar con la Lupe. Hoy por tí, mañana por mí. El luto de Guadalupe lo hacemos nuestro" [Everything people say is a way of being with Lupe. Today for you, tomorrow for me. We make her mourning our own] (114/108). The sentiment conveyed for the family's misfortune, particularly Lupe's pain as a mother, is at once empathetic and also an expression of solidarity. Lupe's loss is the community's loss, not just because Justino was a *campesino*, but also because the tragedy that has befallen him and his family can happen to any one of them. This notion is further drawn out by the manner in which Argueta uses the collective voice to narrate this particular episode. Many of the speakers are anonymous, yet each of them speaks on behalf of the other, thereby complementing each other's stories and highlighting the fact that their experiences could be interchangeable.

Inherent to this representation of a politicized motherhood and domesticity is a struggle by women against the patriarchal order that governs all facets of Salvadoran society. Although the politicization of these women stems primarily from their contact with the domestic sphere, it emphasizes a new, gendered form of resistance that becomes more radical with each generation. Lupe's understanding of the world is different from that of her granddaughter, and it is Adolfina and María Romelia who hold the key to the future. As a matter of fact, although at the close of the novel Adolfina's future remains uncertain, her character considers guerrilla warfare as an alternative, a decision that would take her even further outside the domestic sphere. Thus, the participation and agency of this younger generation is premised not only on their expected roles as wives and mothers but also on their conscious choice to be political and social activists. In opting to publicly engage in a struggle to transform society, they have also embarked on a simultaneous process to transform and imagine themselves beyond traditional social norms.

Despite the fact that Adolfina's introduction to social and political struggle was instilled in her by her father, Helio, the disruption of the family dynamic and the domestic space by the state's repressive forces, also a reflection of the nation's fragmentation, allows her to adopt a new identity and agency. This is exemplified in the novel by Adolfina's affirmation: "Mi papa se llama Helio Hernández. Era el sostén de la familia. Ahora soy yo" [My father's name is Helio Hernández. He was the mainstay of the family. Now I am] (159/152). Whereas María Pía and Lupe could not fully envision themselves as the heads of the family without their husbands, Adolfina does. In her father's absence, Adolfina co-opts his male authority as well as his responsibility, a viable and necessary alternative given the breakdown of the patriarchal familial structure. Unlike the other women in the text, who more than once express the fear that they will be unable to fend for themselves without their spouses, Adolfina willingly takes up that challenge. Moreover, Adolfina, like María Romelia, whose father is also missing, does not yet have a husband or even a boyfriend whom she needs to answer to or take into consideration. Without the burden of these particular concerns and restrictions, Adolfina is capable of making her own decisions as well as choosing different alternatives with regard to her activism and involvement in the civil conflict.

The synthesis of both the plight of the *campesino* population and the underlying liberation struggle being waged by women reaches its apex in the novel's final scene. At the end of her day, Lupe is confronted with the reality that her husband has been captured and severely beaten by the National Guard. As José is held up before her by the soldiers, who ask her to identify him, Lupe claims not to know him: "Entonces dije que no. Tenía que ser un no sin temblor de voz, sin el menor titubeo. . . . Y dios me iluminó la mente, quizás, porque te recordé hablándome: 'Si alguna vez mirás algún peligro, para vos y nuestra familia, no vacilés en negarme'" [Then I said no. It had to be a no without any quavering of my voice, without the least trace of hesitation. . . . And God illuminated my mind, maybe, because I remembered your saying to me, 'If at any time you detect danger to yourself or to our family, don't hesitate about denying me'] (199/192). In choosing to deny her husband, Lupe remains loyal to José and his beliefs for social change. However, her loyalty is not a submissive one. Meeting José's silence with her own and maintaining her composure despite the state of his tortured body denies the authorities the satisfaction of knowing that they have wounded Lupe. And in refusing to affirm the state's power, Lupe strengthens the *campesino* struggle for which her husband is sacrificing his life. Ironically, the act of keeping silent, a trait traditionally associated with her status as a woman and her class, is transformed by Lupe into a viable form of resistance that empowers her and the community. In highlighting this one pivotal act of not speaking out, Argueta draws an important correlation to one of the primary functions of the *testimonio*—that of giving voice to the subaltern and her struggle against oppression. After all, in this instance, it is not Lupe's words, but rather her strategic silence that delivers the clearest message. In effect, she is choosing to fight on behalf of her community, regardless of the consequences to José or herself.

Hence, in this critical scene the novel reveals a decisive confrontation between an old way of life and a new way being forged by the Salvadoran *pueblo*. Once again, the discourse of gender becomes an important way of addressing the immediate relationships of power between men and women as well as social and class dynamics. An authoritarian and patriarchal Salvadoran state will always view and need to treat the peasantry as a feminized sector that must be dominated, silenced, and controlled. Corporal Martínez, as a representative of the state, is incapable of acknowledging that any power can be derived from that position. In fact, Corporal Martínez must continually brutalize *campesino* activists like José in order to assuage his own feelings of inferiority. By contrast, a politicized *campesino* population draws strength precisely from its subordinate and feminized position. The traditional ideological and socioeconomic barriers that define such a position as weak are no longer viable. Not only has the national crisis created a space in which women can rise up and have agency, but it has also allowed for an equally feminized *campesino* class to become a political force. Therefore, in depicting Lupe's unwavering resolve in front of Corporal Martínez, a power that stems from her own presumed inferior role as a wife and mother, Argueta is likewise drawing attention to a potent rural sector whose strength derives from its communal and domestic center, the home. In this transformative era of struggle and imminent war, the old way of life dictated by the state and dependent on the ignorance and political anonymity of the peasantry is no longer possible.

Cuzcatlán's Women of Maize

To a certain extent, *Cuzcatlán* picks up where *Un día* leaves off. In the final pages of *Un día*, Adolfina tells her grandmother about a vision she has had of Corporal Martínez lying dead with his eyes and mouth open while his family mourns him. Adolfina's prophetic vision will come to task in *Cuzcatlán* by way of Lucía, who is depicted in the opening chapter of the novel riding a bus en route to San Salvador, where she will testify against her uncle, Corporal Pedro Martínez. Given the interrelatedness of both story lines and these two characters, one has to wonder if, in fact, Adolfina is not the model for Lucía's character. Lucía's bus ride takes place in 1981, a few years after the events narrated in *Un día* and the same year that the FMLN launched its first major offensive against the state's military forces.[9] Although Corporal Martínez does not die in the novel, nor is he mourned by his family in the same way that Adolfina imagines, his defining encounter with Lucía—which, like his final confrontation with Lupe in *Un día*, also occurs at the end of this novel—will open his eyes to the reality of his crimes.

 Cuzcatlán is also characterized by the use of testimonial forms and the exploration of themes related to the specific reality of *el campo*, including the systematic oppression of the rural sector by the state's military forces, as well as the politicization and growing agency of women. Despite these similarities, however, *Cuzcatlán* differs significantly from its predecessor with regard to its narrative structure. This variation allows Argueta to expand his exploration of the rural reality by situating it within a broader discussion of El Salvador's process of colonization and the country's indigenous origins, while still highlighting the pivotal role of *campesinas* in the civil conflict. Whereas in *Un día* a clear dichotomy is drawn between the voices and experiences of *campesinas* and those of the National Guard, paralleling the oppositions engendered by the war, in *Cuzcatlán* readers are privy to a wider array of *campesino* accounts, namely those belonging to members of the Martínez family. Among the voices included are those of Emiliano (Lucía's great-grandfather), Beatriz (Lucía's grandmother and Emiliano's daughter), and Juana and Jacinto (Lucía's mother and father). The notable exception is that of Pedro Martínez, whose only words are those spoken in the end to Lucía. However, if we are to assume that his was among the voices included in the testimonies of "Lautoridad" and "ellos" in *Un día*, his perspective has already been foregrounded.

Although at first sight these voices seem to not follow a particular pattern, in keeping with Astvaldur Astvaldsson's critical analysis of the narrative structure of *Cuzcatlán*, it is possible to see that these testimonies do adhere to some form of order, and that Lucía is the key to understanding it. In the opening paragraphs of the novel, Lucía introduces herself as if she were giving a formal interview or, perhaps, a military account. She provides a concise list of specific information: her pseudonym, which is Beatriz, like her grandmother, her age, her ethnic origin, her living situation, and her real name. She also reveals other details about herself, such as the fact that her favorite pastime is daydreaming, that her favorite natural element is *metate* [volcanic stone], that she has two children and has recently lost her *compañero*, and her reasons for traveling to San Salvador. According to Astvaldsson, the fact that Lucía is daydreaming is of most relevance, because it is this action of self-reflection and imagining that explains the seemingly incoherent web of voices that appear in the narrative. The accounts narrated by the different members of the Martínez family in the novel are done so "in and through her [Lucía's] imagination" (607). In other words, they are contained within and are to be understood as an aspect of Lucía's daydreaming. Astvaldsson further maintains that the unidentified third-person narrative voice that also appears throughout the text alongside those of the other characters and that ties different threads of memories and thoughts together can also be accredited to Lucía (612).[10]

This conceptualization of the novel's narrative structure posits Lucía as the "central rather than main first-person narrator" (Astvaldsson 612), signaling her as the designated spokesperson for her family and, by extension, for the broader *campesino* community to which they all belong. As such, Lucía gives testimony not only to the current circumstances in which she finds herself as a *guerrillera* and mother who has lost her *compañero* but also to her family's history. The saga of the Martínez family is really the story of all of El Salvador's rural poor and the long trajectory of oppression to which they have been subjected throughout the centuries, beginning with the conquest of Cuzcatlán (the Nahuatl name for El Salvador) by the Spanish and the establishment of the indigo industry during the colonial period, followed by the rise of coffee and of a new land-owning elite whose power is protected by the National Guard. Lucía's bus ride and the daydreaming she engages in throughout its duration acts, therefore, as a site where the present context of civil conflict collides with El Salvador's indigenous and colonial pasts. By the same token, and like the women in *Un día*, Lucía comes to represent a changing *campesino* nation that draws strength from its feminized position and from the domestic space.

Two characters who are fundamental to the elaboration of this greater vision of the country and its *campesinos* are Lucía's great-grandfather, Emiliano, and his daughter, Beatriz or "la Ticha," Lucía's grandmother. One of Emiliano's earliest memories is when his father took him to see the ocean for the first time to witness "donde bate la Mar del Sur" [where the Southern Sea beats], as the title of the novel underscores. As the narrative voice explains, during this visit, Emiliano is cognizant of the five hundred years of colonial struggle and exploitation he and his people have undergone since the arrival of the conquerors' ships and canons (Argueta, *Cuzcatlán* 43/34). The legacy of this victimization has manifested itself not only in Emiliano's impoverished living conditions and lack of access to the lands that once belonged to his people but also in the death of his wife, Catalina, who, according to Emiliano, fell victim to the indigo industry. Having worked as a child in the cultivation and processing of indigo, Catalina had been exposed to toxic fumes that eventually killed her shortly after she gave birth to Beatriz. It is telling that Catalina's death is related to this particular agricultural product, as it formed the basis of the trade economy established in El Salvador in the colonial period, which was sustained until the early twentieth century. However, more than a casualty of indigo, Catalina is a casualty of the process of colonization.

Despite the fact that Emiliano's life has been heavily conditioned by this process and state of marginality, he refuses to become a victim. He swears that neither he nor his daughter will ever work in the fields harvesting indigo or in the processing plants. They will not, as Emiliano tells Beatriz, be slaves to death or to anyone, and instead forge their own way cutting grass and making grindstones from *metate* (39/30). Emiliano's comprehension of his own oppression and the stance he takes against it derive not only from the experience of watching his wife die and being helpless to stop it but also from a deeper sense of knowing. As the narrator reveals, "[a]lguna vez habían sido sabios y poetas los hombres como Emiliano. Después fueron esclavos y siervos" [once men like Emiliano had been poets and sages. Then they became slaves and serfs] (39/31). Emiliano has inherited his wisdom from his ancestors. It is a type of knowledge or historical consciousness transmitted through blood, from generation to generation, and that allows the *campesino* population to survive their misfortunes (Argueta 39; Hansen 31).

Like her father, Beatriz possesses this same understanding of the past and its bearing on the present. Although she tries to follow the rules set forth by the priests who rarely come to visit them, Beatriz knows that there is another historical truth, one that predates the story of Adam and Eve. Beatriz intuits the story of creation recounted in the Mayan *Popol Vuh*. The myth, which is retold in the narrative, details how the god Gucumatz successfully created men from maize after two failed attempts to forge beings from mud and wood. The men of maize were unique in that they had possessed understanding, loved and cried, and lived happily upon the earth (85/73). They also, however, had to endure wars and massacres, hunger and thirst, and as the narrative voice suggests, were able to do so because of their "corazón y entendimiento" [hearts and understanding] (86/73). What Beatriz understands as the Mayan myth of creation is, in fact, the story of El Salvador's *campesinos,* the men of maize who continue to subsist despite the odds and whose social status was not always that of slaves or servants to others.

Inasmuch as Emiliano's and Beatriz's experiences recall El Salvador's process of colonization, they also underscore the equally important indigenous wisdom and spirit of defiance that characterize the rural population. The highlighting of these latter aspects provides another means of understanding the process of *conscientizacion* undertaken by *campesinos* that is discussed in great length in *Un día*. In addition to the influence of labor rights movements, Christian organizations, and the FMLN, *Cuzcatlán* clearly suggests that the politicization of the rural sector is also derived from this community's inherent sense of rebellion and survival given their constitution as "men of maize." By the same token, and given the broader examination of El Salvador's colonial history, the novel's emphasis on indigeneity and resistance also reveals the struggle of the "men of maize" in the current context of the civil war as a significant turning point in their condition as peripheral subjects. The participation and visibility of the *campesinos* in the conflict marks the beginning of another process, that of decolonization. What is all the more telling, however, is who is at the forefront of this process in the novel.

As Frantz Fanon argues in his influential work, *The Wretched of the Earth*, decolonization leads to the "veritable creation of new men" and the need to completely call into question the colonial situation (36–37). It is a process meant to ensure that the "last shall be first and the first last," an inversion of the dominant order that needs to be achieved by whatever means necessary, including the use of violence (Fanon 37). Emiliano's and Beatriz's experiences and the historical consciousness and indigenous wisdom they possesses certainly contest the colonial condition the rural community has been forced to bear through the ages. Yet, in the novel, neither his generation nor his daughter's nor even that of his grandson, Pedro Martínez, is necessarily cast as the "new men" to whom Fanon refers. That is a role not held by men at all, but rather women such as Lucía. She is the "new woman" or, more to the point, the "new woman of maize" born out of the process of decolonization, whose militancy as a *guerrillera* is testament of her resolve to transform El Salvador's stratified social order at all cost, even if that means using arms and engaging in war.

That Lucía is positioned as a leading figure in this new struggle for *campesino* legitimization and freedom is not surprising, as she represents a synthesis of both the belief system of the older generation of *campesinos* and the more progressive views of the newer generations that have come into contact with popular and armed movements. Like the older members of her family, Lucía is cognizant of what it means to be a *campesina*, to be a part of a larger history of colonization, but also resistance:

> Ser *campesina* en Cuzcatlán significa que mis padres, mis abuelos y bisabuelos, fueron *campesino*s. Sus tatarabuelos fueron Señores de estas tierras, las cultivaron y repartieron el producto por igual entre todos. Después, los Señores se convirtieron en esclavos y se fueron difuminando sus características de quienes habían sido formados para la poesía y el combate. (Argueta, *Cuzcatlán* 141)

> Being a peasant girl, a *campesina*, in Cuzcatlán means that my parents, grandparents, and great-grandparents were peasants. Their great-grandparents were Masters of the Earth, they cultivated it and distributed its fruits equally amongst

everyone. Later the Masters became slaves and the talents they
had developed for poetry and combat were suppressed. (123)

She understands that she comes from a long line of workers but also
belongs to a civilization of people who were not always slaves and who
were characterized by their poetry and combativeness. Lucía's involvement
in the popular and armed struggle has only added to this historical
consciousness, allowing her to achieve another degree of politicization and
to take a more definitive stance against the oppression of her community.
As Lucía states, "[s]i no me hubiera organizado ya estuviera muerta entre
miles de gente. . . . Yo no me incluyo entre los inocentes. Trato de
resistir y por eso uso seudónimo" [if I hadn't been organized, I would
have wound up dead like thousands of other people. . . . I don't include
myself among the innocent. I try and fight back, so that's why I use
an assumed name] (14/8). Tellingly, Lucía draws a distinction between
those who have been innocent victims and who have been unable to
fight back, like Emiliano, Beatriz, and the majority of the *campesino*
population, and herself, who has chosen a different path.

Lucía's narrative centrality and ideological positioning as a leader of
her community's resistance reveal her to be more than just a spokesperson
for the rural population. She is its allegorical referent, representing a
campesino nation that has become more politicized with the years and,
broadly speaking, has initiated a new process of decolonization. Lucía's
function as an allegory is further underscored by the direct correlation
made in the text between *campesinas* and Cuzcatlán. Following a
description of Lucía and her sister Antonia that is heavily laden with
metaphorical references to nature, the narrative voice surmises: "Todas
las cipotas son iguales entre sí. Todas las cipotas de Cuzcatlán tienen los
rasgos de su antigüedad poética, sabia y llena de riquezas" [All girls are
equal among themselves. All the girls of Cuzcatlán carry traces of their
ancient poetic lineage, wise and overflowing with wealth] (169/148). It
then goes on to explain the significance of the word Cuzcatlán, a word
that connotes the richness of the land, followed by the reasons why the
conquerors later changed the country's name to El Salvador. Although
Lucía and other *campesinas,* as a part of Cuzcatlán's people of maize,
share an indelible connection to the earth on which that they subsist
and toil, this representation of all *campesinas* stresses a specific type of
gendered association. In keeping with the traditional symbolization of
"woman as nation" or land, *campesinas* embody Cuzcatlán. They represent
a Cuzcatlán of the past, a pristine and rich land untouched by violent
conquest and exploitation, and a Cuzcatlán that is combative at its core.

Outside of her identity as a *guerrillera* and her ancestry, a main source of Lucía's strength to endure comes from her relationship with other women and from the space of the home. It is revealing, for example, that Lucía's *nom de guerre* is Beatriz, that of her grandmother, the most prominent matriarchal figure in the novel. The closeness the two women share does not come from having spent a lot of time together, for, as Lucía discloses, she has never had an intimate conversation with her grandmother because of the different paths their lives have taken. Yet, in spite of this, both women share the common experience of having to bear the misfortune of their impoverished condition and having lost loved ones. Beatriz recognizes this when she asks Lucía, during the only and final conversation the women have prior to Beatriz's death, if Lucía misses her partner, who was killed during a failed ambush by the National Guard. She is concerned that her granddaughter has been left to fend for herself and her two children alone—a reality she knows all too well, having had to do the same when her husband, Eusebio, left to go work in the mines and never returned. Lucía responds to her grandmother's inquiry by asking her about another recent loss they have both endured, that of her great-grandfather, Emiliano, killed during a confrontation between himself and Corporal Martínez.

Throughout the entire conversation, Beatriz has made continuous references to her heart, asking Lucía to feel the palpitations emanating from her chest that seem like "un montón de mariposas enjauladas" [a bunch of caged butterflies] (261). The butterflies trapped in her chest are a metaphor for the truth that Beatriz has had to bear, which is literally breaking her heart, the fact that the famed Corporal Martínez who has committed such grave atrocities against their rural community, including contributing to the death of her father, Emiliano, is none other than her son, Pedro. Yet heartache is not the only affliction from which Beatriz is suffering. During her final moments before her death, Beatriz confesses what she knows to Lucía and her only surviving son, Jacinto. She informs them that what also is killing her is the feeling of rage caused by her impotence, her inability to do anything in the face of these circumstances. Her last request is that her family let everyone know who Corporal Martínez is so as to give testimony of his actions. With her last breaths, then, Beatriz takes the only stance she can on behalf of herself and her family, that of speaking out against her own son, even if it means condemning him in the process.

This pivotal scene reveals the main factor that motivates Lucía to participate in her uncle's popular hearing, one she refers to in the novel's opening chapter when she states explicitly, "La muerte de mi abuela es la que me hace viajar este día. Debo atestiguar para que se castigue al culpable" [My grandmother's death is the reason why I am traveling today. I have to testify so that the person responsible will be punished] (10). It also draws attention to the agency *campesinas* wield as a group in the novel, and to the fact that it is they who carry the burden of defending their families and homes. It is notable, for instance, that upon hearing his mother's words concerning his brother Pedro, Jacinto's response is to remain silent, to try to forgive his brother and forget the past. Moreover, when a neighbor later informs him of the crimes Corporal Martínez has committed, Jacinto claims he does not know who he is despite the similarity in their last names. His daughter, Lucía, however, refuses to remain quiet and suffer from the same sense of impotence that killed her grandmother. Empowered by the knowledge her grandmother has given her on multiple levels, Lucía takes it upon herself to fulfill her grandmother's last wishes, beginning by telling her mother, Juana, what Beatriz has said.

Lucía is, thus, also depicted as a historical agent of change whose actions against the state's patriarchal power are strengthened by her traditional role as a wife, mother, daughter, and granddaughter; this is a result, in effect, of her association with her domestic and feminized position within Salvadoran society. She is the one charged with the task of procuring some form of justice for her family because the male members cannot. The *campesino* community Lucía epitomizes is also depicted in a similar light, occupying a marginalized position from which its members derive a sense of strength. This notion is most discernible in the novel's final scene, when Lucía comes face to face with Corporal Martínez. Although he is Lucía's uncle, Corporal Martínez is completely ignorant of this fact, having completely lost sight of who he once was prior to becoming a soldier. As a member of the National Guard and a lead signifier of El Salvador's oppressive oligarchic state, Corporal Martínez has been forced to erase any vestiges of his former self as "Pedro," a humble and impoverished *campesino*, brother to Jacinto Martínez, son to Beatriz and Eusebio Martínez, and grandson to Emiliano. In turn, he has adopted and internalized a new identity as a corporal, reborn in the barracks of San Salvador and indoctrinated to believe that all *campesinos*, including his family, are the spoils that must be eradicated from the country. He derives his sense of power from his weapon and from thinking himself a part of the "us" waging war against an unlawful and threatening "them."

Therefore, when Corporal Martínez is questioned by the first guerrilla commander regarding his crimes, those recounted in *Un día*, he refuses to admit that he belongs to the same community, claiming that he is not a *campesino* and that he is from San Salvador [279/249]. It is not until he sees Lucía or Commander Beatriz that he breaks down, for he does not see a young woman but a reminder of his mother and the past he has forgotten. As Lucía states, "Para él, yo seré su mamá, la que dejó al sur de la laguna de Apastepeque. Reparará que mis rasgos son semejantes a los de mi abuela. El cabo Martínez volverá a su niñez, retrocederá en el tiempo" [To him, I will be his mother, who left the south side of Apastepeque lagoon. He won't notice that my features merely resemble those of my grandmother. Corporal Martínez will go back to his childhood, he'll go back in time] (282/253). As the embodiment of Beatriz, Lucía is the only person capable of bringing Pedro Martínez back to himself and forcing him to confront the magnitude of the crimes he has committed against his own community. This is an action that is reminiscent of Adolfina's insistence on Corporal Martínez's identity as the son of "la Ticha" in order to save her life. Coming from his niece, his own blood, this return to his identity and roots has a greater effect. Although Lucía informs Corporal Martínez that she is his niece, Jacinto's daughter, he does not believe her and continues to refer to her as *mamá*. In this one moment, the maternal and the familial space of the home and, by extension, the rural community is shown to encompass a greater power than that of the state. It is the feminine and the feminized that rise up and take control, that have now become the dominant.

What is more, and as this final scene also suggests, it is the rural community that will determine the future of the struggle—a notion underscored by the decision Lucía takes and the sentence she gives her uncle. Rather than condemn Corporal Martínez for the crimes he has committed, Lucía chooses to absolve him. When asked by her fellow commander why she has done this, she simply replies that "al absolverlo lo hemos condenado" [by finding him not guilty we have condemned him] (284/255). According to Lucía, her uncle will suffer more having to live with the truth than if he were to be given a quick death. Although Lucía's decision has been influenced by the long history she has been contemplating all along on the bus ride to her final destination, in taking this particular stance she also conveys a deeper message. Lucía understands that despite waging war on opposite sides, all *campesinos* belong to the same community. As she expresses in her last statement—the final sentence of the entire novel—"siempre estaremos unidos en un compañerismo eterno" [we will always be bound by eternal friendship] (285/255). Instead of contributing to the further division of her community, and of the nation, Lucía chooses to foster unity, a unity that is inherent to the *campesino* way of life. Here, then, Argueta seems to deliver the same message as in *Un día* regarding the perseverance as well as the fundamental role of the *campesino* population as the future of not only the struggle but also of the nation. They are to be the embodiment of an alternative ideal of solidarity and nationhood.

Campesino Imaginings of Nationhood

By way of his testimonial novels, *Un día en la vida* and *Cuzcatlán: Donde bate la Mar del Sur*, Manlio Argueta engenders a compelling portrait of El Salvador's *campesino* population during one of the country's most tumultuous and decisive national periods. Rural women are a fundamental aspect of both of these narratives as well as of their thematic structures. By way of their oral accounts and experiences, they give voice to a long-standing history of rural oppression, dating back to the conquest and the colonial period, the current manifestation of which is the context of civil war. It is their struggle to defend their families and livelihoods against members of the state's military forces, in some cases their own family members, that constitutes the core of both texts. In positing women as active agents of social and political change and filtering the plight of the rural sector through the domestic space they inhabit, Argueta affords an alternate view of the conflict that is empowering both to women as well as to the *campesino* population they represent.

Although Argueta employs a fairly conventional understanding of women as allegories for the nation, his representation and construction of *campesina* subjectivity coupled with his use of testimonial elements allow for other possible reworkings of this construct and new ways of portraying and imagining women, as well as the feminine or feminized position of the other. This literary development is particularly significant because it is a direct response to a concrete development in the country's historical context—not only the rise of the popular struggle but also the fact that the war created a space for women to emerge as a viable and important force for change. It is precisely their roles as mothers and wives and their ties to their families that afford *campesinas* the necessary strength to take a stand against the state and undertake the process of decolonization and liberation. These traditional identities associated with the home are likewise the basis for their survival strategies and solidarity. Thus, rural women are represented as a feminine or feminized yet empowered force that is capable of transforming what the patriarchal state assumes to be an inferior position into one of agency. A marginalized and subordinate rural sector is likewise depicted as a new, politically viable power within the popular struggle.

Casting *campesinas* as allegories for the nation, however, also has wider-reaching ideological implications concerning women's national agency and alternative imaginings of Salvadoran nationhood. Argueta's novels show women to be agents not only of communal but also of national change. In the same way, the rural collectivity and majority that they represent is also posited as the base of a future liberated nation that is no longer marked by class hierarchies and that contests the exclusionary notions of the past. As I have hinted throughout this chapter, this alternate concept of *campesino* nationhood significantly contrasts that of the left's socialist ideal of and proposed project of revolutionary nation building. Although advocating the eradication of class hierarchies, the left's project remained plagued by its own limitations with regard to gender and its foundational understanding of a liberated Salvadoran society. It still held the middle-class intellectual and male revolutionary as the key to the future. By comparison to this model of revolutionary nationhood, Argueta's women-centered testimonial novels offer a more nuanced and contestatory vision.

Chapter 2

Making Militants and Mothers

Rethinking the Image of the *Guerrillera* in Women's Revolutionary Testimonios

In the years leading up to and during the Salvadoran civil war, a series of testimonios and hybrid texts that included testimonios as part of their larger narrative projects were authored by or written about female combatants in the left's revolutionary forces. Among these were Ana Guadalupe Martínez's *Las cárceles clandestinas de El Salvador: Libertad por el secuestro de un oligarca* (1996), originally published and circulated clandestinely in the 1970s; Claribel Alegría and Darwin Flakoll's *No me agarran viva: la mujer salvadoreña en la lucha* (1987); and Nidia Díaz's (pseudonym of María Marta Valladares) *Nunca estuve sola* (1988).[1] All of these texts center, almost exclusively, on the experiences of *guerrilleras* from urban and middle-class backgrounds. Martínez's testimonio recounts her capture, torture, and imprisonment in one of El Salvador's secret jails, where she was held for seven months in 1976. In addition to Martínez's narration of her own experiences, her testimonio includes the secondhand accounts of other *compañeros/as* [comrades] imprisoned with her. Díaz's testimonio similarly tells of her detainment in a National Guard prison following her capture in 1985 by a U.S. military advisor and is a composite of her testimony, poems, and drawings. Alegría and Flakoll's *No me agarran viva* differs slightly from these first two texts because it draws on a series of testimonios by different militants, history, photographs, and fiction in order to reconstruct the life of Ana María Castilla Rivas, an urban commander known as "Eugenia" who died in the line of fire.

The fact that these narratives are testimonios or incorporate some form thereof is fundamental to understanding how they engage with the social reality of these Salvadoran *guerrilleras*. As John Beverley and Mark Zimmerman have noted, testimonio was one of the most prevalent literary forms in El Salvador during the 1970s and 1980s. It did not necessarily take one specific form, but varied in expression and focus. Texts like Salvador Cayetano Carpio's *Secuestro y capucha en un país del "mundo libre"* (1979), Martínez's *Las cárceles clandestinas,* and Díaz's *Nunca estuve sola* followed a guerrilla model of testimonio inspired by the writings of Ernesto "Che" Guevara.[2] Such texts centered on the accounts of members of liberation parties, detailing their social activism and participation in warfare and, in some cases, their detainment, imprisonment, and torture by Salvadoran national forces. They constituted, on the one hand, "a form of propaganda for armed struggle directed toward a progressive general public," and, on the other, a "kind of cadre literature internal to the revolutionary organizations" (Beverley and Zimmerman 174). Other forms, less didactic and sectarian in scope and marked by a greater degree of literary experimentation, were also prevalent, especially during the 1980s. Manlio Argueta's testimonial novels, as well as Alegría and Flakoll's *No me agarran viva*, are exemplary of these later manifestations.

All of these texts played a significant role in the popular struggle and the left's revolutionary project. Their immediate goal was to communicate not only the experiences of the individual narrator (whether a militant, a peasant, or a union leader) but also, and more generally, the plight of an oppressed Salvadoran *pueblo* on whose behalf they were also speaking. Such articulations of urgency and resistance helped to promote and raise awareness about the left's revolutionary cause, thereby defining these texts as an "ideological practice of national liberation" (Beverley and Zimmerman, preface ix). In the case of the three aforementioned examples by Martínez, Díaz, and Alegría and Flakoll, they likewise underscored, to varying degrees, the gender-specific struggles faced by women. In *Las cárceles clandestinas,* for instance, Martínez relates several events, including her torture by prison guards. Although it is clear to the reader that her gender plays a key part in the way she is treated—the ideological and physical conflict is played out on her body—Martínez chooses not to explicitly underscore such a factor, giving primacy instead to her unwavering resolve to uphold the revolution's ideals at any cost and to not betray her *compañeros*. By contrast, in Alegría and Flakoll's *No me agarran viva*, it is women who are at the center. This is evidenced by the authors' intentions—to bring to light the heroism and participation of countless Salvadoran women who have given their lives for the revolutionary cause, like their subject, Eugenia—and the dedication of their book to the "miles de muchachas, mujeres y ancianas salvadoreñas que siguen de frente en la lucha, sin claudicar" [thousands of girls, women, and the elderly who are still at the front of the struggle, without giving up] (Alegría and Flakoll, *No me agarran,* prologue 7).

Understanding women's gender-based concerns and oppression to be a central component of these texts, I explore them in greater detail in this chapter. I do so, however, by focusing on a key representational aspect: the construction and depiction of the authors/subjects as *guerrilleras.* This portrayal, which speaks to the individual experiences and perceptions of the authors/subjects, works in tandem with a more popular and idealized image of the *guerrillera* as both revolutionary and mother. As I contend, it is by looking at this twofold representation that we can better understand the social reality experienced by women who participated in the Salvadoran civil war as armed militants and the lasting effects of such involvement. In this sense, this analysis of these women's revolutionary testimonios follows in line with my previous discussion of Argueta's testimonial novels in Chapter 1 in that it emphasizes the importance of looking at the representational capabilities of these texts as opposed to only focusing on the communicative qualities associated with testimonio.

Guerrilleras: The New Women?

Whether an auto-representation of the self or one fabricated by secondary authors, the *guerrillera* depicted in the testimonial narratives by Martínez, Díaz, and Alegría and Flakoll is an individual who is understood to be a courageous and loyal militant who embodies, to a certain extent, a male ideal, and a maternal figure who epitomizes the notion of abnegated motherhood, asking nothing for herself and willing to sacrifice everything for the revolutionary cause and her children. Such a portrayal was, in large part, a product of the broader Latin American revolutionary imaginary of the latter half of the twentieth century. Similar portrayals and symbolic interpretations of the *guerrillera* had been popularized in revolutionary Cuba in the 1950s and 1960s and in the armed movement waged by the Sandinistas in Nicaragua during the 1970s. Within Cuba's revolutionary iconography, female combatants were projected as "examples of the ultimate *compañeras*—women willing to die not only for their own *compañeros,* but for the *commandante en jefe* and the Revolution" (Stoner 91).[3] In Nicaragua, as Lorraine Bayard de Volo contends, women were mobilized by way of a discourse of motherhood that cast them as "Patriotic Wombs" and "Spartan Mothers" (24).

This imagining of the Salvadoran *guerrillera,* however, was also the result of a specific history of women's participation in the country's revolutionary process—a history in which Martínez, Díaz, and Eugenia were to be crucial players. Taking its cue from the successful endeavors of Cuban revolutionaries and those of Nicaragua's Sandinista National Liberation Front (FSLN), the left's militant forces in El Salvador opted to integrate women within their ranks. As such, women came to comprise a third of all militants in the FMLN, composed of the following five organizations: the Popular Forces of Liberation (FPL), the Popular Revolutionary Army (ERP), the National Resistance (RN), the Salvadoran Communist Party (PCS), and the Revolutionary Party of Central American Workers (PRTC).[4] The first women to join the armed resistance were those with an urban middle-class background, followed by women from the working sector and *campesinas*, who quickly became the majority. Many were already members of one of the five aforementioned militant organizations and had been active in Christian-based, university, labor, and peasant movements prior to taking up arms.

The inclusion of women into the FMLN, however, was anything but seamless. In keeping with Cynthia Enloe's observations about women's participation in war, the Salvadoran civil conflict was an "abnormal" circumstance, one that allowed for women's national participation as combatants (*Does Khaki Become You* 123). Women's active presence during the armed struggle was not only perceived as a short-term military strategy but also as an "anomalous" occurrence born out of necessity (Enloe, *Does Khaki Become You* 123). Not surprisingly, the roles assigned to women within the ranks of the FMLN were, for the most part, in keeping with traditional divisions of labor. Few women held positions of high command, whereas the rest were assigned domestic duties such as working in the camp kitchens, in sanitation, or in makeshift clinics. They were also employed as recruiters for other women to join the cause, acting as what Julie Shayne has termed "gendered revolutionary bridges" (43).

Double standards were similarly upheld with regard to women's sexuality. *Guerrilleras* were considered soldiers, as were their male counterparts, but unlike men, they had to be responsible for their bodies and their actions. Female promiscuity was frowned upon, as it "weakened" and threatened the morale of the troops. Pregnancy, by the same token, made women vulnerable and obsolete as soldiers. Should a pregnancy occur, it was women who, more often than not, were expected to assume the sole responsibility of providing or finding adequate care for their children (Vásquez et al. 149, 177).

Contradictions such as these between women's militancy and the gender practices maintained within the armed movement were further entrenched by the left's male-centered revolutionary rhetoric as well as that of liberation theology, a strong undercurrent of the left's ideologies, which emphasized the rights of the poor but did not challenge the traditional roles of women supported by Catholicism. All militants of the FMLN, regardless of gender, were expected to uphold the ideal of the "New Man," in keeping with the writings and conceptualization of the ideal revolutionary elaborated by Ernesto "Che" Guevara (Vásquez et al. 77). A hybrid of the militant fighter and the sensible priest, the "New Man" was dedicated to the struggle but, more importantly, to the people. He was willing to sacrifice himself for the common good of the nation. Despite having to follow this male standard of soldiering, women were still expected to remain women. That is, they had a fundamental obligation to be reproducers and partners to men. Like the nation-building projects of the nineteenth century, the left's revolutionary project of national liberation was premised on a heterosexist model of coupling that cast women as mothers of the liberated nation's "New Men" and, perhaps, not so "new" women. Within the movement, it was also generally assumed that after the triumph of the revolution and once life regained its sense of "normalcy," women would give up their guns and return to their former domestic lives and duties.

Viewed in relation to this complex portrait of women's revolutionary participation and the practical and ideological incongruities that accompanied it, the appeal and critical dimensions of the representation of the *guerrillera* afforded in the testimonial narratives by Martínez, Díaz, and Alegría and Flakoll become apparent. The *guerrillera*'s militancy is indicative of the revolutionary ideal and male-centered notion of soldiering upheld by the revolutionary movement, whereas her maternity is an expression of women's desired femininity and, ultimately, their symbolic role as reproducers of future citizens—in essence, a socialist reformulation of republican motherhood. The coalescing of these seemingly disparate attributes within the same figure gives way to an alternate view of women's national agency and subjectivity. Here, then, I argue that the dualistic image of the *guerrillera* evoked by Martínez, Díaz, and Eugenia not only signals the emergence of a new form of female revolutionary subjectivity but also functions as a strategic point of entry for comprehending the broader social and political implications and consequences of such a development. What, for instance, does the *guerrillera*'s role as an active player in armed insurgency tell us about gender equality and the notion of women's liberation within the revolutionary movement? In what ways did this expression of female public agency challenge or affirm the foundational principles of the left's project of liberation and, by extension, its socialist ideal of nationhood? Ultimately, did women's participation as female combatants and their portrayal as such affirm, contest, or transform existing expectations of gender roles and femininity?

This analysis consequently posits an understanding of these testimonial narratives as critical sites for exploring what was at stake for Salvadoran women who opted to step outside their domestic roles in order to wage war on the front lines. In keeping with Marilyn May Lombardi's critique of the testimonial scholarship produced in the last two decades, this analysis seeks to underscore the centrality of "actual women" and their struggles while also engaging the ideological and literary projects that likewise define these testimonial narratives.[5] I first explore how Martínez's, Díaz's, and Eugenia's representations as *guerrilleras* underscores Salvadoran women's revolutionary subjectivity before undertaking a more nuanced analysis of the *guerrillera*'s two most defining characteristics: her militancy and maternity. In my discussion of the *guerrillera* as a militant figure, I take special note of her identity as a soldier and, more to the point, her codification as masculine. In addition to bringing attention to a topic that has been largely overlooked in the few existing studies written on these testimonial narratives,[6] a focus on the *guerrillera*'s masculinity prompts a rethinking of female combatants not only as heroines but also as potential "threats" to the gendered hierarchies that characterized the revolutionary movement and, more generally, Salvadoran society. By the same token, it calls attention to the latent social anxieties provoked by women's growing agency during this period. My discussion of the *guerrillera*'s maternal nature stresses the notion of revolutionary maternity and heterosexist coupling advocated by the authors/subjects and within the movement itself. An examination of these elements—which offset the female militant's masculinity and are the basis of the *guerrillera*'s conceptualization as a praiseworthy mother figure—calls attention to the limitations of the left's project of national liberation with regard to women—the fact that in spite of their militancy, their main duty still consisted of reproducing "New Men."

Salvadoran Female Revolutionaries "Going Public"

Through their representations as *guerrilleras*, Martínez, Díaz, and Eugenia reveal the emergence of a female revolutionary subjectivity that had not existed in the same way before in El Salvador.[7] This subjectivity was as much an expression of the female combatant's political militancy and activism as it was her experiences and concerns as a woman, especially as a wife or partner, and as a mother on the front lines. Such a notion recalls Jean Franco's discussion about the relationship between women and testimonio, in which she posits that the testimonial genre "lends itself effectively to the story of conversion and *concientización* that occurs once women transgress the boundaries of domestic space" ("Going Public" 53). Many testimonial narratives by women, as Franco clarifies, "bear witness to the breaking of the taboo on 'going public' and their [women's] initial fears" ("Going Public" 53). The female revolutionary subjectivity constructed and depicted in the testimonial narratives by these authors/subjects is precisely a marker of the female combatant's process of "going public." It encompasses both the politicization of women as socialist revolutionaries and as individuals with a growing awareness of gender-based oppression—though the latter does not necessarily result in a radical expression of liberation.

Despite the fact that Martínez, Díaz, and Eugenia attempt to portray themselves or are depicted as one of many women involved in the struggle—as exemplified by Alegría and Flakoll's prologue, which describes Eugenia as an "everywoman" (7)—it is notable that the *guerrilleras* in these texts belong to a more specialized group that sets them apart from their *campesina* counterparts. Like other women from the same middle-class background, Martínez, Díaz, and Eugenia initiated their politicization early on, as student activists at university and as volunteers in Christian-based initiatives focused on aiding the rural poor. They were among the first women to join the armed struggle in the mid- to late 1970s, in the years prior to the official start of the civil war, and who worked and lived clandestinely in urban settings. They were, likewise, part of a limited subset of women who achieved high-ranking positions within their different revolutionary organizations as military strategists and leaders. Martínez and Díaz were both commanders of respective guerrilla organizations, the ERP and FMLN, whereas Eugenia was part of the FPL's Central Command.

Here, then, we are talking about a female revolutionary subjectivity premised primarily on a middle-class and urban sensibility, rather than one that is marked by growing up in *el campo*. This notion is most evident in Alegría and Flakoll's depiction of Eugenia's process of *concientización*, or as it is referred to in the narrative, her process of *proliterización* (coming to understand the concerns and struggles of the proletariat). In 1974, while still a university student, Eugenia begins to work organizing the rural sector alongside another comrade, Javier, who would eventually become her husband. As Javier recalls, it is this initial contact with *campesino* laborers that solidifies their political resolve:

> Los dos, a pesar de que era una relación muy incipiente,
> vimos en ese momento, sobre todo a raíz de nuestra primera

> reunión con los trabajadores del campo, como una opción revolucionaria para siempre. Lo entendimos como el inicio de nuestra reincorporación a la lucha armada de El Salvador, una opción que no tenía regreso. (Alegría and Flakoll, *No me agarran* 37)

> Despite the fact that our relationship was so recently formed, the two of us saw ourselves all of a sudden—and particularly after our first meeting with the agricultural workers—as having taken a permanent revolutionary option. We regarded it as our initiation into El Salvador's armed struggle, a choice that there was no way of denying. (58–59)

Although Eugenia is not certain that taking up arms is the only means possible of ensuring social change, she later becomes convinced of that fact, as Javier later discloses.

The testimonios by Martínez and Díaz include similar narratives of politicization, which are intermittently recounted throughout their texts. Martínez makes passing references to her years at university and as a medical student with aspirations of helping the rural poor, whereas Díaz relates her memories of being a student activist, working with Christian organizations and forging bonds with *compañeros* in both the rural sector and the city. The political awakening of these two women is also clearly connoted in the socialist ideologies that permeate their writing and motivate the publication of their accounts. The prologue to Martínez's *Las cárceles clandestinas* was written by René Cruz, the alias of Joaquin Villalobos, founder of the ERP. Cruz's prologue provides the ideological and political framework for understanding Martínez's testimony. As he states:

> El presente libro es un documento de inapreciable valor para la lucha revolucionaria y contiene experiencias en todos los aspectos de la lucha: la tortura, el funcionamiento de los cuerpos represivos, las contradicciones interburguesas, la lucha armada, la cárcel, etc.; transmitir esto y denunciar a la dictadura son sus objetivos fundamentales. (Martínez 21)

> This book is an invaluable document for the revolutionary struggle and contains experiences from all aspects of the struggle: torture, the workings of repressive structures, contradictions among the bourgeoisie, the armed struggle, prison, etc.; transmitting this and denouncing the dictatorship are its fundamental objectives.

Cruz follows this assertion by emphasizing that the text is written in a simple style, in the language of *el pueblo*, and is free of literary and intellectual pretensions. Martínez's own brief introduction reiterates many of the same points. Moreover, and in keeping with one of the general characteristics of testimonial discourse, she conceives of herself as a type of "spokesperson" for those who, like her, have undergone similar experiences but have not had the same opportunity to transmit their stories to their fellow revolutionaries and to the broader public.

Díaz's prologue to *Nunca estuve sola* echoes many of the same politically driven sentiments and claims while also drawing attention to other dimensions of the civil conflict, which was entering its eighth year at the time of the text's publication in 1988. The writing of her testimonio is motivated by the need not only to support the armed struggle and the fight for human rights, but also to denounce U.S. military and financial aid, which, as Díaz stresses, resulted in the death of thousands of *compatriotas* [compatriots] (5–6). In addition to condemning "Yankee" imperialism and its effects, the text is also meant to convey "la necesidad del diálogo como única salida verdadera al conflicto; la participación de la mujer en la lucha y la toma de decisiones; lo que hace y es capaz de hacer la solidaridad internacional" [the need for dialogue as the only real solution to the conflict; the participation of women in the struggle and in decision making; what international solidarity does and is capable of doing] (6). Notably, among this list of objectives is the need to provide an account of women's participation in the armed movement. Such a claim, which is lacking in Martínez's prologue, underscores Díaz's purposeful attempt to call attention to women's experiences, another crucial element of the female revolutionary subjectivity espoused in these texts.

Throughout her testimonio, Díaz pays homage to female *compañeras* who were killed in battle or prison and who played a decisive role in her formation as an armed militant. These intermittent segments are an important foundation for Díaz's broader narrative of women in combat and provide insight into her understanding of gender politics within the movement. When writing about these women, Díaz not only expresses her feelings of loss and love but also exalts the camaraderie and empathy she feels toward them. She provides poignant observations regarding the importance of these women and herself as role models and as visible markers of the female presence in El Salvador's revolutionary organizations. Even though Díaz speaks about male *compañeros* as well, she does not characterize her connection to them or identify with their experiences with the same level of intensity. Implicit in these commentaries, then, is a shared awareness of women's gender-based struggles as well as the deeper sense of solidarity spurred by that awareness.

In one segment, Díaz writes about her interactions with Ruth, a *guerrillera* who was part of the FPL's Central Command and who spent three days working in Díaz's revolutionary camp. Díaz's description of Ruth underscores the admiration she feels for Ruth "como revolucionaria, como amiga y como mujer" [as a revolutionary, as a friend, and as a woman] (175/155). Following a talk Díaz gave to a group of militants in training, Ruth approached her to congratulate her for having participated in a key meeting of the FMLN in La Palma, in which the majority of the attendees were male. As Díaz recounts, Ruth applauded Díaz's efforts and thanked her for representing women, for evidencing the degree to which women were participating in the struggle, and for being a voice for all of them (176/155). Díaz follows this recollection with the observation that "[u]na a veces no se da cuenta del significado de las cosas que hace" [there are times when we ourselves are not aware of the significance of our actions] (176/155). This statement betrays Díaz's lack of awareness at that precise moment about her potential as a role model and a representative for other women. By deliberately including this memory as part of her testimonio, however, Díaz reveals that that is no longer the case. She is embracing that role and using her testimonio as an avenue to speak on behalf of other *guerrilleras* in the FMLN who, like her, have dedicated their lives to the armed movement but have not achieved the same visibility.

Alegría and Flakoll's portrait of Eugenia takes this notion of an emergent revolutionary female consciousness one step further by specifically addressing the issue of gender equality and women's liberation. Throughout the narrative, strong emphasis is placed on Eugenia's views on gender and her development as an equal participant in the struggle. When Javier is asked to elaborate upon Eugenia's feelings about this issue, he explains:

> La liberación femenina nunca fue un problema para ella . . . Eugenia en sus relaciones como mujer con todo el mundo, en su desarrollo revolucionario, en su relación conmigo, siempre combatió todos los rasgos machistas que encontraba en compañeros e incluso en compañeras. Eugenia sostenía que era por medio de la incorporación a la lucha revolucionaria de nuestro pueblo, que la mujer iba a liberarse, adquiriendo su verdadera y justa dimensión. (Alegría and Flakoll, *No me agarran* 75)

The women's liberation movement was never a problem for her. In her relations—as a woman—with the outside world, in her revolutionary development, in her relationship with me, Eugenia always fought all traces of the *machismo* she had come across in her comrades, including the women. Eugenia maintained that it was through involving our people in the revolutionary struggle that women would liberate themselves, obtaining their true and fair place. (87)

Women's liberation, according to Javier, was never a concern for Eugenia because she was always adept at fighting sexism in her everyday relationships and insisted on equality. The problem of sexism is posited as an issue to be dealt with at the individual level rather than an institutional one. Moreover, given Eugenia's understanding of the revolutionary movement and its aims as all encompassing, she maintains that it is only by fighting against the oppression of all Salvadoran people that women will come into their own.

The topic of women in combat and the gender-specific difficulties such as participation are explored further in the secondary testimonies provided by other *guerrilleras* in the text. Although many of the women interviewed by Alegría and Flakoll admitted that sexism did exist, they made a point of stressing that they had not been personally affected by it. In fact, they had been able to overcome it, even while working with *campesinos*, the segment of the population who had been most resistant to female leaders, according to the women. When asked to specifically address the issue of women's oppression and liberation, Mercedes del Carmen Letona, a member of the ERP, answered:

> En el marco de la represión, que ya después del triunfo no existirá, la mujer tendrá posibilidades de comenzar a reivindicar su propia participación, porque antes de una participación la mujer tiene que luchar por la liberación de su pueblo. Después cuando hayan sido rotas esas cadenas, la mujer tiene posibilidad de aspirar a su propia reivindicación. (85)

> Once victory has been gained, the question of oppression will no longer arise. Women will possess the opportunity to assert their claim to full participation, but until that day women have to struggle for the liberation of their people. Later, when they've broken these chains, women will have the opportunity to stake their own claims. (95)

Del Carmen Letona's statement echoes a similar sentiment to Eugenia's, that only through the revolution will women achieve liberation, and only after it triumphs can women begin to seek their own form of vindication and collective action. The notion of gender equality and women's liberation elaborated by both of these women is one limited by the armed movement's prioritization of class-based struggle and the implicit assumption that "feminism and socialism are opposed to each other" (New American Press 87). Indeed, the idea of developing a feminist agenda and integrating it into the movement from its initial stages is not a possibility either woman can or even feels the need to entertain.

Similar conclusions can be drawn from Díaz's text, because her portrayal and that of other *guerrilleras*, in solidarity with *el pueblo*, are just as heavily circumscribed by a narrowly focused rhetoric of class-based liberation. Martínez's text, which of the three testimonial narratives analyzed here is the least clear about espousing a women-centered view of the struggle, follows suit. References to the specific difficulties women experience are few and far between in Martínez's testimonio, as they are not meant to detract from the text's political dogma and collective notion of resistance. For this reason, they tend to stand out, as does Martínez's harrowing account of her rape and the crippling anxiety she feels at the thought of having become pregnant: "Sólo pensarlo me provocaba una desesperación indescriptible" [just thinking about it provoked in me an indescribable desperation] (119). In this account, Martínez showcases her precarious position as a prisoner of war and a woman subject to the destructive power of the National Guards. In line with Vicky Román-Lagunas's analysis of Martínez's testimonio, such revelations can be interpreted as indicative of a "broader notion of Latin American feminism," which does not primarily focus on the victimization of women (as does its First World counterpart), but on the predicament of "all exploited individuals—both male and female—who have been oppressed by a system characterized by both social imperialism and patriarchy" (114). Even so, this feminist attitude or consciousness remains subject to Martínez's revolutionary indoctrination—a fact that is all the more apparent in her observations about women's participation in the movement. As Martínez claims, within her organization it is common for women to engage in armed activities in the same way men do (129). Like Eugenia, Martínez does not allow for any accountability at the institutional level with regard to sexism because for her, women are, for the most part, equal participants in the struggle and are treated as such.

The gender consciousness that is brought to bear in all of these testimonial narratives is one plagued by a series of problematic assumptions and a narrow view of women's oppression. These shortcomings do not overshadow, however, the fact that in these texts women manifest a certain understanding of their gendered positions within the movement and are, in essence, initiating an important dialogue about gender equality and women's liberation. It is this aspect, and not just the visible politicization of women as militants, that makes the expression of female subjectivity and agency in these texts a novel and "revolutionary" occurrence. This was an occurrence that did not go unperceived and that at the time had important implications for the revolutionary movement. It also had, and continues to have, key implications for women and their changing roles in Salvadoran society, as the following section details.

Women with Guns

One of the best-known cultural studies on Central American guerrilla narratives and women's representation is Ileana Rodríguez's *Women, Guerrillas, and Love* (1996). A central focus of Rodríguez's analysis is the peripheral position women occupied by contrast to that of the male militants within the movements, a premise she mostly explores in the diaries and political essays of male combatants, specifically Guevara and Mario Payeras.[8] According to Rodríguez, this power differential is transmitted and inscribed in the very language of revolutionary ideology because "[t]he narrative of the revolution is a narrative of the construction of self first as *guerrillero*, and then as vanguard, party, leader, and government. All those subject positions could then be formulated in a masculine I, aiming at narrating a collective subject that does not include women" (Rodríguez, introduction xvii). Because of this predetermined formulation, women remain marginal even in revolutionary texts that attempt to posit them as equal participants in the struggle, like that of Alegría and Flakoll's *No me agarran viva*. The discourse of gender equality espoused in these texts, for instance, is one that forces women to equate themselves with men and, in essence, become "men," thereby devaluing their identities as women and their specific contributions (158). This form of incorporation into the struggle does little to challenge the patriarchal order that supports male superiority and, as Rodríguez suggests, disregards the *guerrillera*'s "femaleness" (158).

Rodríguez's observations are imperative to any exploration of male and female revolutionary subjectivity and the mutually constructive relationship between the two. Yet her insistence on the *guerrillera*'s femaleness leaves something to be desired, as this focus elides the critical potential of the *guerrillera*'s masculinity and the notion that women can still have agency even when inserted as "men" into a male field of action such as armed warfare (158).[9] Judith Halberstam's provocative book *Female Masculinity* speaks precisely to this overlooked subtext and its analytical possibilities. As Halberstam maintains, female masculinity, like other minority masculinities such as those of men of color, provides an informative means of contemplating the links between power, hegemonic masculinities, and patriarchy (2). Furthermore, it is a "fruitful site" for examining the gendered divisions and taxonomies such associations foster and maintain (9). Following Halberstam's theories, the *guerrillera*'s masculinity underscores male dominance within the revolutionary movement and the heteronormative-gendered binaries on which it was premised. In so doing, it also highlights the ways in which the *guerrillera* not only "threatened" the masculine power of the National Guard and the revolutionary movement but also undermined normative conceptions of femininity. It allows for an understanding of the *guerrillera*'s masculinity in its own right and as an element that may not necessarily eradicate gender hierarchies and, in some instances, even reinforces them, but can also destabilize them, as Halberstam claims (29).

As previously noted, the notion of militancy fostered by the FMLN was heavily dictated by a socialist dogma of class-based struggle and modeled in the image of Guevara's "New Man." Hence, like other military organizations, the FMLN was an institution that reproduced gender norms by stressing the important connection between soldiering and men, maleness and masculinity despite its integration of women (Herbert 10). Being forged in the image of the "New Man," which included being armed at all times and, in some cases, fighting in combat, fierce loyalty, and a willingness to die for *la patria* [homeland], coded female militants, to a certain extent, as masculine. Although this codification of women by way of their soldiering tended to reinforce stereotypes of masculinity and reaffirm heteronormativity, it was also capable of simultaneously subverting those same social constructions. In the testimonial narratives by Martínez, Díaz, and Alegría and Flakoll, this double function of the *guerrillera*'s masculinity is evidenced most clearly by the depiction of the authors/subjects as "women with guns," soldiers with a mastery of weapons and unwavering valor, even in the face of extreme adversity such as imprisonment, torture, and certain death. Although the abilities to successfully wield a weapon and be courageous would seem to be obvious characteristics of an ideal soldier, it is necessary to emphasize them here, for they were instrumental in marking hierarchies of power among female combatants. As the study by Vásquez et al. suggests, even though all *guerrilleras* were obligated to carry guns, those who fought in combat were valued far above those who were radio workers and all the more over those assigned to domestic duties (115). Those who were adept with their weapons and had proven their valor on the battlefield were considered not only more revolutionary but also more like their male peers.

Martínez's testimonio opens with an account of her capture by the government's secret police on July 5, 1976. This moment is etched in her mind because at the time of her arrest she was unarmed and felt "impotent" because she was unable to defend herself (27). Her specific use of masculine terminology to describe her disadvantaged state and, later, to refer to herself—she declares to one of her captors that to be a *guerrillera* takes real *huevos* or "balls" (29)—illustrates Martínez's identification with and, by the same token, affirmation of the male-centered ideal of soldiering upheld by the FMLN and, similarly, by the National Guard. It is not surprising that it is the lack of a weapon that most bothers Martínez, for it is one of the key signifiers of her identity as a revolutionary or "New Man" fighting for the people's liberation (Vásquez et al. 92). It also symbolizes the phallic power she wields as a *guerrillera*. Without it, she feels herself to be not only an inferior adversary to the state's military forces but also an ordinary woman subject to the sexual abuse and will of the armed men who have taken her captive. Therefore, when during one of her initial interrogations Martínez sees an opportunity to steal the weapon of one of her interrogators, a guard known as Castillo, she does not hesitate.

The incident is narrated in great detail by Martínez, who begins by specifying what kind of weapon Castillo carried—a Walter 380— and noting that Castillo had previously taunted her about having the same gun she used to carry. Although Martínez manages to slip Castillo's weapon out of the holster around his waist, she fails to kill him because the gun's chamber is empty and she is unable to reload it before Castillo realizes what is happening and wrestles the gun away from her (104). This power play between Martínez and Castillo in the interrogation room and its outcome are highly gendered exchanges that reveal more than just Martínez's tenacity as a political prisoner. They highlight the *guerrillera*'s multiply subversive positionality. Martínez's armed militancy and affiliation with the left's revolutionary forces define her as a threat to the National Guard and the Salvadoran state it represents and protects. Her soldiering as a *guerrillera* also posits her as a menace to the patriarchal symbolic order that permeates all aspects of Salvadoran society and renders men the privileged sex. The struggle between Martínez and Castillo for possession of his weapon (the same gun Martínez also had as a *guerrillera*) is really a struggle for the phallic power afforded to men within that patriarchal symbolic order. The fact that Martínez momentarily gains access to Castillo's gun and that she also holds a certain degree of phallic power disrupts the presumed relationship between men, masculinity, and supremacy. With her acts of defiance and transgression, Martínez reveals such associations to be mere social constructions, the products of patriarchal discourse.

Castillo's punishment of Martínez is equally telling, as it speaks to the anxieties provoked in him by Martínez's female masculinity and agency. After regaining possession of his gun and thus control over the phallus, Castillo orders two of his agents to take Martínez back to her cell. Once there, Martínez is chastised by another group of guards for having taken Castillo's weapon away from him and for attempting to kill him (104). She is forced to undress, handcuffed, and made to feel helpless. Forcing Martínez to strip and remove all vestiges of her public persona as a *guerrillera* and even as a civilian makes her subordinate, once again, to male and military control. In its naked and bound state, her body becomes a visible marker of her female sex, serving to restore the general perceptions of masculinity upheld by the National Guard (including that of Castillo's manhood and authority), which Martínez's presence and actions unsettled. Castillo's need to debase Martínez in this way is symptomatic of his fear, and that of the other guards, of the *guerrillera*'s ability to co-opt phallic power and, in essence, displace men.

Martínez's account underscores a similar angst among men within the revolutionary movement, though its expression is not as extreme. Among the prisoners being held with Martínez is Valle, a former militant who deserted the ERP and whom Martínez holds in low regard for having collaborated with the National Guard in her capture. Within the fraternal revolutionary order to which Martínez belongs, the gravest offense a guerrilla can commit is that of giving up information to the enemy. Doing so not only constitutes a grave tactical error, but also shows that the enemy has defeated you both physically and mentally (117). Not giving in, even in moments of extreme duress such as torture, is intrinsically linked to one's (masculine) strength, for a traitor is also a weak individual who lacks the power of his convictions and courage. This association is readily seen in Martínez's description of Valle, whom she describes as an uncommitted adventurer "[que] había caído en todas las tretas y trampas puestas por el enemigo para obtener información, aprovechándose de las debilidades, de los conflictos políticos y personales de los militantes y ex militantes" [who had fallen for all of the enemy's tricks and traps for obtaining information, taking advantage of all of the weaknesses, the political and personal conflicts of the militants and ex-militants] (130). Valle's behavior is contrasted with that of Martínez, who refuses to provide the enemy with information despite being tortured repeatedly with an electric probe and raped. She appears, then, as the more capable revolutionary and, by extension, the better man. According to Martínez, this, along with her high-ranking position within the same organization, is the source of Valle's resentment toward her (129). Although Valle is the only example of this kind in Martínez's narrative, his presence in the text and her awareness of the resentment of other male combatants toward women are suggestive of the latent anxieties women's masculine power provoked within the movement as well.

Díaz and Eugenia are also portrayed as women who are skilled combatants, yet it is their courage and heroism that most underscore their militancy/masculinity. Unlike Martínez, Díaz was wounded during combat prior to being taken hostage. Having sustained burns and multiple gunshot wounds to her back, right arm, and left leg, Díaz was taken prisoner by a "Yanqui," a U.S. military advisor (Díaz 15/19–20). Díaz's capture is a difficult reality for her to face not only because of the pain but also because of the anger she feels at having been captured by a "symbol" of Reagan's oppressive administration (16/20). She chastises herself for not being able to remain conscious while being transported by helicopter to the Air Force base and impresses upon herself the need for courage: " 'Nidia, no debes volver a desmayarte; estas en las garras de ellos . . . debes hacer un esfuerzo por sobreponerte. Ahora debes asumir con valentía, como debe ser, la lucha más grande de tu vida' " ['Nidia, I told myself, you mustn't faint again! You are in their power. . . . You must make an effort to overcome. Now is the moment to fill yourself with courage and prepare to wage the greatest struggle of your life'] (17/21–22). This notion of valor is one that Díaz will sustain throughout her narrative, most notably in the first days of her imprisonment, during which time she was denied any medical treatment for her wounds.

In an attempt to resist both the pain and the continued verbal assault by her interrogators, Díaz seeks strength and comfort by singing a popular song that likens the *guerrillero* to a bull caught in the midst of a storm and ends in the following manner:

> Me hirieron,
> me mataron,
> me capturaron,
> y hasta la muerte me dieron.
> Pero nunca me doblegaron . . . (42).

> They wounded me,
> they killed me,
> they captured me,
> and even gave me death.
> But they never broke me . . . (40).

Inasmuch as these verses evoke Díaz's predicament, they also stress the most important element of being a prisoner of war, that of never giving in or yielding to the enemy. As in Martínez's testimonio, a strong distinction is made between the courage of the "true" revolutionary and the coward who submits to the enemy's power—a notion that is also brought to bear when Díaz learns that one of her *compañeros*, Miguel Castellanos, has betrayed their cause. Díaz's response to this information, which the guards purposefully make her witness on the television, is one of extreme rage. Not only does she express the desire to kick Miguel in the groin but also informs the guards that she will kill Miguel if they bring him to see her (72/65). According to Díaz, Miguel is a "cobarde" [coward] and a "gusano" [worm], an individual even worse than the guards (73/65). Once again, a strong correlation is made between revolutionary courage and masculinity. It is telling that Díaz wants to injure Miguel by kicking him in the testicles, thereby emphasizing his lack of manhood while asserting her own. It is she, the woman, who does not succumb to the enemy, who embodies the notion of the true revolutionary, and who, by contrast with Miguel, is the better man.

Even the guards, who are her oppressors, are privy to this fact. Following a visit to Díaz by the International Red Cross, the military is pressured to provide her with a medical exam to determine the extent of her injuries, particularly the nerve and muscle damage to her wounded arm. The exam, conducted by way of needle electrodes and extremely painful, is held in front of various members of the National Guard and secret police. As has been the case throughout most of her imprisonment, Díaz is determined not to give her spectators the satisfaction of knowing that she is in pain, stating that "mi orgullo es mayor que el dolor y no doy muestras de ello" [my pride was stronger than the pain—I did not flinch] (119/108). Upon witnessing Díaz's unwavering resolve, one of the guards tells her, "Vos si tenés huevos, Nidia" [You really do have balls, Nidia] (119). In acknowledging that Díaz has "balls," the guard conveys a certain sense of admiration for her. She is no longer just a *guerrillera*, but rather a woman who has reached the status of a male revolutionary.

This exaltation of the *guerrillera*'s masculine valor reaches its apex in Alegría and Flakoll's rendering of Eugenia's death in *No me agarran viva*. Notably, this is the only part of the text that is told by way of a fictional account—what the authors imagine must have been Eugenia's last moments. While on a clandestine mission to transport weapons, Eugenia and two other *compañeros* are ambushed by vigilante groups working in league with government forces. Rather than surrender, Eugenia heroically calls out, "¡Que no nos agarren vivos!" [They won't take us alive!] (Alegría and Flakoll, *No me agarran* 16/40). Eugenia had maintained her resolve not to be taken alive throughout her militancy, according to the testimony of a fellow guerrilla commander,

Ricardo. Whenever he would stress to Eugenia that as a revolutionary one could not determine the circumstances of one's death, she would always answer: "No me importan las condiciones, a mi no me agarran viva" [Circumstances don't matter to me. They won't take me alive] (148/144). This was the credo by which Eugenia lived and obviously died, and the inspiration for the text's title.

More than an a portrait of a fearless *guerrillera*, this depiction of Eugenia's heroic death marks her as the revolutionary *par excellence*, an embodiment and affirmation of the "New Man" that, perhaps, even supersedes that of Martínez and Díaz. One of the more salient characteristics of the "New Man" as envisioned by Guevara is his willingness to sacrifice himself for a just cause, thus purging himself of his "bourgeois egotism, arrogance, and ambition in order to become the humble, loving new [man] who will have the moral authority to build a new world" (Treacy 85). This understanding of the "New Man" is reminiscent of the discourse of "popular martyrology" promoted by liberation theology, for in becoming an example for others to follow and in giving up his life for the common good, the *guerrillero* personifies a Christ-like ideal that elevates him to the status of a public or political saint (Peterson 100). Alegría and Flakoll's depiction of Eugenia's life— her transformation from middle-class woman to exemplary militant— and death closely adheres to this model of revolutionary service and martyrdom. What is more, her dying for the cause is seen as the pinnacle of her militancy, a fitting end to what was a fulfilling life. As Ricardo surmises: "Eugenia's muerte no es sino coronar con heroísmo una vida profundamente entregada, sin ninguna reserva" [Death merely bestows the crown of heroism upon her profoundly committed life, without reservations] (Alegría and Flakoll, *No me agarran* 147/145). Eugenia, then, is shown to epitomize the "New Man," her heroic death codifying her all the more as male.

Díaz and Eugenia's female masculinity gives way to similar tensions with regard to women's agency and its threat to male power, both in and outside the revolutionary movement. In Díaz's testimonio, the government's military forces respond to her militancy in the same ways they did to Martínez, by imposing their authority through verbal and physical abuse and by rendering Díaz's wounded body the focus of their need to reaffirm the established gender hierarchies her phallic power calls into question. In Díaz's case, the affirmation of this male dominance is further fueled by her public imprisonment and by her reputation as one of the FMLN's leading military strategists. The threat of Eugenia's masculinity is not as readily discernible in Alegría and Flakoll's text, yet it is clearly a factor in the sexism she observes and experiences during her process of politicization in the movement. This glimpse into the generalized male anxieties and patriarchy that permeate Salvadoran society, however, is not the only critical view of the struggle that can be ascertained through an exploration of the *guerrillera*'s masculinity in these texts. This expression of female masculinity also brings into contention the traditional and middle-class sensibilities concerning femininity and sexuality that the authors/subjects subscribe to and uphold despite their actions on the battlefield.

It is telling that none of the authors/subjects discusses or even entertains the potential ramifications of her codification as a soldier and her phallic power outside the context of the revolution, even as she is shown to exemplify both as a *guerrillera*. In fact, they all take great care to not seem overtly masculine, mainly by underscoring their traditionally feminine positions as wives and mothers. This dynamic speaks to the potential risk female combatants run of being perceived as sexually aberrant if they cross the boundaries of what is clearly perceived as feminine or masculine. Women's militancy and, to a certain extent, their masculinity as soldiers are tolerated as long as they retain some semblance of traditional femininity—in essence, as long as they remain "real women." To not do so, as Melissa S. Herbert observes in her study of women in military organizations, would constitute a true deviation from the norm, resulting in the censorship of women "in the form of having their sexual orientation questioned" (19).

The notable silence with regard to female masculinity and other forms of queer identification within the testimonial narratives by Martínez, Díaz, and Alegría and Flakoll is indicative of the author's/subject's fear of being perceived not as capable soldiers but as "mannish"; even worse, still, of being perceived as lesbian, as homosexuality was considered one of the biggest taboos, and not readily accepted, within the revolutionary movement (Vásquez et al. 189). Indeed, the only explicit reference to homosexuality that appears in all three of these testimonial narratives is in Díaz's testimonio when she makes a passing comment about the placement of homosexuals in the cells of male prisoners (Díaz 141). Díaz stresses the fact that some of these individuals are dressed as women—as if noting the horrifying nature of this practice—and registers this action by the National Guard as another form of torture that she feels she needs to denounce, as it denigrates and leads to the psychological torment of the detainees (144). Her observations in this regard betray the homophobia rampant within Salvadoran society as well as her own narrow views and "fears" with regard to sexualities that threaten the gendered order and heteronormative standards sanctioned within the revolutionary movement and in keeping with her middle-class and Christian upbringing.

Revolutionary Maternity or Republican Motherhood Redux

The *guerrillera*'s maternal attributes and her portrayal as a mother figure are as revealing as her representation as a militant who embodies a masculine ideal of soldiering. This other side of the *guerrillera*'s dichotomous image can serve to further highlight many of the same social anxieties spurred by the militancy/masculinity exhibited by female combatants, especially those of the authors/subjects with regard to sexuality and female desire. As Mary Jane Treacy argues in her analysis of *No me agarran viva*, the depiction of the *guerrillera* as both mother and wife serves a specific ideological function within the text, that of offsetting the *guerrillera*'s masculine attributes as a soldier and bringing her "back into the feminine domain where she is less likely to challenge conservative notions about women's nature or to disturb the reader as an example of the monstrous woman warrior" (83–84). Insisting on the *guerrillera*'s maternal attributes neutralizes not only her masculinity but also her understanding as a sexual being, for inasmuch as she is able to procreate and nurture, she lacks the ability to express individual sexual desire.

Treacy's argument does not only ring true for Alegría and Flakoll's text but also for many of the literary and popular representations of the *guerrillera* that emerged during the span of the war.[10] Take, for instance, the following verses from a tribute poem titled "Compa Guerrillera" written by a male combatant fighting on the front lines:

> Muchacha guerrillera de mi pueblo.
> estás aquí, allá, en todo lugar,
> en la cocina, en la clínica,
> en las montañas, en las compañías.
> Aquí y allá eres madre,
> Portadora de alegrías,
> Confianza y valentía
> (Alegría and Flakoll, "On the Front Line" 42)

> Guerrilla girl of my people.
> you're here, there, everywhere,
> in the kitchen, in the clinic,

> in the mountains, in the companies.
> Here and there you're mother,
> bearer of happiness,
> confidence and valor (43)

In these lines, the *guerrillera*'s service in the mountains and as part of the revolutionary troops is duly noted. However, it is her domesticity and ability to mother all those in need that are truly praiseworthy, thus far outweighing and overshadowing her masculine capabilities. She also remains an asexual and abnegated being whose primary role is to serve others.

This same evocation of the female combatant as a universal mother figure is discernible in the testimonial narratives by Martínez, Díaz, and Alegría and Flakoll. More than a means of offsetting the *guerrillera*'s masculinity, however, the emphasis on the female combatant's maternal nature in these texts serves to underscore the limitations of the left's project of national liberation with regard to women. Within these texts there is little discussion of female sexuality that is not related to motherhood or marked by a specific revolutionary ethic. Even Díaz's recollections of her fallen partner, which are among the most open with regard to physical desire and love, succumb to this tendency. Díaz characterizes her relationship with her partner, another *guerrillero* and the father of her son, as a passionate affair, one without borders or limits (50). In the loneliness of her cell, she brazenly admits to being "plenamente mujer" [fully woman], longing for his touch and the feel of their bodies together (Díaz 51/48). Yet, in the midst of these emotions and memories, Díaz is careful to not lose sight of what is of most importance: upholding her revolutionary ideals. Combatants may fall in love and experience life-changing relationships, but they are also aware that other issues take priority, such as national liberation (51/48). Such politically motivated affirmations stress Díaz's resolve, while also helping to curtail any real expression of individual wants and sentiments.

Not all female desires, however, are meant to be censored or repressed. Wanting to be a mother and have a family are not only highly regarded by all three of these authors/subjects but also are posited as an experience all *guerrilleras* aspire to have. None of these testimonial narratives entertains the possibility of a revolutionary subjectivity that is not defined by a woman's reproductive capabilities or affords any examples of women who do not want to have children or get married. When Martínez wrote and published her testimonio, she was not yet a mother.[11] However, as Román-Lagunas highlights, Martínez does espouse a " 'feminine' way of raising children, one that stands in contrast to "the machista methods practiced by the jailers" (119). This assertion of maternal instincts is discernible in Martínez's observations regarding the adolescent boys, Califa and El Cancasque, who work for the National Guard and who have internalized their ways of treating prisoners. As Martínez observes, the submersion of these boys into the world of the secret jails and of the guards, a world in which they are treated without tenderness, kindness, or goodness, makes them calloused, replicas of their adult role models (Martínez 226).

Martínez discloses more explicit thoughts on the matter of motherhood in a telling interview that appears in Alegría and Flakoll's *No me agarran viva*. Her responses, as well as those of other *guerrilleras*, appear in a chapter of the text dedicated specifically to the topic of children. When asked whether or not she would like to have children, Martínez answers: "Yo creo que todas las mujeres aspiramos a tener hijos y bastantes" [I believe that all of us women want to have children, and plenty of them] (Alegría and Flakoll, *No me agarran* 105/109). Martínez stresses this seemingly universal truth by adding, "Todo el mundo, por lo menos las compañeras de dirección hemos discutido cuántos hijos queremos. Decimos que unos ocho. A lo mejor tener uno o dos, pero vamos a adoptar cinco por lo menos" [All of us, at least we women comrades within the leadership, have discussed how many children we want. Some of us said eight. At least to have one or two, but we'll go on to adopt at least another five] (105/109). Martínez's comments emphasize motherhood both via physical reproduction and through adoption, recalling the more generalized sense of "mothering" and servitude connoted by the poem "Compa Guerrillera." Women are meant to be mothers both to their biological children and to those disenfranchised by the nation. Moreover, her answers are indicative of the general sentiments held by all of the women who appear in the text, especially the main protagonist, Eugenia. As Javier reveals, one of his and Eugenia's greatest desires was to have a child, so much so that Eugenia became pregnant almost immediately after they got married (89/97).

By all accounts, motherhood is understood to be a norm, one that is necessary for all female combatants to reach their full potential as women. Among the other voices featured in Alegría and Flakoll's narrative is that of Mélida Anaya Montes, more commonly known as Commander "Ana María," one of the founders of the National Association of Salvadoran Educators (ANDES) as well as the second in command of the FPL. In her testimony, Montes draws attention to the fact that the revolutionary movement "pone todas las condiciones concretas y reales para que la mujer se desarrolle de acuerdo a sus capacidades y a su potencialidad" [provided all possible real and concrete conditions

for women to develop according to their capacities and potential]
(82/93). When Montes speaks of women's potential, she is referring
to more than just the *guerrillera*'s promise as a militant and her equal
treatment within the different revolutionary organizations. Her follow-up
statement, "No es contradictorio ser madre" [Being a mother doesn't
present contradictions], and the example she provides of how both men
and women must negotiate their domestic responsibilities, implies that
the revolutionary movement also facilitates the necessary conditions for
women to reach their full capabilities as mothers (82/93). Militancy
and the upholding of revolutionary ideals are, according to Montes,
not antithetical to being a good mother.

Ironically, it is Eugenia's martyrdom that best serves to illustrate
this point. As I argued in the previous section, within the context of
her militancy and identity as a soldier, Eugenia's death on the battlefield
is the ultimate affirmation of her heroism and male-defined courage.
However, given the duality of the *guerrillera*'s image and her depiction
as a mother figure, her martyrdom can also be construed as the greatest
expression of maternal self-abnegation. Eugenia's final letters to her
husband convey her sadness at being apart from him and their child,
but more importantly her commitment, above all else, to liberating El
Salvador. In one letter, in which Eugenia describes in detail how to care
for and what to feed their daughter, she writes, "No sé cuanto durará
esto, pero, mi amor, estoy dispuesta a todo y a sacrificar todo, aunque
me duele" [I don't know how much longer this can last but, my love,
I'm ready for anything and to sacrifice everything, even though it hurts]
(135/135). By her own admission, Eugenia is prepared to give her
life for the revolutionary cause, thus seemingly prioritizing her military
duties over her domestic and reproductive responsibilities. However, by
fighting and dying for her country, Eugenia is procuring a better future
for all Salvadorans. Looked at from this perspective, Eugenia's martyrdom
positions her as a mother not just to her daughter but also to the entire
nation, a fierce protector of *all* children and of her country (Bayard de
Volo 247). Montes's observations and Eugenia's depiction as a universal
mother are key examples of how the left's revolutionary rhetoric co-opted
discourses of maternity and traditional perceptions of femininity—women
as inherently domestic beings defined by their tenderness, kindness, and
self-sacrifice—resulting in a "new" understanding of motherhood as a
"revolutionary act" (Treacy 82).

As Díaz reveals in her testimonial account, self-sacrifice is not the
only characteristic that defines *guerrilleras* as "revolutionary" mothers.
While in prison, Díaz, who was a mother at the time of her capture,
often dwells on the memories of her son and the difficulties of being a
mother amidst the uncertainty of the struggle:

No me fue fácil decidir tener a mi hijo en la guerra, más con las responsabilidades que una tiene. Una desea tener un hijo, varios, que nazcan y se desarrollen en la lucha. Verlos crecer en el proceso. Casi nunca se gozan, pero sabés que están ahí, que viven y que son semillas que fructificarán y se desarrollarán en el ejemplo de sus padres. (126)

It wasn't easy for me to decide to have a child in the midst of the war, especially with the responsibilities that one has. You wish to have a child, many, who will be born and develop in the struggle. Watch them grow alongside the struggle. There will never be enough time to enjoy them, but you know that they are there, that they live and are seeds that will bear fruit and that they will develop following the example of their parents.

What is striking about this passage is not necessarily Díaz's affirmation that all women want to have children—which echoes the opinions of the combatants interviewed in Alegría and Flakoll's text—but the reasons why she believes all *guerrilleras* aspire to have them. As she claims, female combatants want children so that they can raise them within the movement and inculcate them with revolutionary ideals. Díaz's postulation of revolutionary maternity recalls the notion of republican motherhood, albeit reimagined through the left's revolutionary discourse. Female militants are cast as reproducers of new citizens, in this case, of "New Men," the foundation of the left's socialist ideal of nationhood. Tellingly, whenever Díaz refers to her son, she lovingly calls him "mi pequeño gran hombre," or "my little big man," signaling him to be both a humble member of *el pueblo* that she is fighting for as well as one of the "great men" of the future nation.

Following nationalist narratives that cast women as the reproducers of future citizens, the *guerrillera*'s function as a republican mother cannot be divorced from another corresponding social construction, that of heterosexual coupling. Diaz's references to her fallen partner underscore this fact, as does the representation of Javier and Eugenia's marriage as the ideal of a revolutionary foundational union. In his description of their relationship and eventual marriage, Javier highlights the vital role their involvement in the revolutionary struggle played in deepening the love he and Eugenia had for each other:

Todo el proceso de nacimiento del amor nuestro—nos dice—, a partir no sólo de una simpatía, sino de una sintonía muy grande en los valores, la manera de ver al pueblo, las inquietudes

> que teníamos desde el 74, en fin, todo el desarrollo, o sea
> nuestra incorporación al proceso revolucionario de la lucha
> de liberación de nuestro pueblo, lo hacemos junto. (Alegría
> and Flakoll, *No me agarran* 65)

> The whole situation surrounding the birth of our love sprang
> not only from a mutual liking but also from a close sharing
> of values. Our way of relating to people, the worries we'd
> had ever since 1974, ultimately the whole development of
> our involvement in the revolutionary struggle as part of our
> people's liberation. All this we had in common. (80)

Javier and Eugenia's bond is both fueled and cemented, above all else, by their political consciousness and by their commitment to *el pueblo*, a commitment that becomes all the more defined upon getting married and choosing to live clandestinely (66/80).

Assuming a clandestine existence, however, is more than just a marker of how profound Javier and Eugenia's revolutionary commitment truly is. It is testament to their disavowal of their middle-class upbringing and beliefs. Although Javier and Eugenia were and remain rooted to the bourgeoisie—another marker of the traditional narrative of foundational coupling—they are also different in that they have been politicized and will, therefore, also produce children with a different understanding of the world. As Javier explains, Eugenia's education of their daughter was in keeping with their socialist beliefs: "[Eugenia] le va imprimiendo a la niña una serie de actitudes que ahora son bien manifiestas. La niña se va acostumbrando a que si uno le regala dulces, ella inmediatamente los reparte entra toda la gente que está allí" [She implanted a series of behavior patterns that can now be clearly seen. The girl has learned that if someone gives her sweets, then she immediately shares them out with the assembled company] (113/115). The ideological education Eugenia gives to her daughter is another example of the notion of revolutionary motherhood detailed in Díaz's account. It also serves to further stress the configuration of her and Javier's relationship as a prototype of a revolutionary foundational couple responsible for physically and ideologically engendering a new socialist alternative of nation.

The *guerrillera*'s representation as a mother figure thus calls attention to the key underlying contradictions of the left's project of national liberation with regard to women's equality and expected roles. Uncritical of its own affirmation of gendered divisions, the revolutionary movement and the alternate notion of socialist nationhood it championed still depended on the sublimation of any female forms of agency that fell outside traditional norms. Individual desires and, more generally, women's sexuality were topics better left unexplored; they needed to be repressed so as to not detract from male dominance as well as what was to be the more crucial role of women—that of being reproducers. The *guerrillera* was reinscribed into the popular revolutionary imaginary as an alternate type of republican mother, whose presence on the battlefield did not necessarily alter social expectations concerning her domestic duties. Furthermore, it set an important precedent for justifying women's relegation to the private space if and when the revolution triumphed.

Beyond the *Guerrillera*'s Image

To be sure, the representation of the *guerrillera* fostered in these testimonios brings to the fore many of the complexities and contradictions that characterized women's involvement in the Salvadoran revolutionary movement. Although hindered, in many respects, by the left's privileging of class-based struggle and its failure to conceptualize women's oppression as part of this same process, the participation of women as female combatants was instrumental in fomenting a new understanding of female agency and consciousness. The popular and idealized image of the *guerrillera* as both militant and mother is testament precisely to this significant transformation in many women's lives. The dualistic portrayal of the female combatant, however, also acts as a broader signifier of the larger issues at stake for women who chose to mobilize by taking up arms and, as such, assumed a new role as public players in one of the most defining moments within Salvadoran history.

As "women-at-arms," women were expected to live up to a male-centered view of revolutionary soldiering, one that, in many respects, codified them as masculine. Those who excelled as military strategists and rose within the ranks of their militant organizations, as well as displayed the heroism and loyalty characteristic of the ideal of the "New Man," such as Martínez, Díaz, and Eugenia, were proof of women's ability to be equal to, if not better than, men in the role of soldier. However, excelling in this capacity and displaying their own brand of female masculinity also marked female combatants as a "threat" to male authority and the traditional notions of hegemonic masculinity and femininity upheld within the revolutionary movement and, more generally, Salvadoran society.

In addition to the expectations women were expected to meet with regard to their militancy, they also had to fulfill another key role, that of being revolutionary mothers. As such, they were expected to be "women-at-arms," partners to men with whom they could live an alternate ideal of revolutionary coupling and engender "New Men" whom they would also literally nurse and carry in their arms. The notion of women being revolutionary mothers was a fundamental base of the left's project of national liberation, as it was dependent on the birthing of a new generation of citizens who would be educated in keeping with a socialist doctrine of class-based equality. Yet this specified role for women, one that recalled the ideal of republican motherhood, also revealed the narrow view held by the revolutionary movement concerning women's national agency, as it did not allow for other conceptions of femaleness that were not rooted in the institutions of marriage or motherhood. Furthermore, it left no room for the exploration of women's concerns with regard to gender inequality, sexuality, and their own liberation.

The broader social implications brought to bear by the image of the *guerrillera* elaborated in these texts is one of the most significant literary and political contributions of these testimonial narratives. Inasmuch as they underscore a vital moment of Salvadoran women's politicization, these texts also foreground the tensions between the left's socialist ideals and women's liberation that would come into play in the years following the end of the civil war, as discussed in the proceeding chapter. To read these texts as solely political propaganda and valid only within the context of the Salvadoran revolutionary process—a trend that Joanna O'Connell first noted in the late 1990s among Latin American critics—would be to disregard the insight they provide about the livelihoods of women during this period. Without them, it would be difficult to understand the new struggles women currently face and whose roots are to be found, in large part, in the activism and participation of women in the Salvadoran popular and armed movements.

Chapter 3

Setting *La diabla* Free

Women, Violence, and the Struggle for Representation in Postwar El Salvador

The signing of the Peace Accords in 1992 marked the end of El Salvador's twelve-year civil war and initiated a new phase of "reform." Similar to Southern Cone countries that had begun the process of national reconstruction a decade earlier, El Salvador adopted a neoliberal model of modernization consisting of political democratization by way of open and competitive elections and the introduction of new economic policies and initiatives.[1] The latter, which include "trade liberalization, devaluation of the currency, privatizations, the lifting of subsidies, the promotion of non-traditional exports, and the expansion of free trade zones and maquiladora activities," have been implemented under the auspices of the right—in particular, a faction of young entrepreneurs and technocrats within the ranks of the Nationalist Republic Alliance Party (ARENA), which has displaced the long-standing oligarchy (Robinson 96). Despite what seem to be positive changes in the Salvadoran political and economic systems, recent studies suggest that the new neoliberal agenda has not only failed to ameliorate existing social and economic problems but also has reproduced and, in many cases, exacerbated them.[2] The demobilization of both the FMLN and the National Guard, coupled with the failure to properly implement the stipulated agrarian reforms, has led to an increase in unemployment and poverty. The growth of the informal sector and remittances from abroad, phenomena well established during the civil conflict, continue to be integral parts of the national economy. All the while, violence continues to escalate, and severe cutbacks in government programs and social services, especially at a time when popular demands

71

are at their highest, have led to an individualist mentality of "sálvese quien pueda" [everyone for themselves] (Vilas 317).

In addition to the social and political changes spurred by the advent of neoliberalism, the postwar period in El Salvador has been characterized by a significant cultural renovation, which has, in turn, prompted a questioning and reconfiguration of Salvadoran national identity.[3] Along with the promotion of Salvadoran classics by privately funded printing presses, there has been a resurgence of literary magazines and cultural supplements in daily periodicals.[4] State-funded institutions such as the *Consejo Nacional para la Cultura y el Arte* (CONCULTURA) have also taken a prominent role in the dissemination of new and well-known literary texts. Perhaps one of the most notable occurrences, however, has been a rise in literary production, particularly works of fiction. Whereas these new texts do not share the sense of socialist purpose or exhibit the urgency of the testimonial narratives and poetry of the 1970s and 1980s, they are still very much engaged with the precise historical moment from which they emerge, providing a critical view of neoliberal modernization, the basis for projects of national consolidation in the postrevolutionary period.

For literary critic Beatriz Cortez, this critique takes the form of "an aesthetic of cynicism" (*Estética de cinismo*). Gone are the utopian and idealistic notions of rural communal action and solidarity promoted by revolutionary movements and prevalent in texts from that period. The disillusionment, pessimism, and violence that permeate El Salvador's postwar literature call into question the so-called successful implementation of neoliberal alternatives and "reforms" as well as the type of citizen and emergent nation that have resulted. With their often stark and disparaging portrayals of neoliberal social reality, these narratives suggest that free-market doctrine has created rather than attenuated disparity and that the transition toward democracy is plagued by the persistent discriminatory and oppressive practices of the past. Not all Central Americans are conceived of as equal citizens, nor are they all viewed as part of the Central American identity that is being redefined and reimagined.

Among the peripheral figures who inhabit these texts are ex-soldiers turned drug traffickers or assassins for hire, ex-guerrillas turned "shady" cops or bodyguards, emigrants disgusted with their fellow countrymen, and corrupt politicians. Women also figure among these protagonists, but unlike their male counterparts, they are often depicted as passive victims of male violence and abuse. Furthermore, they continue to be cast in traditional gender roles such as mother, wife, or prostitute. Ironically, even though many of these texts use women to question the neoliberal project of modernization and national reconstruction, they do not necessarily challenge the exclusion of those same women from these processes. Given these limiting portrayals of women, one of the main concerns of this chapter, in addition to exploring the critique of neoliberalism expounded in these texts, is to address what such depictions imply about women's social roles and their active political and cultural participation in the postrevolutionary period. According to Joan Wallach Scott's understanding of gender as a category of historical analysis that provides "insight into the reciprocal nature of gender and society" (46), looking at the representation of women in contemporary Central American fiction can help to elucidate the particular ways these texts, in their capacity as a space for imagining the nation and critiquing the neoliberal process of modernization, use and construct gender and what such constructions reveal about issues of equality and representation specifically related to women.

Women from all backgrounds were pivotal to the revolutionary process in El Salvador. Through their efforts as activists, writers, and armed militants, the struggle acquired a new dimension. As Kampwirth and Shayne argue, the mobilization of women during this earlier period was also a key factor in the development of a feminist movement. Given that these "new identities threatened traditional gender relations," however, in the postwar period, women have had to face new obstacles characterized by attempts to consign them to the subordinate positions they occupied prior to the war (Luciak 49). This observation highlights a fundamental conflict inherent in the Salvadoran neoliberal project of modernization with regard to women. Neoliberal policies that were meant to democratize and that have led to the incorporation of more women into the global economy by way of their participation in free-market enterprises, in the formal sector, and through emigration continue to oppress, exploit, and marginalize women. This is largely because these policies are premised on and reproduce in the public sphere the gender inequality that governs the private space of the household. Consequently, within the neoliberal project, the new economic status acquired by women as producers has not necessarily resulted in their inclusion in the political and cultural arena precisely because they continue to be identified by their traditional roles as reproducers and viewed as secondary citizens.

In El Salvador, the persistence of this gendered inequality and the limitations placed on women's political agency have led several women's organizations, such as Mujeres por la Dignidad y la Vida [Women for Dignity and Life] (DIGNAS) and the Movimiento de Mujeres "Mélida Anaya Montes" [Mélida Anaya Montes Women's Movement] (MAM), to seek independence from the leftist groups with which they were affiliated during the war. Realizing that their participation in the popular and armed struggles did not necessarily equate with their emancipation and that the 1992 Peace Accords did little to enhance women's rights, these groups have pursued a feminist-based agenda focused on women's legal, political, and domestic subordination. Other organizations that had been previously dedicated to human rights issues, such as the Comité de Madres y Familiares de Presos Desaparecidos y Asesinados Políticos de El Salvador "Monseñor Romero" [Monseñor Romero Committee of Mothers and Relatives of the Political Prisoners, Disappeared, and Assassinated of El Salvador] (CO-MADRES), also began efforts to raise awareness around concerns such as domestic violence, reproductive rights, sexuality, education, and land reform.[5]

While Salvadoran women struggle to gain access to a male-dominated political arena, the scarcity of female literary production and the portrayals of women in postwar narratives reveal a similar difficulty in the cultural sphere. According to a recent study of Salvadoran literature by Rafael Lara-Martínez, six important novels were published in 1996: *Baile con serpientes* by Horacio Castellanos Moya, *Libro de los desvaríos* by Carlos Castro, *Lujuria tropical* by Alfonso Kijadurías, *Tierra* by Ricardo Lindo, *Amor de jade* by Walter Raudales, and *Bajo el cielo del Istmo* by Armando Molina. This list of novels is devoid of any contributions by women, suggesting, as does Lara-Martínez, that the narrative renovation taking place in El Salvador is marred by the same exclusionary practices of the past with regard to female authors (*La tormenta entre las manos* 246). More to the point, although in many of these narratives women are central or noteworthy characters, they are still confined to traditional roles such as that of "republican motherhood" or function as an allegory of the postwar Salvadoran nation. Rather than the hopeful portrayals of a feminized and empowered *campesino* nation that characterized Manlio Argueta's novels, these allegories more often than not rely on limited and stereotypical portrayals of women as a means of depicting a corrupt Salvadoran society. Consequently, many of these depictions are dismissive of the diverse experiences and gains of Salvadoran women during and after the war.

My analysis of the literary representations of female protagonists in postwar Salvadoran narratives and the obstacles confronted by women in the neoliberal era focuses on four works: *La diabla en el espejo* [*The She-Devil in the Mirror*] (2000) by Horacio Castellanos Moya, "La noche de los escritores asesinos" [The Night of the Murderous Writers] (1997) by Jacinta Escudos, and "Vaca" [Cow] (1999) and "Mediodía de frontera" [Midday Border] (2002) by Claudia Hernández. Despite a shared focus on women's experiences, these texts differ significantly in their constructions of female subjectivity and agency. Castellanos

Moya's novel is premised on a traditional conceptualization of woman as an allegory for the nation and as a "republican mother." Although he is critical of the Salvadoran neoliberal agenda, his portrayal of the elite housewife upholds a patriarchal view of female subordination. By contrast, in their short stories, Hernández and Escudos develop depictions of women that defy this representation. They portray female protagonists who dare to imagine an alternative existence to the one upheld by neoliberalism and, in many instances, fight for access to the public sphere. Moreover, their narratives signal an important intervention in what has been an exclusionary cultural practice and literary forum dominated by men.

The use and manifestation of violence is an integral part of these conflicting depictions. As noted in the introduction to this chapter, one of the more critical aspects of El Salvador's neoliberal reality has been the escalation of violence, particularly physical assaults against other human beings and crimes against property. For many scholars, this rise in violence and the lack of efficient structures and measures to deal with it can be seen as symptomatic of a "culture of violence" characterized by the creation of value systems and social norms that legitimize and privilege the use of violence over that of other social behaviors in any given setting (Instituto Universitario de Opinión Pública 33). Although El Salvador's long history of state-sanctioned violence and repression— most recently during the civil conflict—are not the only factors that have contributed to the propagation and "normalization" of violence in the postwar period, it has been instrumental. As Edelberto Torres-Rivas argues, in the transitions toward democracy that have taken place in Latin America in the late twentieth century, it has been difficult to overcome the "residues" of authoritarian regimes, including political violence and impunity, fear, and the trivialization of horror and despair, all of which feed other antisocial behaviors and give way to new forms of violence (294–95).

In the works by Castellanos Moya, Escudos, and Hernández, the pervasiveness of this "culture of violence" is not only visible in the everyday life of the public sector but also within the domestic space of the home. The ultimate form of female marginalization is enacted in Castellanos Moya's novel by the killing of a socialite and housewife in the living room of her residence in front of her two young daughters. Similarly, in the short pieces by Escudos and Hernández, violence is a significant aspect of women's personal lives, is inherent in the private sphere, and serves a critical function. However, in these narratives the female protagonists are not necessarily passive victims of male violence but are violent aggressors in their struggles to gain access to the public sphere. Following Nancy Duncan's discussion of the political practices of marginalized groups that destabilize the public/private divide, the violent measures taken by these female protagonists become a "countervailing force working to open up not only private space but to reopen public space to public debate and contestation" (127).

Construed in this manner, violence calls into question the private/public dichotomy upheld by a neoliberal agenda that continues to marginalize women despite the agency they have acquired through their participation in the civil conflict and their economic viability as part of a new international workforce. To a certain extent, then, the violence experienced in the private space is a means of contesting the contradictions of the neoliberal reality with regard to gender oppression and equality, and by extension female empowerment. Reading these texts in dialogue with each other and in connection with postwar violence makes possible a critical exploration of El Salvador's new neoliberal reality and provides a basis for understanding the role of women in national reconstruction and democratization. The physical, literary, and symbolic violence that is produced in these narratives, especially by women, speaks to a need for a greater awareness of the cultural and political struggles that women have undertaken in the postwar era.

Neoliberal Gossip, Mayhem, and the Elite Housewife

In *La diabla en el espejo*, Horacio Castellanos Moya depicts a postwar world in transition and disarray, rife with cynicism, violence, and fraud. His scathing yet humorous portrayal of Salvadoran neoliberal reality is brought to life through Laura Rivera, an upper-class housewife. As a divorcée and member of an oppressive oligarchy that has lost control over the country's economic and political structures, she seems to unravel in the course of the novel, and so does the Salvadoran nation. More than just a commentary on Salvadoran neoliberalism and its inconsistencies, however, the construction of Laura's subjectivity and her representation as a madwoman serve as a testament to women's peripheral status in the burgeoning national project.

Like many of the male protagonists of Castellanos Moya's best-known novels, including *El asco: Thomas Bernhard en San Salvador* (1998), *El arma en el hombre* (2001), *Donde no estén ustedes* (2003), and *Insensatez* (2004),[6] Laura's opinions and experiences dominate the text. This focus on Laura's sole perspective, one that recalls the individualistic neoliberal mindset, is underscored by the fact that the entire novel is narrated by Laura in the form of a long-winded diatribe that she relates to an unknown and silent partner.[7] Although the identity of this listener is not disclosed until the end of the novel, Laura continuously refers to her as "niña" [girl], a term of familiarity or endearment employed between women. The reader becomes cognizant that Laura is speaking to a female auditor and learns what is motivating Laura's narration: gossip. It is through Laura's *chismes* or gossiping, a practice that is traditionally associated with women, that the reader is made aware of the myriad infidelities and political corruption that typify the Salvadoran elite. It is also by way of these unreliable commentaries that Castellanos Moya constructs Laura's subjectivity, because she herself is a product of her own story and, as Miguel Huezo Mixco underscores, her own tongue ("La diabla en el espejo").

The novel opens with the murder of Olga María Trabanino, supposedly one of Laura's closest friends. Olga María's death at the hands of a hired assassin, an ex-sergeant of the Acahuapa battalion by the name of "Robocop," spurs a series of rumors and hypotheses about the possible motive and perpetrator of the crime that implicate several members of the Salvadoran elite, including Laura. What begins, however, as a formulaic mystery novel turns into something completely different, aimed at highlighting the interpersonal and professional relationships within a rising powerful entrepreneurial class and a waning coffee oligarchy. Solving Olga María's murder is of secondary importance to all of the characters except Laura, who becomes obsessed with it. In fact, the murder is never solved and is subsumed by another significant event in the text—the bankruptcy of FINAPRO, one of the country's core financial institutions, whose investment capital totals more than U.S. $100 million belonging to El Salvador's wealthiest families. Although it is later revealed that FINAPRO's bankruptcy is due to a fraud perpetrated by the company's leading executives, as in the case of Olga María's unsolved murder, no one is brought to justice.

Complicating the plot of this interrupted murder mystery is the fact that Laura is a paranoid schizophrenic—a detail revealed to the reader only in the last chapter. Her mental illness undermines the questionable events recounted by Laura by way of the many rumors she has heard and passed on to her invisible confidante, "la diabla en el espejo," who is none other than herself. The entire novel, then, is revealed to be a complicated web of gossip and assumptions, the veritable conjecture of a madwoman. This disclosure, however, does not necessarily invalidate Laura's perception of postwar El Salvador or the critical nature of her observations. If anything, it serves to affirm the text's critique of neoliberalism's negative impact. Laura is incapable of subsisting in this new violent and marginalizing social order, and this is the cause of her mental breakdown. By the same token, her social fall from grace and the revelation that she has been talking to herself all along make her marginalization from the public and cultural sphere all the more apparent.

Exposing the persistent corruption of El Salvador's political and economic systems during this key transitional moment is essential to the novel's critique of postwar society. Laura's social formation as a member of the once-dominant coffee oligarchy and her former marriage to Alberto Rivera, financial consultant and vice president of FINAPRO, make her representative of the country's economic and political transition. Her comments regarding her father are vital to understanding her class background and her values. At Olga María's thirty-day vigil mass, Laura remarks: "Mi papá tiene razón: todos los curas son retorcidos, sucios" [My father is right: all priests are twisted, dirty] (Castellanos Moya 103). She expands on the topic by saying, "Nunca he aprendido nada de los santos. Mi papá dice que la mayoría son farsantes o criminales. . . . Son cosas del pueblo, de gente tonta o de pícaros, dice mi papá" [I have never learned anything from the saints. My father says that the majority of them are fakes or criminals. . . . Those are things of *el pueblo*, of dumb people or of the mischievous, my father says] (111). Her conviction that all priests are twisted and all saints are criminals and imposters stems from her father's belief that all priests are in league with communists, a sentiment reminiscent of the oppressive ideologies of the conservative oligarchy during the war. The derogatory way in which her father expresses himself about the clergy's relationship with *el pueblo* alludes to the role of liberation theology in the years of the struggle and the right's opposition to its dissemination. Clearly, Laura has internalized her father's ideologies and therefore represents the interests and discriminatory practices of the waning Salvadoran oligarchy.

By contrast, Laura's ex-husband, Alberto Rivera, and his business partner, Toñito Rathis, are prime examples of the new entrepreneurial class that has taken shape in the postwar period. Together, they run the investment firm FINAPRO, where the majority of El Salvador's landowning families and military have invested their money. Alberto has been educated in the United States, whereas Toñito belongs to one of the original "fourteen families," the generation that has displaced the coffee oligarchy. According to Alberto, it is Toñito's financial exploits that are responsible for FINAPRO's demise. He confesses to Laura that Toñito has used money from FINAPRO not only to finance political campaigns for the right and run his soccer league but also to cover his family's business debts (143). Toñito's actions highlight serious inconsistencies within the neoliberal economic and political model implemented by the new elite and, as Carlos Vilas observes, the corrupt financial practices dictated by linage, race, and social class that persist despite the transition from an oligarchic to a seemingly democratic state (297).

Laura's marriage to Alberto Rivas is symbolic of economic and political change, given her affiliation with the defunct coffee oligarchy and her husband's role as a neoliberal entrepreneur. The Salvadoran nation, once dominated by a powerful oligarchy, has succumbed to a new elite class of neoliberal entrepreneurs. In this context, Laura's divorce is symptomatic not only of the inability of the oligarchic order to persist in the postwar era but also of the failure of the neoliberal model that has replaced it. What served as the basis of nineteenth-century liberalism and nationalism is no longer valid. The Salvadoran civil war transformed the concept of nation and facilitated its reconceptualization, and despite its centrality to neoliberalism, this traditional model and the gender norms that define it are continuously undermined by the economic and political practices introduced by that same project. Thus, the corruption that plagues the financial and political arenas also characterizes the private space of the home.

Infidelity is a constant in the marriages in the novel. Both Laura and Olga María have conducted a series of sexual liaisons, and as Laura discloses, she has been Olga María's confidant and accomplice throughout many of them. At first, Laura justifies her friend's illicit relationships, claiming that they were a natural response to the fact that Marito, Olga María's husband, had alienated her and also been unfaithful. Laura alludes to this set of circumstances when discussing the details of Olga María's first affair with a Spanish associate of Marito's, whom she and Olga María nickname "Julio Iglesias" after the famed singer:

> No es que aquella fuera infiel, al contrario, por eso le costó tanto, porque era la primera vez que le atraía de esa manera un hombre desde que se caso con Marito, era la primera vez en que iría más allá de su coquetería natural, culpa del propio Marito, te quiero decir, porque en esa época él tenía abandonada a Olga María . . . supo por lo menos de dos mujerzuelas. (Castellanos Moya 20)

> It wasn't that she was unfaithful, on the contrary, that is why it was so difficult for her, because it was the first time that she was attracted to a man in that way since she married Marito, it was the first time that she went beyond her natural flirting, which was Marito's own fault, I want to tell you, because during that time he had abandoned Olga María . . . she knew of at least two mistresses.

The "solidarity" Laura claims to share with Olga María is called into question later in the novel when Laura learns that Olga María has also had an affair with her husband, Alberto. Laura's perception of Olga María quickly changes from one of a "helpless" victim forced into infidelity to that of an antagonist who knew exactly what she was doing (134). Much like the financial frauds that plague the enterprises of the new Salvadoran elite, Olga María's and Laura's marriages as well as their "intimate friendship" are also farces.

By way of these infidelities, betrayals, and failed unions, Castellanos Moya reveals the demise of the traditional family unit, a microcosm of the postwar Salvadoran nation. However, more than merely functioning as allegories for a dysfunctional neoliberal project of modernization, these negative portrayals of Olga María and Laura seem to suggest that their questionable behavior is also part of the problem. By defying their prescribed gender roles, these women are also to blame for the demise of the postwar nation and must somehow pay for their wrongdoing. In her analysis of Southern Cone literature and neoliberalism, Mary Louis Pratt contends that the breakdown of the fraternal social order, the foundation of which is the sexual contract, has made women expendable or superfluous ("Tres incendios"). Women who do not conform to their traditional gender roles not only encounter resistance but also are violently punished for their actions. Given Pratt's analysis, Olga María's murder and Laura's schizophrenia and institutionalization can be read as punishments for having betrayed or undermined the traditional family unit and defied their prescribed gender roles.

Olga María's numerous extramarital affairs are not her only form of threatening behavior. As a small-business owner, she exemplifies one way in which upper-class women have been able to become part of a male-dominated political and economic sphere. On account of her transgressions, however, Olga María is punished. Her assassination by Robocop in front of her two daughters, no less, and the lack of interest in solving her murder not only mark her as expendable but also "send a message" to future generations concerning women's place in society. Olga María's role as an economic reproducer must be policed when it destabilizes the subordinate status of women within and outside the home and becomes a threat to the patriarchal social order, thereby underscoring one of the many contradictions and shortcomings of the neoliberal agenda.

Similarly, Laura's schizophrenic tendencies, aside from being representative of a postwar Salvadoran nation in decline, raise questions regarding her participation as a woman in that nation. Precisely because Laura is divorced and has no children, she is expendable, like Olga María.

As a woman who has refused to function as a wife and mother—that is, to embody "republican motherhood" and engender a new male nation— she must too be expelled and punished. She is committed by her father to a mental institution, with only her reflection in the mirror to listen to her. Although she does not suffer a physical act of aggression, as in the case of Olga María's murder, Laura is subject to an institutionalized form of violence and victimization that ultimately renders her silent. In true Foucauldian fashion, her disciplining and punishment, which are condoned by patriarchal society, are orchestrated through the asylum where she is confined against her will, albeit under the guise of it being for her "own good."

Violence, then, becomes a means of punishing Olga María and Laura for their failure to abide by neoliberal social norms that are premised on traditional gender hierarchies and roles. Olga María becomes another female casualty whose murder is of no consequence to the male-dominated world of public politics and corrupt business dealings, and Laura is cast as the "madwoman" of El Salvador's weakened coffee oligarchy. The fact that this violence occurs within the private sphere of the home or the isolated space of the asylum, and that it is enacted against female victims without impunity, serves to legitimize male privilege and to reinstate patriarchal authority.[8] Consequently, Laura's and Olga María's attempts to become part of a political, economic, and cultural center are subverted, and like the she-devil trapped in the mirror, they are denied access to the realm on the other side.

Warring Pens and Literary Murders

Although Jacinta Escudos's short story "La noche de los escritores asesinos" participates in a larger discussion of neoliberalism and its negative effects, her portrayal of female agency, use of violence, and desire brings to the forefront issues of gender and female empowerment that are lacking in other literary works of the postwar period. Included in the collection *Cuentos sucios* (1997), this story recounts the ill-fated and destructive relationship between a young writer named Boris and his ex-lover Rossana.[9] Both former guerrillas, they meet years later in a corrupt and crime-ridden postwar San Salvador while working for the same newspaper. Although Boris is suffering from writer's block, Rossana possesses real talent and writes with ease. His creative frustration and continuous sexual rejection by Rossana culminate in efforts not only to keep her from getting published but also to kill her. At the story's end, the reader becomes aware that Boris has been telling his account to a fellow inmate while in prison for having killed Rossana. He is eventually set free and acquitted of all charges, having claimed that it was Rossana who was obsessed with him and that he had killed her in self-defense. The story, however, does not end there. In a surprising turn of events, the reader learns that what Boris has been telling his cell mate in the previous pages is the story he has been writing within the story the reader has been reading. In a final twist, when Boris finishes typing his story and steps outside to enjoy a smoke, he encounters Rossana, holding a revolver, at the door. She shoots and kills him, and at this point a third narrative voice ends the story with the phrase "Y termina la historia" [And the story ends] (Escudos 123).

Boris and Rossana's conflictive relationship is symptomatic of the crime and desperation as well as the loss of revolutionary ideals that characterize El Salvador's postwar reality. As Boris observes, "[a]quí te matan a cuchilladas por un reloj de plástico, de esos que valen una nada! . . . La vida de una persona en este país vale tan poco" [here they stab you to death for a plastic watch, those that aren't worth anything! In this country, a person's life is worth so little] (107). Ironically, the meaningless crime and the trivialization of life that exasperate Boris do not keep him from attempting to kill Rossana, thereby incurring her revenge—a fact that becomes all the more significant when one considers that both were former militants of the left's guerrilla forces. Recalling the testimonials produced during the war, especially those discussed in the previous chapter regarding *guerrilleras*, Boris and Rossana's relationship was once emblematic of the model of socialist coupling upheld within the armed movement, which was to give way to a future alternative of nation once the revolution triumphed. In the war's aftermath, Boris and Rossana are anything but a foundational couple. Rather, they are its dark underside, revealing an embittered and sexist state of affairs that underscores the limitations of the previous paradigm of coupling and, more generally, the demise of and disillusionment with the left's project for social change.

The physical and verbal power struggle that characterizes Boris and Rossana's relationship also allows for an exploration of the obstacles and limitations women face in the new neoliberal reality and, in particular, those that the woman writer faces in a profession dominated by men. Fueled by his own sense of impotence both as a writer and as a scorned ex-lover, Boris uses his editorial position at the newspaper to exert the only degree of control he has over Rossana. He deliberately rejects Rossana's contributions, claiming that they are uninteresting, too long, or vague (109). Yet this is not the only way in which Boris attempts to overpower and silence Rossana. Complicating Boris's written account is the presence of an italicized voice that *seems* to belong to Rossana and manifests itself as an entry in her diary. Upon a closer inspection of the text, however, this is a tenuous and problematic reading. How do we know that this is Rossana's voice? Boris says that Rossana did not write about him in her diary: "No. No escribía mucho sobre mí. En realidad, no escribía nada sobre mí en sus diarios. Y eso me era tan extraño" [No. No, she did not write a lot about me. Actually, she did not write anything about me in her diaries. And that was so strange to me] (90). The only alternative Boris has is to imagine what Rossana could have thought about him; he is desperate to take up some part of her life, given that thoughts of her dominate his own. In addition, in several instances Boris's voice expresses an idea or thought that Rossana's entries later confirm. This is most evident when Boris narrates his final encounter with Rossana in the story he is writing. As Boris threatens Rossana with the revolver, he says:

—pongámonos cómodos querida, lo que quiero hacer contigo require de una luz más sensual.

—*Y la sola idea de que este tipo vaya ponerme la mano encima me produce un asco tal que*

—tengo que ir al baño, déjame levantarme—me dice. (116)

—let's get more comfortable, dear, what I want to do with you requires a more sensual light.

—*And the very thought of this guy putting his hands on me sickens me in such a way that*

—I have to go to the bathroom, let me get up—she tells me.

Rossana's literary murder solidifies the subjectivity that Boris has created for himself at Rossana's expense. He needs to silence her to make his story palpable and allow himself to make sense of the reality that surrounds him. Although he is successful in killing her on the written page, he is unable to do so outside his own story's reality. Rossana is in fact not dead, and it is she who kills Boris. We realize that Boris is an unreliable narrator—that his version is a fabrication.

Boris's appropriation of Rossana's thoughts and negation of her voice through his ventriloquism are the basis for the story's social critique with regard to women. Although both Boris and Rossana are struggling to exist within a new neoliberal reality that has rendered their previous roles as guerrillas void, Boris's writing of Rossana, like his dismissal of her work at the newspaper, is exemplary of his need to restore and maintain patriarchal control over the public sphere—a control that Rossana now threatens, given her success as a writer and her economic independence. In his construction of Rossana's subjectivity, which is a reflection of his own, Boris is only capable of viewing Rossana as an object of male desire. He describes her as the heroine of a *telenovela*, a romantic figure in need of rescuing. In this way, he is capable of keeping himself the "Subject" of his own story, making himself the hero and relegating Rossana to a secondary and marginal position—the position of the "Other," a position that Lucía Guerra Cunningham maintains women have traditionally held in narratives by men (5–16). Read more broadly, this verbal power play echoes the limitations placed on female militants by male-dominated leftist organizations and the sexual discrimination exhibited against them during and after the peace process.

At the conclusion of Boris's story, he is redeemed and acquitted of any wrongdoing. Society has chosen to believe Boris, and he uses the privilege he has always had in the male-dominated world of communications and literature to superimpose his version of the events on Rossana's in an article titled "La justicia triunfa de nuevo" [Justice Triumphs Again] that he has written about his own vindication. With no other alternative, Rossana—the Rossana who exists outside of Boris's account—resorts to violence to create a space for her voice to be heard. The final words Rossana whispers to Boris as she prepares to shoot for a second time are "La única manera de sacarte de mi camino para siempre, la única manera de terminar con todo este ridículo cuento es ésta" [The only way to get you out of my path forever, the only way to end this entire ridiculous story, is this one] (Escudos 123). Finally, Rossana's story or version of events is liberated. Ironically, what Rossana cannot achieve with her pen because there is no room for her in a male-dominated sphere, she must achieve with a revolver, a token of the war and their previous existence together. This last scene is suggestive, then, of the possibility that this entire narrative has been orchestrated and written by Rossana—that Boris's story is not contained within the account of an omniscient narrator but framed by Rossana's narrative. By appropriating Boris's voice, Rossana inverts and parodies the male appropriation of female voices in literature. Escudos's employment of a framing narrative technique can be seen as "an act of framing power, of enclosing it within a female voice which not only deconstructs it but also inverts the phallologocentric meaning usually assigned to the 'Center'" (Cunningham 11).

Although at heart "La noche de los escritores asesinos" is a story about writing and creation, it is a story about writing in a postwar era, a period of transition in which El Salvador is still coming to terms with the "failure" of the left and the persistence of social and gender inequalities. It is also a story about redefining a woman's place in a Salvadoran society that continues to negate her by appropriating her words. Few alternatives exist for women like Rossana who refuse to be silenced or conform to the prescribed gender roles that not only marked the revolutionary ideal of couplehood but also characterize the neoliberal social order. The story calls into question the type of national identity that is being forged and that will result in the postwar era if only male voices are heard and if women's participation in the public and cultural sphere continues to be limited.

The Perversion of Republican Motherhood

As in Escudos's fiction, Claudia Hernández's short stories "Vaca" and "Mediodía de frontera" give way to a critique of women's marginalization and limiting options within El Salvador's new neoliberal reality. It bears mentioning, however, that Hernández's pieces are characterized by two significant differences that set them apart from the narratives by Escudos and Castellanos Moya. One is the fact that Hernández does not explicitly draw attention to the vestiges of war that have and continue to condition, to a great extent, the country's questionable transition to democracy.[10] As such, her work encompasses the trials and tribulations of common citizens, in some cases anonymous individuals, who confront everyday forms of oppression,[11] though the backdrop for these stories is, oftentimes, anything but "ordinary." The other distinction is that the violence enacted by the female protagonists in Hernández's stories is not directed toward another person, but rather toward their own bodies. Violence, in this case, is doubly embodied, as these women are both victim and aggressor. Nevertheless, it remains a means by which these women are able to liberate themselves while also underscoring the broader social circumstances that have influenced and led to their conscious decisions to injure themselves.

"Vaca" recounts the story of Aleída Maza, a small-town woman who has been mysteriously impregnated by an unknown stranger.[12] At the age of forty and having outlived six husbands, she finds herself expecting. Because of the dismal fate of her husbands and her childlessness up to this point, the townspeople speculate about the possible malignant origins of her unknown lover. The enormous size of her stomach helps to confirm their belief that "el padre no podía ser humano" [the father could not be human] and "al único que ella podría tener dentro era a un animal o al mismísimo Anticristo" [the only being she could have inside of her was an animal or the Anti-Christ himself] (Hernández 152). Tired of the rumors and her alienation, Aleída takes matters into her own hands and induces an abortion. She aborts eight fetuses, seven of which are underdeveloped and one of which is born with horns and a tail. Aleída proudly exhibits the seven malformed fetuses in jars of formaldehyde in an act of defiance against the townspeople and their rumors but buries the eighth.

Hernández provides little information regarding the identity of Aleída's lover. Although the townspeople go so far as to suggest that he is the Devil, Aleída claims that he is a foreigner. No one believes her, because "no habían transitado por allí extranjeros desde que la bananera había desaparecido a causa del sindicato viento años atrás" [no foreigners had traveled through there since the banana company had disappeared because of the union twenty years before] (152). This passing commentary is the only reference in the story to a political and social context. Could it be, then, that the advent of neoliberal political and economic structural adjustments paved the way for a foreigner to return and once again lay claim to the land and industry that he had lost? In this interpretation, Aleída is representative of a Salvadoran nation whose "affair" with the United States has produced an "abnormal" pregnancy. On the one hand, the union of the two has resulted in malformed and underdeveloped fetuses—the continuous reproduction of a Salvadoran nation defined by economic dependency, political corruption, and social inequalities. On the other hand, it has produced a child that has horns and a tail and needs to be hidden away. Whereas previous versions of the Salvadoran nation have been incomplete, the new neoliberal model seems to be a true perversion.

Although the prior reading of Aleída seems to limit her role in the text's critique of neoliberalism to that of an allegory for the Salvadoran nation, her characterization and actions reveal a deeper questioning of women's agency and participation in the public sphere. From the beginning, Aleída is regarded by the townspeople as a female perversion. Not only is she not a good wife—her previous husbands are all dead, and no one else is willing to marry her because "estaban seguros que guardaba una trampa de muerte en la cueva baja de su cuerpo" [they were certain that she hid a death trap in the lower cave of her body]— but she also has not borne any children (152). In a postwar era dictated by a neoliberal mind-set that continues to define women as mothers of the new nation, Aleída has failed to perform her designated role and is a social outcast. Moreover, her pregnancy outside of wedlock and with a stranger serves to further marginalize and exclude her. According to the townspeople, Aleída "[e]staba marcada. Como mala semilla" [was marked. Like a bad seed] (152). Her abnormally large stomach, like a scarlet letter, only helps to accentuate that fact.

Unlike Laura and Olga María in *La diabla*, Aleída is represented as a strong woman with a significant amount of agency. She is accustomed to taking care of herself, capable of performing the same duties as a man and not dependent on a male partner. Despite attempts to dismiss and exclude her, she forces the townspeople to acknowledge her existence and her version of the events by aborting her unborn offspring and displaying the aborted fetuses in the front window of her house.

Aleída's choice to abort her children—to do violence to her own body—signals a conscious effort to "unmark" and empower herself. The strategic exhibition of the fetuses and the burial of the eighth one allow Aleída to defy the town and its perception of her, thus, as Beatriz Cortez suggests, shifting blame and guilt from herself onto the town ("Estética de cinismo" 9). People who saw the fetuses "pensaban que los niños habían muerto a causa de ellos y sus comentarios" [thought that the children had died because of them and their commentaries] (153). However, Aleída's decisión also stands as a claim to her own body—her sexuality and her reproductive rights. In many ways, the rumors about her and the surveillance of her actions are linked to her disavowal of social norms regarding women's expected behavior as domesticated, submissive, and nonsexual beings. Not only does Aleída call into question all of these traditional associations, but through her self-induced abortions, she also challenges society's control over her body and sexuality. A stark commentary on the deformed versions of Salvadoran nationality that the neoliberal project is fomenting, Aleída's pregnancy and violent action are also a poignant remark about this agenda's toll on women's lives.

Women in the Borderlands of the Nation

The vision of neoliberalism and female agency afforded in "Mediodía de frontera" is no less critical. The story, included in Hernández's collection by the same title, *Mediodía de frontera* (2002), begins with a matter-of-fact description of a wayward dog searching for food in a public bathroom located at an undisclosed national border exactly three minutes before noon. Having first gone into the men's bathroom to lick some urine, the dog then ventures into the women's bathroom because, as the omniscient narrator states, "Se le ha antojado algo más. Algo femenino" [He craves something more. Something feminine] (113). Once inside, the dog encounters a woman who has cut out her own tongue and holds it in her hands. Disgusted and a bit fearful, the dog decides to leave, for he knows that "una mujer que es capaz de cortarse la lengua es capaz también de acabar con la vida de un perro de frontera" [a woman who is capable of cutting out her own tongue is also capable of ending the life of a dog from the border] (113). However, when the woman asks him not to leave her, he reconsiders. She explains to the dog that the reason she has cut out her tongue is that she is planning to commit suicide by hanging and does not want anyone to be "horrified" by the sight of her tongue hanging from her mouth. The dog tells her he understands and does not ask her why she wants to kill herself out of some sense of respect for her privacy (114). He proceeds to stay with her until she is dead, which is how the story ends.

Instead of focusing on the specific reasons why the woman chooses to take her own life, Hernández draws attention to the peripheral status and alienation that plague the protagonist. The emphasis on the woman's marginality—and in a more general sense, that of Salvadoran women—is underscored from the very beginning of the story. As the dog approaches the women's bathroom, the narrator makes it a point to inform the reader that the sign on the door reads "ellas" [them-female] instead of "damas" [ladies] (Hernández 113). This designation, which is different from the sign of *caballeros* [gentlemen] or *hombres* [men] that most likely hangs on the men's bathroom door, posits women as a female "them" or collective "other" that stands in contrast to a male "us." The gendered division drawn here is made all the more paramount by the fact that the events of this story transpire in the "borderlands" of both time and the nation. When the dog walks from one bathroom to the other, it is close to noon, an hour that significantly divides the day. By the same token, the woman's suicide signals her crossing of another temporal border, one from life into death. More important, however, is that the bathroom that serves as the site of these "crossings" is located in the geographic and metaphorical borderlands of the nation, indicating women's literal exclusion from a male-dominated Center and their relegation to the margins. Recalling Gloria Anzaldúa's well-known theorization of *La frontera*, the border is a "dividing line" that marks difference, the borderlands a place of constant "transition" (3). Women are among the "prohibited and forbidden" individuals who inhabit the borderlands, in this case, of the Salvadoran neoliberal nation (Anzaldúa 3).

The protagonist's act of cutting out her own tongue and hanging herself likewise contributes to this view of female marginality. However, these acts of self-violation are also what afford the woman the limited amount of personal and national agency she claims for herself in the story. In *Violence and Democracy*, John Keane argues that suicide can serve as a "public affirmation of civility" (140). It can be a rational choice that empowers an individual living under repressive conditions by allowing her to be in control or to be the "conqueror" of herself (141). As the woman explains to the dog, "[L]os ahorcados no se ven mal porque cuelguen del techo, sino porque la lengua cuelga de ellos. Es la lengua que causa horror. La lengua es lo que provoca lástima. . . . Y ella no quiere horrorizar a nadie. Sólo quiere ahorcarse" [Those who hang themselves do not look bad because they hang from the ceiling, but because their tongue sticks out. It is the tongue which causes horror. The tongue is what provokes sympathy. . . . And she did not want to horrify anyone. She only wanted to hang herself] (Hernández 114). Inasmuch as the woman's self-mutilation signals the lack of voice and representation of Salvadoran women in the public sphere, it also constitutes a transgressive act that denounces that very silencing and exclusion. Rather than be the passive victim of a patriarchal order that requires her to be subordinate and conform to the role of either mother or wife, the woman chooses an alternate path by determining the conditions of her death.

Tellingly, the protagonist stages her death in such a way as to make a statement about the limitations imposed upon her life. In addition to cutting out her own tongue, the woman changes her clothes and glues her mouth shut in the shape of a smile so that people will know that she is "una ahorcada feliz" [a happy hanged woman] (115). The semblance of "happiness" the protagonist insists upon conveying to her "audience" is suggestive of her contentment with being able to control at least one aspect of her existence, even if it is her death. Furthermore, because her suicide, an action generally associated with the private space of the home, is staged in a public restroom where her hanging body will be on display, it works to destabilize the public and private divide that upholds gender hierarchies. In fact, as both the dog and the narrator observe, after the woman dies and the authorities are informed of the suicide, the women's bathroom stops being, if only for a brief moment, "un baño sólo para mujeres" [a bathroom only for women] (116).

Maintaining some sense of civility, especially in what may seem to be an irrational situation, is also apparent in the interactions between the woman and the dog. Not only does the dog respect the woman's choice and discretion regarding her motives—granting him a certain air of decorum—but he also mourns her death, crying and refusing to leave her side until after her body has been cut down and taken away by the authorities. For her part, the woman is grateful to the dog to the degree that when she hears the dog's stomach rumbling from hunger, she offers him a piece of herself: "Corta en trozos la lengua y se la ofrece. Aún está caliente, buena para comer. Le extiende el primer trozo con la mano derecha mientras, con la izquierda, cubre su boca con el trapo que el perro le ha alcanzado" [She cuts the tongue into pieces and offers it to him. It is still hot, good for eating. She extends him the first piece with her right hand, meanwhile with her left, she covers her mouth with the rag the dog had reached for her] (115). Undoubtedly, Hernández is making an important statement here, because only a dog is capable of granting this woman some semblance of the dignity and humanity that has been denied her by her human contemporaries. However, another reading is also possible regarding the woman and the dog—one that speaks, to a certain extent, to the question of Salvadoran national identity in the postwar era.

Hernández's portrayal of the "perro abigarrado y flaco" [motley skinny dog] can be seen as a modern manifestation of a key figure of Salvadoran folklore, the *cadejo* (113). In keeping with Salvadoran oral and indigenous traditions, these supernatural beings resemble dogs and emphasize duality, because it is believed that there are white *cadejos*, which follow women, and black *cadejos*, which follow men (Gutiérrez 49). Although *cadejos* can be regarded as being either good or evil, more generally they are believed to help people avoid or ward off harm (49).[13] Although in the story the dog does not prevent the woman from killing herself, he does initially crave "something feminine" and provides a certain degree of comfort to the woman as she dies. Hernández's use of anthropomorphism—the dog's ability to speak, his nobility, and the compassion he feels for the woman he befriends—likewise lends him an otherworldly quality. To include such a figure in this narrative stresses the importance of El Salvador's indigenous past and identity, which is an essential aspect not only of Salvadoran culture, but also of El Salvador's rural peasantry, a sector of the population that has undergone a process of *descampesinación*, or class displacement in the postwar period (Robinson 98).

Understood in this manner, it is not a coincidence that a dog from the borderlands is the only companion and witness to the female protagonist's death, for he too is representative of a segment of Salvadoran society and culture that occupies a tangential, if not precarious, position in the neoliberal project of modernization. Whereas he is incapable of acting out against this fact because he is a dog, the woman in this story does take a stand. Like Aleída in "Vaca," she chooses to empower herself through the use of violence. Although she may not be able to dictate the terms of her peripheral existence within the new neoliberal order, she can and does choose the conditions under which she exits life. In so doing, she disavows the gender roles upheld by neoliberalism, which women are expected to undertake throughout their lives.

Waging New Revolutions

The works of Horacio Castellanos Moya, Jacinta Escudos, and Claudia Hernández offer an incisive look at the new Salvadoran neoliberal reality. This cynical world is plagued by crime, corruption, and growing disparity but also defined by efforts to reconstruct and reimagine the nation. It is no wonder, then, that all four of these texts also raise issues concerning notions of Central American identity and participation in the political and cultural spheres. Moreover, they do so by way of specific literary representations, in some cases traditional ones, of female subjectivity and agency and the use of violence.

In *La diabla en el espejo*, Castellanos Moya presents his critique of the neoliberal project of modernization in terms of the mad musings of Laura, a schizophrenic upper-class woman confined in a mental institution. In this text, women once again function as an allegory for the nation. However, in addition to limiting women to this foundational role, the narrative reveals an equally problematic vision with regard to female agency. Women who defy their expected roles as "republican mothers" of a new postwar nation are not only violently punished but also perceived as part of the problem, contributing to the demise of the postwar nation. Their dysfunction and thus the corruption of the traditional bourgeois model of the family is in part also to blame for the shortcomings of the neoliberal model and perceived as among its negative effects. Inasmuch as it provides a critical view of the Salvadoran transition with regard to economic and political matters, Castellanos Moya's rendering of Laura fundamentally reaffirms the patriarchal stance of the neoliberal project.

By contrast, in Escudos's "La noche de los escritores asesinos" and Hernández's short stories, the representations of women attempt to defy a traditional allegorical representation while at the same time contesting the limited agency of women in a male-dominated cultural and public sphere. The marginalization of women is also shown to be a hindrance to the process of national reconstruction and modernization. In Escudos's "La noche de los escritores asesinos," this is made clear by Rossana's violent measures against Boris. By killing a man (like Castellanos Moya) writing women into the traditional role of wife and mother, Rossana (along with Escudos) violently negates and refutes such positions. Furthermore, as the "real" writer of their story, Rossana is able to reclaim her voice and thus empower herself.

Whereas in "Vaca" the anecdote of Aleída Maza lends itself to a limiting allegorical reading, it also problematizes such depictions by way of self-inflicted violence to the very body that marks her as such. Aleída's power lies precisely in her ability to pervert the discourse of "republican motherhood" and liberate herself from the townspeople's rumors while also making a statement about women's rights to their bodies. A similar reading can be made of the anonymous woman who kills herself in "Mediodía de frontera" with only a dog as her witness. Rather than accept the peripheral existence prescribed to her under neoliberalism, the female protagonist opts for a civilized death that denounces her oppression and, in the process, also "frees" her from her expected social roles.

Consequently, although these texts participate in a broader critique of Salvadoran neoliberalism and its negative effects, they also reveal an important aspect of women's political and cultural participation. Their literary representations of women and their nuanced use of violence against others and/or themselves bring to the surface the tensions that exist between the agency women exhibited during the struggle and hope to retain in the postwar era and a neoliberal agenda that in many ways stifles and rejects any efforts focused on gender equality. Set against the type of violence enacted against Laura and Olga María in Castellanos Moya's narrative, the particular use of violence in the pieces by Hernández and Escudos produces a metaphorical means of self-liberation. In this sense, the extreme measures taken by these women are suggestive of the new revolutions women have undertaken and are being forced to engender in the neoliberal postwar era.

Chapter 4

¿Hermanas lejanas?

Female Immigrant Subjectivities and the Politics of Voice in the Salvadoran Transnational Imagined Community

En route from El Salvador's international airport in Colapa to the capital city of San Salvador stands the Great Arch of the Emigrant Alliance. Erected in 1994, barely two years after the signing of the Peace Accords, the monument pays tribute to the hundreds of thousands of Salvadorans who reside abroad and whose remittances during the war and in the current era have been vital to El Salvador's financial livelihood. Although officially inaugurated with a sign post that reads "Hermano Lejano ¡Bienvenido!" [Distant Brother. Welcome!], a name underscoring fraternal ties but also distance, this phrase was eventually changed to "Hermano bienvenido a casa" [Welcome Home Brother], a sentiment of welcome rather than alienation. Ironically, the insistence on changing the phrasing on the monument came from the very community it was meant to praise—Salvadoran immigrants residing in the United States.[1] According to Reynaldo Alvergue, director of the Association of Salvadorans in Los Angeles (ASOSAL), Salvadorans residing in various parts of the United States resented the official title, arguing that their financial contributions created a closer bond between them and their country of origin (qtd. in Miranda, "Cambiarán el nombre" par. 5).

Although it attests to the complex relationship El Salvador maintains with its migrants and the influence these foreign compatriots wield on the basis of economics, this dialectal exchange also draws attention to another notable factor: an overtly male vision of Salvadoran migration that went uncontested. As the emphasis on the word *hermano* [brother] implies, the image of the Salvadoran emigrant conjured by the monument is male, in keeping with traditional understandings and depictions of migration that privilege men's experiences over that of women.[2] Because remittances are also an underlying current of this homage, the structure likewise seems to imply that men are not only at the forefront of this endeavor but also that they define and speak for the Salvadoran immigrant community in the United States. Such observations inevitably beg the questions: What about the *hermanas lejanas* [distant sisters]? Do they not also factor into the process of Salvadoran migration and transnational community building? And if so, where are their voices, and what are the stories they have to tell? This problematic erasure of women speaks to a key tension that characterizes Salvadoran migration, a tension that is also at the center of the literary analysis in this chapter. Although women are a significant portion of the migrant population and have acquired new forms of agency via their involvement in this process, it is men who continue to be hailed and depicted as the principal journey takers and/or "heroes."

Like the monument, literary works by Salvadoran writers residing in and outside El Salvador·are also marked by similar debates concerning identity, migration, and gender in a transnational context. Whereas the works of Berne Ayalá and Claudia Hernández speak of the multiple border crossings Salvadorans undertake to get to the North,[3] novels such as *El asco* (1997) by Salvadoran author Horacio Castellanos Moya examine the social and cultural role of emigrants who return to El Salvador and their oftentimes conflicted relationships with their homeland.[4] By the same token, the cultural production of Salvadoran-American writers and artists including Mario Bencastro, Quiqué Áviles, Marcos McPeek Villatoro, Leticia Hernández-Linares, and Carolina Rivera underscore the multiple types of negotiations Salvadoran immigrants and second generations make as they attempt to incorporate themselves into U.S. society. Here I focus on two such texts, centering my analysis on the representation and construction of female immigrant subjectivities: the novel *Odisea del Norte* [*Odyssey to the North*] (1999) by Mario Bencastro and Leticia Hernández-Linares's chapbook of poetry *Razor Edges of My Tongue* (2002). Although both "give voice" to the Salvadoran experience of migration, calling attention to the oftentimes oppressive conditions under which migrants are forced to travel and coexist in the United States, they do so in contrasting ways that either reaffirm or destabilize gendered notions of women's participation in this process. In Bencastro's novel, men factor as the main protagonists of El Salvador's history of migration and immigrant life in the United States, whereas women remain secondary and obscured figures with little or no agency.

Hernández-Linares's spoken-word poems challenge such depictions by reclaiming Salvadoran women's voices and underscoring the oppression and exploitation of female immigrants at home and in the public sphere. Read in dialogue with each other, these texts bring to the fore key issues regarding the gendered dynamics of Salvadoran migration and immigrant life.

The differing representations of female immigrant subjectivities that Bencastro and Hernández-Linares afford, as well as the politics of voice—meaning who speaks and for whom—in which these texts engage gain greater significance when read in the broader context of Salvadoran international migration, transnational community building, and women's participation in both of these phenomena. Salvadoran migration to the United States, especially by women, is not a new occurrence. However, the outbreak of the civil war in the 1980s propelled this process to new heights.[5] Those who were not escaping possible repercussions or death threats from government forces such as the National Guard, paramilitary groups, or in some cases ex-guerrillas were in search of new job opportunities, given the continued disruption of industries and production as the conflict intensified. Unlike previous migratory flows, which were minor and mostly composed of urban groups including educated professionals, skilled laborers, and female domestic servants recruited by U.S. employers, these newer waves of refugees had a primarily rural base and a different context of emigration and reception in the United States (Repak 37). The Reagan administration's monetary and military support of El Salvador's government, which it deemed "democratic," created a conflict of interest that led to the denial of the majority of applications filed by Salvadoran refugees for political asylum. Rather than acknowledge that these individuals were fleeing from an oppressive regime, as it did in the case of Nicaraguans escaping a leftist Sandinista government, the U.S. government categorized Salvadorans as economic immigrants, subject to deportation. Consequently, fewer than 3% of the applications filed for political asylum by Salvadorans during this time were granted (García 113).

One of the lasting effects of the large-scale emigration prompted by the armed conflict—a phenomenon that persists today—and the subsequent U.S.-based Salvadoran communities that resulted was the development of new and differing relationships between Salvadorans at "home" and those residing abroad. In addition to remittances that are helping to sustain family members in the postwar era, Salvadoran immigrants living in the United States have been instrumental in the development of small businesses, hometown civic committees, and art festivals in El Salvador.[6] Economic, political, and sociocultural enterprises such as these that cut across multiple borders and class lines and are capable of being initiated by both migrants as well as Salvadoran government agencies are suggestive of what Landolt et al. argue is the "creation of a transnational social field" by way of a "dialectical process" (292). The undertaking of transnational practices and the correlating existence of the transnational social fields in which they take place have similarly given way to a broader social organization—namely, that of a Salvadoran transnational community (Guarnizo and Smith 27).

Identity—as it is constructed and negotiated at both the individual and communal levels—is an inherent aspect of this process of transnational community building. Underlying many Salvadoran transnational practices is the need by migrants to participate in and feel part of the Salvadoran nation they left behind. This desire for the homeland speaks to the diasporic elements that mark the waves of Salvadoran international migration spurred by the civil conflict and that are a pivotal aspect of the Salvadoran transnational identity being elaborated. Indeed, if, as James Clifford argues, "[d]iasporas usually presuppose longer distances and a separation more like exile: a constitutive taboo on return, or its postponement to a remote future" and "also connect multiple communities of dispersed populations," then the Salvadoran migrants who fled the civil war and established immigrant communities throughout urban centers in the United States can certainly be classified as such (246). The diasporic cultural forms in which these populations engage, such as "longing, memory, and (dis)identification," are inherent to their construction of a transnational identity that straddles both "home" and their new surroundings in their host country (Clifford 247).

However, as with other Salvadoran transnational practices, this renegotiation and formation of identity is also premised on a dialectical exchange. As such, the issue of identity is not one mediated only through and by the Salvadoran diasporic populations that reside outside the nation. Recalling the aforementioned example of the *Hermano lejano* monument, Salvadorans at "home" are also participating in a process of reimagining El Salvador's national space as transterritorial and themselves as part of a broader transnational family or community that links them to their *hermanos lejanos*. This is not to say that Salvadoran nationalism and ties to the nation are no longer of consequence, for, as I contend below, the Salvadoran transnational community that has emerged is simultaneously characterized by new ways of defining identity and community *as well as* by the persistence of gendered nationalistic discourses and identifications that are exclusionary to women. As Eduardo Guarnizo's and Peter Michael Smith's discussion of the complexities of transnational identity politics stresses, the identities forged by transnational actors "from below" (as opposed to hegemonic identities imposed from above) continue to be marked by the essentialist and "hegemonic projects of nation states" (23). Consequently, the Salvadoran transnational community in question can be understood more broadly as an interstitial site that enables new forms of contestation and resistance (to prevailing structures), of identity and agency, but that also has the potential to adapt and reproduce dominant discourses (Guarnizo and Smith 9).

Women's involvement and contributions to both of these processes of migration and transnational community building have been and continue to be significant. Recent studies by scholars working on Central American migration highlight the significant extent to which Salvadoran women have participated in international migratory flows to the United States—in some cases as pioneers—and call attention to the positive changes that have resulted from such involvement, including the altering of perceptions regarding expected gender roles.[7] For many women, living and working in the United States has provided them with increased social independence as well as a greater sense of empowerment as both "productive workers and wage earners" (Mahler, "Engendering Transnational" 295). Oftentimes, female immigrants are able to acquire jobs more readily than their male partners and do not have to rely on them for monetary support (Repak 159). In some cases, women are the major contributors or sole providers within their family units and are equally responsible for regularly sending remittances home (Menjívar, "Intersections" 109). Like their male counterparts, many women are thus *hermanas lejanas*, vital economic mainstays not only for their families but also for El Salvador.

The reconfiguration of immigrant women's roles in the United States as "breadwinners" is suggestive of the fact that, similar to the Salvadoran civil war, international migration affords women opportunities to incorporate themselves into a male-dominated public sphere. Women are privy to different forms of inclusion and activity that they did not experience prior to emigrating. Furthermore, and perhaps as a consequence of this newfound mobility, many female immigrants also gain a greater awareness with regard to gendered oppression. Few Salvadoran women living in the United States consider going back to El Salvador. As Mahler's study reveals, many women have reservations about returning home given not only the violence and sense of disillusionment that they feel with the state of affairs, but also the lack of economic opportunities available to them in El Salvador—what many believe will result in their having to once again become dependent on men ("Engendering Transnational" 303). In other words, they are unwilling to give up the limited independence and freedom they have acquired in the United

States in order to return to an "old way of life" that is premised on their subordination and disempowerment. At stake, however, are not only how women are navigating these changes to their livelihoods at the individual and personal levels, but also what effects the new roles Salvadoran immigrant women have adopted are having on the broader transnational community and the notion of Salvadoran identity that is being elaborated.

Bencastro and Hernández-Linares's texts allow for a deeper exploration of these multifaceted and complex negotiations. Authored by first- and second-generation Salvadoran-Americans, these narratives are, in many ways, a product of Salvadoran migration. However, in keeping with Arjun Appadurai's discussion in *Modernity at Large* concerning the role of imagination in social life, these literary texts also constitute a form of social practice (31); that is, they provide an avenue by which Salvadorans imagine themselves and others as part of a Salvadoran transnational collective. In this sense, these narratives function as a terrain for exerting as well as contesting different forms of agency, both at the individual and communal levels. Viewed from this theoretical perspective, the contrasting representations of female immigrants and the politics of voice that characterize Bencastro's and Hernández-Linares's texts do more than merely call attention to the plight of Salvadoran women in the United States. Rather, they constitute mediated and varied responses to the growing agency and participation of women, thereby speaking to wider-reaching issues—namely, the gendered contours of the Salvadoran migratory process and the complexities of transnational community building and identity formation.

In Bencastro's portrayal of the Salvadoran odyssey, women appear in one of two roles, either as the wife left behind in El Salvador by the male migrant hero or as the disenfranchised refugee. Marking both of these characterizations of women is not only the fact that each occupies a problematic, if marginal, position within the immigrant reality and process of transnational community depicted in the novel, but also that they are both represented in traditional ways. Lina, the wife of the protagonist, Calixto, is rendered an idealized model of *campesina* womanhood, both loyal and submissive, and an allegory for the Salvadoran "homeland" that male immigrants yearn for. Similarly, the plight of Teresa, an undocumented refugee seeking asylum, allows for a poignant critique of U.S. foreign and immigration policy toward El Salvador, yet fails to significantly destabilize the novel's predominantly male image of Salvadoran migration. As I argued regarding the *hermano lejano* discourse, Bencastro's limited depictions of female immigrants elide women's actual participation and changing roles in Salvadoran migration—and are ultimately suggestive of the patriarchal underpinnings of the process of Salvadoran transnational community building and construction of new identities.

Hernández-Linares's spoken-word poetry draws a considerably different picture of the Salvadoran migratory process. Her narrative-driven poems highlight women's endeavors as both migrants and economic providers, oppressed by the need to work under precarious conditions in maquiladoras or other such venues in order to ensure the steady flow of remittances and goods to their loved ones in El Salvador. In keeping with the notion of " 'representative verse' in which the poet chooses to speak to, for, or from a particular community or identity" (Crown 217), it is the poetic "I" of Hernández-Linares's text that serves as a conduit for these female voices and experiences. As in Bencastro's novel, the female immigrant subjectivities and voices disclosed in these poems are also linked to those of women in El Salvador. Yet, in this context, tracing this genealogy serves to un-silence women rather than to reinscribe their traditional roles as wives or mothers. This historical act of un-silencing calls into question the persistence of oppressive social norms while at the same time validating the participation of Salvadoran women in past and present undertakings such as migration and transnational community building. Moreover, it explicitly renders the notion of Salvadoran transnational identity as a gendered and intergenerational construction that women also influence and help to define.

The Salvadoran (Male) Odyssey

Mario Bencastro's novel *Odisea del Norte* depicts a Salvadoran migratory experience of epic and heroic proportions. As the author states, the impetus for writing the novel was to provide an account of this history not only so that Central Americans would know and embrace their own past of migration but also so that those who were not Central American and who did not speak Spanish could better understand how much Central American immigrants suffer and endure in order to come to the United States ("De Ahuachapán" par. 7). Thus, through an eclectic array of newspaper clippings, letters, elements of playwriting, and testimony, Bencastro constructs a collage-like portrait of Salvadoran migration that is anchored by the plot of the protagonist, Calixto, an undocumented immigrant living in Washington, D.C. Calixto's story fluctuates back and forth between his present-day reality in the United States and a series of linear flashbacks that narrate his migrant journey. As Lara-Martínez observes, Calixto is posited as the heroic figure of this odyssey, a new

Ulysses whose return to Ithaca is more subjective—rooted in memory and Salvadoran identity—than physical ("Mario Bencastro" 29).[8] The casting of Calixto as such calls to mind the role of women in the novel, for if he is to be the Ulysses of this epic, then who is his Penelope? And how do women, in general, factor in this voyage away from the homeland with no certain return?

Not surprisingly, it is Lina, Calixto's wife, who embodies Penelope. However, unlike Calixto, Lina's rendering as Penelope is not necessarily new, depicted in the novel as an idealized female who is nevertheless disempowered and reliant on her husband. Her lack of agency is all the more emphasized by her figurative representation as an allegory for the Salvadoran nation, one that, like Lina, has also been left behind. Although she is not an immigrant, Lina functions as a vital subtext for understanding the male and, more explicitly, female immigrant subjectivities that are portrayed. Coupled with the representation of the political refugee, Teresa, who is deported back to El Salvador, Lina's representation reveals a static view of women's roles and agency in and outside migration. When read against the grain or as a means of "counter-narrative" to the dominant discourses of nationalism and a male-focused migration, the seemingly marginal representations of these two women are vital. Not only do they underline the reaffirmation of a Salvadoran migratory history that continues to be defined and rendered in male terms, but they also call into question notions of transnational community and identity construction that are equally problematic.

Calixto's narrative of migration is, in many ways, a prototype of the Salvadoran immigrant experience of the 1980s. A *campesino* laborer, Calixto is suspected by the government of subversive activities and is therefore forced to flee from El Salvador, leaving his wife, Lina, and children behind. While in Washington, D.C., he struggles to find work wherever he can, finally acquiring a job as a dishwasher in a hotel working alongside other undocumented immigrants from various parts of Latin America. Among these workers, Calixto finds a makeshift community, bound by the oppressive conditions they all are forced to withstand as well as their struggles to acclimate to a different social environment that is unlike the ones they are accustomed to in their countries. The sense of community shared by the men is underscored in the text by Bencastro's use of dialogue as well as elements from the theater. In addition to indicating which characters are participating in the conversations—spread out in different segments throughout the novel—Bencastro includes stage directions that offer insights into Calixto's facial expressions and the actions of the other men. The setting for most of these conversations is the kitchen in which the men work, an ironic domestic space that in this context is an important site of male homosocial bonding and memory making, a point I return to in what follows.

Though not physically, Lina constitutes a consistent presence in Calixto's new life in the United States. She factors as a key undercurrent of the recollections and nostalgia that condition Calixto's present, notable in the conversations he engages in with his fellow coworkers. However, Lina's representation is similarly pivotal for what it reveals regarding the affirmation of traditional gendered norms and female immigrant subjectivities. On one such occasion, Calixto recalls an incident involving himself and Lina. Despite having been bitten by a snake and being ill, Calixto insisted on going to work, and his wife, rather than challenge him, opted to follow him from a distance. After falling ill, it was Lina who helped carry him back to their ranch. Calixto's description of the event is noteworthy, for he makes a point to praise Lina not only as a strong woman of *el campo*, "fuerte de carácter y de cuerpo" [strong of character and of body], but also for being a good wife who knows when to keep quiet and not argue with him (Bencastro 69/65). Through recollections such as these and related perceptions of women's roles in Salvadoran society, Bencastro posits a Salvadoran female subjectivity that is rooted in rural life and defined by a predisposition for hard work and loyalty, but also by submissiveness and domesticity.

This is elaborated further in another conversation between Calixto and his coworkers regarding the *doble jornada* [double shift] women must contend with—having to work outside and inside the home. Calixto contributes to the conversation, offering his own observations about Salvadoran women: "En mi pueblo las mujeres trabajan como burros de carga, a la par de los hombres. Cortando algodón o café, de sol a sol" [In my hometown, the women work like beasts of burden, right alongside men, harvesting cotton from dawn 'til dusk] (85/83). Once again, Calixto emphasizes the strength and character of *campesinas*, as he did in the previous recollection of his wife, Lina—and, as before, the qualities being praised are also explicitly associated with women's roles as wives and mothers. It is noteworthy, after all, that this contemplation of the hardships that afflict women in particular is taking place as part of an exchange focused on Mother's Day, which reinscribes gendered binaries and prevents any real critical commentary regarding how patriarchy operates in Salvadoran society or as part of the new immigrant reality. Consequently, the issue of gender equality, though referenced, is not posited as a social problem that needs to be explored further. Rather, it becomes a mere observation that is easily dismissed by describing women as courageous and "seres muy especiales" [special people] deserving of admiration for their work and suffering (86/83).

Lina's characterization as the ideal Salvadoran woman, a hardworking and brave *campesina* who does not question her husband, is inherently linked to her construction and function in the text as an allegory for El Salvador. Annette Kolodny's analysis of the "land-as-woman symbolization" suggests that for the early explorers and settlers of the American continent, characterizing the new uncharted territory as Woman was a means of civilizing and "casting the stamp of human relations upon what was otherwise [an] unknown and untamed" environment (9). The use of this linguistic as well as psychosocial mechanism allowed colonizers to gender the landscape in such a way as to make it capable of being not only dominated but also potentially nurturing. On the one hand, there existed the notion of the American landscape as a virgin territory that did not pose a potentially emasculating threat, and on the other, there was the idea of land as a welcoming mother. Bencastro's rendering of Lina, as it pertains to Calixto, is premised on a similar gendered construction of "woman as nation." However, within the context of Salvadoran migration to the United States, this particular characterization becomes a means of depicting the sending nation rather than the unknown foreign soil. For Salvadoran migrants, the United States is neither a conquerable territory nor a hospitable one, because undocumented immigrants are part of a disempowered minority group who lack rights. As such, for men like Calixto who occupied a dominant position in their own patriarchal societies, the encounter with the North is emasculating. Unable to adjust in the same way that the early European settlers did, Calixto must gender El Salvador, the nation he has left behind, as female in order to help reaffirm his cultural identity and his masculinity.

This mutually reinforcing construction of Lina as both the wife and nation left behind is limiting in that it is premised, on multiple levels, on a traditional notion of female agency that is inherently tied to the home—be it the family domain or the nation. What is more, it works to exalt and reaffirm the primacy of men in the public sphere— here, Calixto's role as the principal historical agent in this narrative of migration. Although Calixto evokes Lina in his memories and relies on her as his link to their homeland, she invariably remains a tangential figure. Ironically, her centrality in Calixto's recollections and worldview is precisely what marks her exclusion, as well as that of many Salvadoran women, from the immigrant reality—and by extension, the notion of Salvadoran transnational identity elaborated in the novel. Few are the women who embark on the perilous journey to the North—and those who do meet difficult fates, often being raped and then imprisoned in detention centers, after which they are eventually deported back to El

Salvador. The experiences of these women are treated as cursory, minor additions to the central narrative of Calixto's trials and tribulations and do not have a strong bearing on the everyday livelihood of Salvadorans attempting to survive in Washington, D.C. Perhaps the most developed story regarding a female immigrant is that of Teresa, a twenty-year-old political refugee seeking asylum in the United States. Still, despite being one of the few female immigrants to be depicted, she, like, Lina, also remains on the margins of this odyssey.

As with the other fragmented storylines that characterize the text, Teresa's predicament unfolds through a series of individual segments dispersed throughout the novel. These episodes—written in a style akin to official court reporting—center on Teresa's deportation trial, including her initial hearing. Aided by her attorney, aptly named Mrs. Smith, Teresa pleads her case to the judge, explaining the reasons why she left El Salvador. According to Teresa, her husband, an ex-soldier, was a prime target of both enemy guerrilla forces and the National Guard, which punished deserters with death. Both organizations had threatened to kill him, Teresa, and their families. Independent of her husband's actions, Teresa had also been caught in a similar catch-22 when the guerrillas begun to use her house as a prime source of water. As Teresa elaborates, to deny the guerrillas water would have put her in danger. Unfortunately, providing the guerrillas with this type of forced help also made her "guilty by association" as far as the National Guard was concerned (Bencastro 83/80).

Teresa's testimony recalls the plight of a significant portion of the Salvadoran immigrant population during the 1980s. However, it also serves as a platform for Bencastro's poignant critique of U.S. foreign and immigration policy, a critique that becomes all the more explicit if the reader understands the broader global context of the Salvadoran civil conflict. As Teresa discloses, her husband was not only a soldier but also part of a special military battalion trained in the United States (104/100). This seemingly innocuous fact is a direct allusion to the School of the Americas located in Fort Benning, Georgia. The training center was responsible for the creation of infamous battalions such as El Salvador's Batallón Atlacatl, which carried out the massacre of El Mozote in 1981, during which more than one thousand men, women, and children were murdered.[9] Although Teresa is the one who has been forced to take the stand, it is the U.S. government that is being put on trial for its role in perpetuating the violence of the Salvadoran civil war and for "washing its hands clean"—an idea exemplified by the judge's lack of response as well as the general failure of either of the attorneys present to acknowledge this aspect of Teresa's testimony.

Related to this indictment of U.S. military intervention in El Salvador is an equally critical view of U.S. immigration policy that also contributed to the repression, and in some cases death, of Salvadorans. One of the most striking aspects of Bencastro's portrayal of Teresa's court proceedings is the manner in which he employs different linguistic modes to emphasize Teresa's undue treatment by the U.S. judicial system as well as her sense of alienation in a foreign country. Noticeable throughout Teresa's trial are not only the distinctions made between Spanish and English formal and informal modes of language, but also an emphasis on social disparity (Lara-Martínez, "Mario Bencastro" 28). Teresa is an illiterate *campesina* who despite being assisted by an official translator has trouble understanding the legal rhetoric being used against her and who is likewise incapable of effectively negotiating bureaucratic procedures that require a base knowledge of the U.S. court system. As the following exchange shows, Teresa's testimony is easily manipulated by the prosecuting attorney so as to undermine the very circumstances and fear that forced Teresa's exit from El Salvador and to suggest that she is an economic migrant—making a stronger case for her deportation.

FISCAL: Su solicitud dice que aparentemente una de las razones por las cuales salió o uno de sus problemas era que el trabajo era muy incierto de un día a otro en su país, ¿es cierto?

TERESA: No, el motivo verdadero era por la ayuda que les dábamos a los guerrilleros, lo cual representa un peligro sin regreso.

FISCAL: ¿Pues la declaración en su solicitud es verdadera o es falsa?

TERESA: Bueno, eso es verdad, no hay tanto trabajo. Uno trabaja allá, sólo para la comida, eso es todo, pero el motivo no es ése. Es que mi vida peligra si regreso a mi país, por la única razón de haberle ayudado a los guerrilleros. (Bencastro 161)

TRIAL ATTORNEY: Your application says that apparently one of the reasons for which you left or one of your problems was that work was very uncertain from one day to the next in your country. Is that true?

TERESA: No, the real reason was because of the help we gave the guerrillas, which puts me in danger if I go back.

TRIAL ATTORNEY: Well, is the declaration on your application true or false?

TERESA: It's true. There isn't a lot of work. When you work there, it's just for food, that's all, but that's not the reason I left. My life is in danger if I go back to my country, because I helped the guerrillas. (159)

The strict legal parameters imposed on Teresa's testimony and experience leave no room for considering the political and social reality of the Salvadoran civil war without which Teresa's case cannot be fully understood; namely, that *any* connection to the guerrillas, whether voluntary or not, was cause for the National Guard to label someone a "subversive" and kill them, along with their families. The underscoring of Teresa's economic situation by the prosecution is equally telling, for though it is meant to render illegitimate Teresa's plea for political asylum, it calls attention to the economic strife that plagues El Salvador's rural populations. In stating, as Teresa does, that when one works there it is only for food, she bears witness to the exploitative conditions under which *campesinos* work and live—a fact that is inherently linked to the political situation and oppression that Teresa is fleeing. Central to the Salvadoran conflict was the attempt to restructure an economic system that kept a long-standing oligarchy in power while rendering the rural populations a cheap source of labor without basic human or political rights. Like the earlier mention of her husband's involvement in a U.S.-sponsored military unit, Teresa's words in this exchange also call for a deeper or alternate interpretation of the facts.

Ultimately, Teresa's application for asylum is denied and she is deported back to El Salvador, where she is eventually murdered. This last detail concerning Teresa's unfortunate end is revealed to the reader by way of a short newspaper article published with the headline "Encuentran cadáver de una mujer" [Body of a Woman Found]. As the article states, the apparent motive for murdering Teresa was "represalias políticas" [political retaliations] (191). While underscoring the seriousness of Teresa's predicament, this unfortunate news further inculpates the United States for its unjust treatment of refugees like her who faced a similar uncertainty and probable death if deported back to El Salvador. However, focused through a gendered lens, Teresa's portrayal is also suggestive of other acts of silencing and dismissal. Teresa is a refugee, but she is also a woman, a fact that comes to bear most noticeably in the judge's final ruling when he cites that "[l]a evidencia parece, francamente, establecer un caso para el esposo, más que para la acusada" [the evidence appears, frankly, to establish a case for the husband more than for the respondent] (177/175). Ironically, the judge acknowledges that Teresa may have established a just cause of fear for her husband given his role in the military, but not for herself. The underlying implication in this ruling is that because Teresa is a wife and therefore not seen as involved in any significant way in the conflict, her case has no grounds.

Teresa's double dismissal on account of her being a refugee and a woman is not only visible in her treatment by the U.S. court system. When juxtaposed against Calixto's immigrant saga, Teresa's struggles and eventual death are indicative of her marginalization within the immigrant reality and the novel's larger conceptualization of the Salvadoran odyssey. Both Calixto and Teresa are *campesinos* and undocumented refugees, working menial jobs to try to subsist. Whereas Calixto's job allows him to be part of a network of male immigrants who, despite working in a hotel kitchen, are still capable of maintaining their sense of male privilege, Teresa's work bars her from any form of social participation and upholds her subordinate status as a woman. As Teresa explains during her trial, her job in the United States is cleaning offices at $3.35 an hour (162/160), a form of work that literally marks her invisibility both as an undocumented employee and as a woman, because working as a "cleaning lady" or a form of "corporate maid" is in keeping with a traditional division of gendered labor and notions of female servitude. Teresa's deportation and death likewise mark her exclusion from the immigrant reality because, by contrast with Calixto, she is incapable of successfully undertaking the journey to the North in search of the elusive "American dream" and exerting any real form of agency. Like that of Lina, Teresa's story is subsumed by the meta-narrative of the male migrant hero. Her depiction is another example of how women's participation and roles are narrowly defined in the text and how women's experiences are easily dismissed.

This problematic construction of female immigrant subjectivity is all the more stressed by the male bonding and sense of Salvadoran transnational identity and community elaborated in the novel. In "Mario Bencastro's Diaspora: Salvadorans and Transnational Identity," Craft posits that among the ways Bencastro constructs a "Salvadoran identity 'away from home'" is through the discourse of nostalgia, the "remembering [of] suffering and other shared experience, and [by] narrating transformations" (157). Calixto's recollections of Lina, which are inherently linked to his longing for his homeland, exemplify Craft's point regarding the function of nostalgia, as do the interactions between Calixto and his Salvadoran friends outside their job environment. One such example is when Calixto, Juancho, and Caremacho eat at a Salvadoran restaurant and discuss El Salvador's Independence Day, September 15. As they reminisce, they observe a drunken compatriot walk over to the jukebox and select the Salvadoran national anthem from among the "canciones típicas" [typical Salvadoran songs] available, after which he proceeds to cry. The parenthetical stage directions that accompany this episode describe the communal response of the other patrons to the emotional man: "Conmovidos por su (el hombre) actitud y por las familiares estrofas, [s]e ponen de pie y, con tono destemplado pero con gran respeto y entusiasmo, entre ruidosos hipos y estornudos, corean las pocas palabras que recuerdan" [Moved by his attitude and the familiar strains, others stand and, off-key but with great respect and enthusiasm, amid noisy hiccups and sneezes, they chorus the few words they remember] (110/106). Here, too, there is a shared nostalgia. However, there is also an overt emphasis on Salvadoran identity and belonging. Partaking in these nationalist activities, especially in a restaurant that serves *pupusas*, a food staple of Salvadoran cuisine consisting of a thick corn tortilla filled with cheese and/or other ingredients such as pork, is a means by which Calixto and his companions evoke their Salvadoranness and maintain their sense of community beyond national borders.

Calixto's insistence on retaining his Salvadoran customs and traditions as opposed to assimilating to the United States' mainstream culture exemplifies Craft's point regarding the "narrating of transformations" in Bencastro's text as a means of constructing identity. When Calixto's coworker, Juancho, begins to call himself "Johnnie" and brag about his new *gringa* girlfriend and Trans Am, Calixto reminds him of his Salvadoran roots. "Mirá, yo te conocí como Juancho desde pequeño allá en el pueblo, y para mí, con carro o sin carro, con gringa o sin ella, siempre vas a ser Juancho" [Look, I've known you as Juancho since we were little kids back home, and to me, with or without your car and your *gringuita*, you'll always be Juancho], he tells Juancho (Bencastro 141/138). The more Juancho insists on his new North American identity and the need to progress by forgetting the past and one's Salvadoran origins, the more Calixto affirms his own Salvadoran identity and pride. He states: "[. . .] cada día soy más de allá. Porque una cosa es progresar, tener trabajo, vivir mejor, pero la tierra se lleva en el corazón. Puedo vivir cien años fuera de mi país pero nunca renunciaré a él" [every day I'm more Salvadoran. Because it's one thing to make progress, have a job, live better, but your home is always in your heart. I could live away from my country for a hundred years but I'll never renounce it] (141/138).

Missing from Craft's analysis of Bencastro's elaboration of a transnational identity is a contemplation of the fact that it is also a gendered process. Calixto's nostalgia is premised on a problematic and nationalist discourse in which woman (Lina) is coalesced with nation (El Salvador). Moreover, in both of the examples previously mentioned, the process of Salvadoran transnational identity formation is being carried out by men in male homosocial environments. With the exception of the waitresses, the crowd of spectators moved by their compatriot's drunken display and the national anthem at the restaurant are described as predominantly male. Similarly, Calixto and Juancho's exchange occurs in the kitchen where they work, a familiar and notable male space. Male immigrants such as Calixto are thus cast as the heroes of this epic because they undertake the journey to the North and are able to withstand the difficulties that come with this endeavor, not to mention that they also function as the bearers of Salvadoran identity. As such, they become the founders of a Salvadoran transnational community that rearticulates sexist nationalist discourses.

Within this particular construction of the Salvadoran immigrant reality, women such as Lina and Teresa can only exist as secondary citizens with limited participatory roles. In Teresa's case, her limited presence and contribution to the immigrant experience shared and defined by the men in the novel is undermined by her deportation and death, acts that exclude her from the process of transnational community building and the construction of identity. The insistence on these limited depictions of women underscore a more complex gendered dynamic operating at the transnational level. Despite the predominant role of Salvadoran women as migrants and economic providers for their families both in the United States and in El Salvador, men continue to be portrayed as occupying a primary and privileged place within the Salvadoran transnational community. As the representations of women in this novel of Salvadoran migration disclose, the Salvadoran transnational community being forged is permeated by a patriarchal social order that excludes women and affirms oppressive gendered binaries.

Women Speaking in Tongues

As the opening poem of Leticia Hernández-Linares's innovative *Razor Edges of My Tongue* suggests, this chapbook of poetry is about finding a woman's voice so that she may speak and reclaim her sense of self:

> My voice
> I lost it
> So I won't take it with me
> I'm going to find it ("Invocation" 8–11)

This proves to be more than an individually focused pursuit, however, because in order for the poetic "I" to find her missing voice, she must summon forth all the experiences and the words of women that have preceded her—an objective further underscored by the message that lines the inside of the front and back covers of the book. A mixture of cursive and typewritten graphics, the graffiti-like wallpaper reveals the poet's quest to write so that her descendants—her daughters—will be able to find the women they did not expect to find. Included among these women are not only the poet, but also her Salvadoran ancestors and the immigrant women that form part of the poet's everyday reality. By calling out to these otherwise silenced and unknown subjects and evincing their personal narratives throughout the collection, the poet outlines an important genealogy of Salvadoran women while at the same time providing these women with a means of speaking. It is by way of this channeling of voices that Hernández-Linares's verses draw attention to Salvadoran female immigrants and their struggles, providing a complex view of this particular subjectivity rooted in Salvadoran women's history and linked to newer generations of Salvadoran-Americans.

Hernández-Linares describes her writing as "teatro-infused poetry" (44). Strongly influenced by a spoken-word aesthetic, the performance-based aspects of Hernández-Linares's poetry are fundamental to fostering this intimate relationship between the singular poetic voice and the collectivity of women it is dialoging with and, ultimately, representing. Zoë Anglesey explains that spoken-word poetry is a "fulcrum between opposite points," bringing together a more traditional understanding of poetic voice with an emphasis on expression that draws from different elements of the performance arts such as "voices, dance, music, visual and media arts," poems or texts that "transmute into monologues or fully developed scripts," and hip-hop (xvii). As a relatively new poetic practice emerging in the 1990s and characterized by its urban-ness, this poetry is linked to younger practitioners and "is of necessity involved in the social conditions that the peoples of the world are in" (Algarín 10). Moreover, as has been the case with the spoken-word movement inspired by the Nuyorican Poets Cafe in New York's Lower East Side, the intermingling of languages such as Spanish and English has also become an important marker of this poetic form.[10] Although with this chapbook of poetic works Hernández-Linares provides what Morris calls a more "page-oriented voice" (qtd. in Crown 215), her poems continue to be defined by many of these performance-related attributes of spoken word. It is oftentimes difficult to divorce the poetic voice speaking from that of the poet herself, who would otherwise embody the poem and the different personalities being channeled or performed on the stage.

Moreover, given her literary background, Salvadoran heritage, and upbringing in East Los Angeles, Hernández-Linares's poetic project also incorporates a wide range of Latin American literary traditions, Chicano and guerrilla street theater, and Salvadoran culture and history, which infuse her poetry with a uniqueness all its own (Rodríguez, "Second-hand Identities" par. 1).

Many of these aspects come into play in Hernández-Linares's poem "La Sibila, La Cigua, y La Poetisa (Conversaciones)" [The Prophetess, the Cigua, and the Poetess (Conversations)], one of two poems in the collection that are written entirely in Spanish. Recalling the opening invocation, in this poem the poetic voice conjures forth the life of Prudencia Ayala, a Salvadoran poet and activist who ran for president of El Salvador in 1930 as a means of protest against the fact that women lacked the right to vote. That Prudencia's voice, including segments of her poetry, is one of the Salvadoran women's voices the poet chooses to invoke is not surprising, given the dedication that appears in the preliminary pages of the collection: "For Prudencia Ayala, foremother, writer, organizer, seer, presidential candidate of El Salvador in 1930" (Hernández-Linares 3). Prudencia, however, is not the only woman who speaks in the poem. Ciguanaba, a figure from Salvadoran folklore, also known as "Sihúan," a Nahuatl water spirit, is also a key presence. As the title suggests, the conversation at hand is taking place between Prudencia, the *sibila* or prophetess, and Ciguanaba, an indigenous precursor of all Salvadoran women. Lastly, there is the poet, herself, who joins the dialogue toward the end of the narrative and who speaks with a *mestiza* tongue. Adding to this interplay of voices is the inclusion of song lyrics by artists such as Totó la Momposina, a Colombian singer who intermixes traditional indigenous and Afro-Latin styles, and Atahualpa Yupanqui, a well-known artist of *Nueva Canción* in Latin America.[11] While attesting to the lyricism and versatility of the spoken-word form, the incorporation of these specific references linked to indigenous cultures and social protest also echoes the poem's critical commentary with regard to Salvadoran women's oppression and silencing.

From its opening lines, Hernandez-Linares's free verse weaves an image of Prudencia Ayala as a strong and socially defiant woman:

ese día el domingo veintitrés
caminó hacia la alcadía y pidió en voz alta
su ciudadanía (lines 5–7)
that day, Sunday the 23rd
she walked toward the mayor's office and asked in a loud voice
for her citizenship

By demanding equal citizenship, Prudencia's decisive step to claim rights for all women also signals her intention to be "muda / no más" [silent / no more] (lines 9–10). But Prudencia was more than just a political activist; as the poetic voice declares, she was also a writer and prophetess whose defiant writings and prophecies were buried under concrete and published no more (lines 27–29). Tellingly, the poetic voice stresses the "burying" and lack of circulation of Prudencia's words despite and perhaps because of their power—a gesture that Hernández-Linares undoes in this narrative of Prudencia's life through the inclusion of a verse from Prudencia Ayala's poem "Lamentación" [Lamentation]. Here, then, Hernández-Linares creates a pivotal interchange between the disclosing of Prudencia's political and artistic contributions, which led to her imprisonment, and the recovery of her silenced voice, because to contend with and make visible the first is to give way to the latter.

In this poetic rendering, Prudencia is deemed a seer capable of looking into the future on account of her acts, which paved the way for women to gain the right to vote in El Salvador. Her links to the past, including El Salvador's folkloric traditions incarnated by Ciguanaba, are just as integral to these qualities as a visionary. Prudencia makes an offering of "pedazos de calabaza / para Sihuán / mujer, espíritu de agua esperando con boca abierta / las semillas" [pumpkin pieces / for Sihuán / woman, wáter spirit waiting with open mouth / for the seeds] (lines 12–15). Referring to this folkloric figure as "Sihuán," the Nahuatl name meaning "woman of water" (Espino 37), emphasizes her identity as a woman first and as a water spirit second. A mutual connection is drawn between Prudencia and Sihuán on the basis of gender as well as the fact that each of them attempted to defy the patriarchal societies that repressed and rendered them voiceless. According to one version of the legend, Sihuán was punished by the gods for turning away from her husband and child, condemned to roam the rivers looking for wayward men for all eternity, appearing at first to be a beautiful woman and then turning into a frightful demon with a wicked laugh (Espino 37). Markedly, when Sihuán appears before Prudencia later in the poem, it is as this second form, as "*Cigua-naaa-baaa*," the trickster water spirit or "*espíritu burlón*" of Salvadoran folklore (lines 62–63).[12] Rather than a frightening entity, Hernández-Linares renders Ciguanaba a spirit in solidarity with Prudencia.

Rising from the ashes in Prudencia's prison cell, Ciguanaba provides her with the following words of support:

¡Qué ondas hermana!
dale dale con mucha gana

> no te preocupés porque a todas nos castigan
> pero con nuestra persistencia continuaremos siendo
>   chingonas! (lines 64–68)

> What's up sister!
> keep going
> don't worry because we all get punished
> but with our persistence we will continue to kick ass!

More revealing than the solidarity that Ciguanaba expresses in these lines is the language with which she speaks—an observation that is noted in the following interruption by another voice, that of "grammar" that is literally personified:

> LA GRAMÁTICA: !¿Pero, qué pasa aquí, estas palabras no son salvadoreñas?! (lines 69–70)

> GRAMMAR: What is happening here? These words aren't Salvadoran!

Implicit in "Grammar's" asking of this question is the juxtaposition between what is considered a more "formal" and structured way of writing that adheres to a specific set of rules and Ciguanaba's use of slang and profanity. "Grammar's" question is answered by the *poetisa*, who is neither Prudencia nor Ciguanaba, but presumably the speaker/ poetic voice that has been narrating all along. In an unruly tone and syntax echoing that of Ciguanaba, the female poet interjects, "Ahhh, largate gramática de mierda, esta poeta mestiza / no se traga ni eructa / ninguna lengua, ninguna patria" [Ahhh, get out of here fucking grammar, this mestiza poetess / does not swallow or burp / any language, any native country] (lines 71–73). The *poetisa's* words provide a nuanced intervention in the initial dialogue between Prudencia and Ciguanaba, bringing into the fold a new voice and perspective that speaks from the now and is not bound to a specific country or language. Linked to the notion of women rebelling against patriarchal norms is, thus, the idea of the poet also breaking free from the confines of "formal" language or traditional poetry, exemplifying what Anglesey notes as the production of a "freeing free verse" through spoken word (xvii).

Following this expressive interlude, the *poetisa* resumes her storytelling, though in a much more familiar manner: "Bueno, como les contaba . . ." [Well, as I was saying] (line 74). She stresses the transformation that Prudencia undergoes after her visit from Ciguanaba, depicting an excited Prudencia who has been infected by laughter, a trademark of the female-trickster, and who imagined herself "dirigiendo como presidenta / a todos los hijos de puta hombres / como sólo pueden ser en El Salvador" [leading like a president / all of those men sons of bitches / as they only can be in El Salvador] (lines 80–82). Prudencia embodies the spirit of Ciguanaba, and it is this possession of sorts that allows her to imagine herself as the future president of El Salvador, indicating what will be one of her historical legacies. The poet is also part of this syncretism, for it is her *mestiza* tongue that is filtering Prudencia's newfound voice and thoughts inspired by Ciguanaba. Ultimately, the poem concludes with a vindication of Prudencia and her actions:

> No era monstrua, ni mala
> nada, nada de esas pendejadas que definen y trauman
> era naba, era cigua, mujer de espíritu y agua
> que inspiró espirales de palabras
> revelaciones como tales (lines 85–89)
> She was not a monster, nor evil
> none of that bullshit that defines and traumatizes
> she was *naba*, she was *cigua*, woman of spirit and water
> that inspired spirals of words
> revelations like that

The fusion of Prudencia and Ciguanaba is once again nuanced in these last lines. There is also a call to see Prudencia (implicitly, also the figure of Ciguanaba) as the inspiring poet and groundbreaking activist she is, as opposed to the forgotten and silenced woman she has been in Salvadoran political and literary history. As such, the poem ends by repositing its social critique regarding Salvadoran women's transgressive agency in a patriarchal society.

Although seemingly unrelated, the poem "La Sibila, La Cigua, y La Poetisa (Conversaciones)" is essential for understanding Hernández-Linares's treatment of Salvadoran female immigrant subjectivities. Commenting on the importance of the "Native Woman" to Chicana feminism and writing, Norma Alarcón argues that this "pivotal indigenous portion of the *mestiza* past may represent a collective experience as well as 'the mark of the Beast' within us—the maligned and abused indigenous woman (Anzaldúa 1987, 43)" (67). Invoking the "'dark Beast' within and without" brings into focus the "cultural and psychic dismemberment that is linked to imperialist racist and sexist practices," allowing Chicanas to come to a new consciousness with regard to their individual as well as collective subjectivities (67). Hernández-Linares's portrayal of Ciguanaba in the previous poem functions in a similar way, for it is this indigenous figure/spirit that constitutes the "dark Beast" for Salvadoran women and signifies the systemic silencing and abjection of Salvadoran women throughout history. Yet Ciguanaba's presence and words are equally empowering, as they bring into focus this oppression and afford Prudencia as well as the *mestiza* poetess a new consciousness in reference to this reality. What is more, this is an understanding that is not limited to the individual women conversing in the poem but one that extends to other Salvadoran women. It is in this sense, then, that "La Sibila, La Cigua, y La Poetisa (Conversaciones)" grounds and at the same time functions as a key point of departure for looking at Hernández-Linares's representations of female immigrant subjectivities and the marginalization that these Salvadoran women likewise face. Only by first understanding the past and the ancestral voices of Ciguanaba and Prudencia can the silencing of these present-day Salvadoran women be understood and undone. Moreover, with this look to the past—free of any nostalgia—Hernández-Linares also foregrounds a broader understanding of Salvadoran transnational community and identity formation.

With her poem "Sweat," Hernández-Linares offers a scathing critique of the proliferation of "sweatshops" or maquiladoras not only in so-called Third World countries such as El Salvador but also in the United States that depend on the necessary erasure and exploitation of its female employees. As with the previous piece, the subject of writing and the notion of voice are central to the poem's narrative about Salvadoran women's lives. Yet here the immigrant reality adds a new dimension to this struggle for voice, bringing to the fore issues related to the gendered oppression these women suffer in the workforce and at home. Added to this complex portrait of female immigrant subjectivity is the ways these women must negotiate their hopes for a better future—encompassed in their pursuit of an illusory "American dream"—and the sense of disillusionment they feel about El Salvador. Like the male characters who predominate in Bencastro's novel, these female immigrants also straddle two worlds and are coming to terms with their own sense of belonging and not belonging, though with varying outcomes. In this way, Hernández-Linares's poems give way to a view of Salvadoran transnational community building and identity formation that validates and accounts for women's experiences and perspectives.

The opening verses of the poem draw a parallel between the routine work undertaken by women in garment factories, in many cases immigrants with little recourses, and the process of writing:

> Writing her life on a hem line
> Hilda watches through the door
> . . . .
> sewing machines in unison
> sound like typewriters
> just one word written over and over (lines 1–15)

While introducing the central character or female subject of the poem, a Salvadoran woman named "Hilda," these first lines emphasize the stifling nature of sweatshop labor and the alienation it engenders. Without another outlet, Hilda and other immigrant women like her are forced into silence, their work absorbing the words that could otherwise line a page. The stories these women have to tell are not only being "stitched under seams / along button holes" (lines 16–17), they are also lying in waste on the cutting room floor, appearing as scraps of fabric or "letters / written to no one in particular" (19–20). One such letter reveals the loss of physical beauty and love:

> Querido:
> Las agujas sacan sangre de mis dedos
> pequeños y cada día menos
> femeninos, más torcidos
> aún así . . . ¿me seguirás queriendo? (lines 22–26)

> Dear:
> The needles make my fingers bleed
> small and everyday less
> feminine, more twisted
> still . . . will you keep loving me?

As an anonymous letter indicative of the experiences of many, the sentiments expressed in this correspondence attest to the corporeal and emotional hardships endured by a female workforce that, without an effective means for speaking out about their lives and exploitation, remains relatively invisible. By literally incorporating this letter into the fabric of the poem, however, Hernández-Linares does more than just underscore the silencing of these female immigrant subjects on the basis of gender and their social and economic circumstances. The visual display of these women's otherwise suppressed thoughts and words keeps this correspondence from becoming another piece of forgotten fabric and instead transforms it into a symbolic outlet for these women's voices and plight.

Likening sewing to writing is only one of many critical comparisons Hernández-Linares employs in her representation of Salvadoran immigrant women. In the latter half of the poem, clothing tags are likened to "flags," while the workers themselves are posited as a new brand of Betsy Ross: "Hilda, Betina, Rosa, and the women next to them / follow in Betsy Ross's footsteps" (lines 43–44). Unlike Ross, however, these women lack the same state of belonging and iconic stature in history; they are "missing rocking chairs / songs museums in their honor / art exhibits displaying charcoal silhouettes" (lines 45–47). Moreover, the "flags" they are sewing—labels such as "Made in El Salvador," "Made in L.A.," and "Made by a slave"—are neither patriotic emblems nor symbols of freedom. Rather, they are markers not only of the marginalization the women endure as immigrant laborers but also of the multiple ways and to what degrees multinational corporations and free-market enterprise have sustained the continued subjugation of foreign economies such as that of El Salvador to that of the United States. Like the unheard stories of these women, the sending countries from which they emigrate also amount to little more than "discarded pieces of the past / that they throw out / at the end of the endless day" (lines 54–56).

Still, despite the oppressive conditions under which they labor, these women continue sewing not only because they have to but also because they hope to achieve and become a part of the illusory "American dream." Leaving behind "offerings in silk and cotton blue" to the "santita de la fábrica" [saint of the factory] (lines 58, 60), they pray, "[P]lease let me trade my m-a-i-d / for a m-a-d-e in the u.s.a label" (lines 61–62). The key wordplay between "label" and the notion of "labeling" underscores both the gendering of this workforce through the categorization of these women as maids as well as their aspirations to become American citizens—a status that would seemingly transform them from foreign others into legitimate members of the U.S. national imaginary. Implicit in these women's pleas is thus the internalization of a traditional and, in many ways, problematic assimilationist discourse for their wanting to be "m-a-d-e in the u.s.a" that requires that they discard their previous national ties and affinities in order to be "American." What is more, being "American" is not necessarily an option available to all given the undocumented status of many of these women, nor does it guarantee that they will be "delivered" from their sweatshop servitude and alienation.

In the poem's final lines, Hernández-Linares extends her critique of gendered servitude and the "American dream" by connecting these to the added labor these female immigrants perform as wives and mothers in their own homes. Returning its focus to Hilda, the poetic voice narrates, "Hilda goes home to thirsty plants / and hungry grandchildren" (lines

67–68). She goes home to another set of responsibilities that await her at the end of her workday, including cooking and cleaning. As such, Hilda's sewing at the factory and her life at home are defined by the same gendered division of labor and become an extension of one another, perpetuating the continued silencing of her words and the stifling of her life. However, within this domestic context, the oppression and sense of hopelessness that pervade Hilda's existence at the factory are also laden with a deeper cynicism linked to Hilda's Salvadoran background. Here, then, Hernández-Linares introduces another vital aspect of this gendered immigrant reality—the conflicted sentiments immigrants have regarding their own countries, which they must negotiate in light of their new lives in the United States and wish for the "American dream."

While in her kitchen, Hilda is doing more than just "cooking up history," she is "burning pieces of her country's flag" (lines 74–75), a flag "stained with dead children's questions hungry farmers dejection" (line 81). The stains that have soiled the Salvadoran flag Hilda is symbolically burning are key allusions to the legacy of war and economic strife that plague El Salvador—motivating factors that propelled many Salvadorans to migrate to the United States. Making Hilda's actions and her disillusionment all the more pronounced is the ironic juxtaposition between her outlook and the lyrics of the Salvadoran national anthem that are also included on the page: ". . . *saludemos la patria orgullosa / quemando la tierra, hechos pura* . . ." [let us salute the proud homeland / burning the earth, made pure] (italics in the original, lines 78–79). Far from exhibiting the pride in El Salvador that the anthem is meant to inspire, Hilda is hoping to be able to trade in her old flag for a new one, to become something other than a Salvadoran national. She is waiting, as the poetic voice tells us, "for the day when she can become 'an american city' / as she likes to say / and have a new flag / a new flag / to put into the flames" (lines 83–87). It is on this note of disappointment yet want for something more that Hernández-Linares ends the poem.

However, it is with these final images of Hilda wishing for a new flag to burn that Hernández-Linares also initiates a discussion regarding Salvadoran transnational identity—one that posits gender, and in particular, women's experiences as central to this process of self and communal identification. Unlike Calixto and his compatriots, Hilda's understanding of what it means to be Salvadoran in the United States is conditioned by her alienating reality not only as an immigrant but also as a woman. If anything, Hilda's double shift reveals that the domestic space of the home (whether in the United States or El Salvador) is also a source of oppression, like her workplace. Inasmuch as Hilda's identity is a product of her country's past of civil war and her culture, it is also affected by the subordinate position she holds in a patriarchal Salvadoran nation and, by extension, Salvadoran transnational community. Interestingly, in this poem the Salvadoran national anthem does not evoke the same nostalgia or sense of community that it does for Hilda's male counterparts in Bencastro's text. In fact, as the last lines of the poem suggest, Hilda wishes to trade in her Salvadoran nationality for one that is more "American," as problematic as that may be. Culture, history, and nationality are all aspects of Salvadoran transnational identity, but, as this portrait of female immigrant subjectivity articulates, they are not the only markers, nor are they conceived of in the same ways by men and women. To contemplate Hilda's struggles, as Hernández-Linares does, gives way to a more nuanced understanding of Salvadoran transnational identities that complicates and calls into question the notion articulated in Bencastro's novel.

As with "Sweat," Hernández-Linares's poem "Cumbia de salvación" [Salvation Cumbia]—perhaps the most poignant commentary about the Salvadoran immigrant reality in the collection—centers on the difficulties women face in their attempts to live the "American dream" and navigate their precarious circumstances in the United States while also providing for their dependent family members in El Salvador. Like many Salvadoran immigrants, the nameless woman being narrated in the poem is caught in a vicious circle of earning and spending in order to meet the demands of loved ones back home—a situation indicative of how in the postwar era consumer culture has become a new trap that makes economic progress for Salvadorans in and outside El Salvador an almost impossible endeavor. Hernández-Linares's use of a female figure to relate such a phenomenon—a representation that calls into question the limited view of immigrant men as the main financial providers—emphasizes the important contributions women make to the upkeep of the Salvadoran transnational economic structure. This representation of female immigrants, however, also allows for a reconceptualization of women's expected social roles and behaviors given their experiences as immigrants.

"Cumbia de salvación" opens with the lyrics of a popular *cumbia* titled "Sabrosa cumbia" by a well-known Salvadoran musical group, Marito Rivera y su Grupo Bravo: "Cumbia sabrosa cumbia / para ti yo bailo hasta amanecer" [Cumbia savory cumbia; I'll dance for you until morning] (lines 1–2). While in and of themselves the lyrics of the song are significant, as they foreground the constant economic "dancing" Salvadoran immigrants must do, the fact that this song is a *cumbia* and is sung by Marito Rivera y su Grupo Bravo, a group known internationally as "la furia musical de El Salvador" [the musical fury of El Salvador] is equally noteworthy (www.maritorivera.com). As one of the most prominent forms of music in El Salvador, *cumbia* is an important marker of home for many immigrants. Like the national food they consume to remind them of home, Marito Rivera's *cumbias* are yet another export that allow Salvadoran immigrants to identify with their Salvadoran culture. Incorporating the music of this entertainer at the beginning and throughout this piece is therefore an important means of establishing one of the pivotal subtexts driving the poem—the complex financial and cultural transnational exchanges that these immigrants maintain with El Salvador.

The initial lyrics of the *cumbia* give way to a sultry scene of a couple dancing, swaying in unison, "caderas [hips] to the right, caderas to the left" (line 6). The erotic overtones of this image, however, are quickly undermined by a woman's statement about El Salvador's financial reality, one characterized by economic dependency:

> and what it is that en realidad *manda en mi país*
> no es
> *el ritmo sabrosón de El Salvador*
> it's el dólar, el peso, el colón (lines 7–10)

> and what it is that really rules in my country
> is not
> the savory rhythms of El Salvador
> it's the dollar, the *peso*, the *colón*.

The affirmation that it is money that rules in El Salvador and not *cumbia* renders the provocative scene of the couple dancing a questionable illusion that hides the reality of life as a Salvadoran immigrant in the United States. As this poetic "I" reveals, "[. . .] that painful inflammation in my hips, my feet / isn't from dancing / but from scrubbing the greed from the corners of the room" (lines 13–15). The *cumbia* that characterizes the lives of many Salvadoran immigrants is anything but *sabrosa*, nor is it a pleasurable mix of inspired rhythms and beats. Rather, it is a never-ending dance propelled by the constant need to sustain a continuous flow of goods and money to loved ones in El Salvador.

As the poem progresses, the poetic voice invites the reader to witness her "dance," to see her "body move through all kinds of beats" (line 18). She describes an endless routine that keeps her saving her money "7 days a week" so that before she visits her family in El Salvador she can "stop by the neon lit duty free store" and buy them the "tommy hillfiger striped american feel" they all need, want, and desire (lines 23–25). Like her, many Salvadoran immigrants are in the same predicament, unable to better either their economic situation or that of their families. Instead, they find themselves purchasing and accumulating useless items that give them a false sense not only of financial advancement but also of being "American." It is no coincidence that it is the Tommy Hilfiger brand, identified by its patriotic red, white, and blue logo as well as its affirmation of an iconic and "classic American style," that Hernández-Linares alludes to as a means of underscoring the "american feel" Salvadorans crave. Echoing the sentiments expressed by Hilda and the other immigrant women in "Sweat," Salvadorans, in and outside El Salvador, are similarly depicted as desperately yearning to be part of the "American dream." Here, too, however, that notion is criticized and challenged by Hernández-Linares when the poetic voice emphasizes the delight of vendors who have "clients dancing right into their arms / deseos de El Salvador trailing after them" (lines 37–38). When viewed from this perspective, the "American dream" amounts to little more than capitalistic greed and consumerism.

Unable to free herself, this unknown immigrant ultimately "dances" to her tragic end, and as another anonymous voice asks, "¿para qué?" [for what?] (line 41). Notably, this last aspect of this immigrant woman's unfortunate experience is no longer related by her, the poetic "I," but through the *chismes* [gossiping] of two anonymous speakers who are also members of the same Salvadoran immigrant community:

> hey did you hear about fulanita [so and so]
> heard she is out of work
> and never goes dancing anymore
> . . . ¿y eso [what]?
> . . . es que [well],
> she danced right into the store
> and choked
> on her debt (lines 44–51)

In this exchange, the immigrant subject of the poem is characterized as a universal "so-and-so," one of the many *fulanitas* who have danced or continue to dance to the beats of the "Cumbia de salvación," which despite its ironic title does not lead to the salvation of Salvadorans either in El Salvador or in the United States. On the contrary, as Hernández-Linares's critical portrayal reveals, this *cumbia*—dictated by the constant demands of El Salvador on its migrants—is, ironically, the perdition of many.

Using the *chisme* [gossip or rumors] as a means of closing the poem is, likewise, telling given the association of this popular oral form with women. Despite the fact that the dialogue between these unknown speakers seems to be devoid of any sympathy for the immigrant woman who "choked on her debt," the discussion of her ordeal in and of itself holds a potential subversive quality. Rather than detract from the narrative that the *fulanita* tells of her own predicament, these *chismes* draw out the politics of voice and gendered representation that are in play in the poem. Akin to what Yolanda Broyles-González terms "contra-decir," the gossiping in which these two speakers are engaged acts as a means of contesting a masculine history (117). In this instance, the historical narrative in question is that of the male migrant hero—the *hermano lejano.* Through these women's words, it is the narrative of Salvadoran immigrant women who are vital to the Salvadoran transnational community as both economic and cultural carriers that takes precedence.

For Hernández-Linares, the invocation of women's voices such as those of Prudencia and Ciguanaba, Hilda, and the anonymous *fulanitas* forced to dance tragic *cumbias* is not merely a means of fostering the poet's own voice and sense of self. Rather, it is an effort to trace a genealogy that bears witness to Salvadoran women's endeavors and contributions throughout history. Only by understanding the struggles for voice as well as the different forms of agency enacted by the poet's predecessors can the hardships of immigrant women and second generations be fully contextualized within the present. In doing so, this chapbook of poetry affords an alternate understanding of Salvadoran women's roles and participation within the current context of Salvadoran migration and transnational community building. What is more, it posits new ways of regarding the construction of Salvadoran transnational identities by underscoring the vitality of women's perspectives and contributions to this process.

Defining Anew Transnational Migration and Identity

Bencastro's *Odisea del Norte* and Hernández-Linares's poems offer an engaging look at the Salvadoran immigrant experience from the "other side." Bencastro's rendering of women as secondary figures who lack voice and participate only tangentially in the migratory process speaks to the persistence of patriarchal norms and gendered divisions that are rearticulated within the Salvadoran transnational community. With the nuanced focus on women's voices and the centering of a female poetic "I," Hernández-Linares lays claim to a different politics of voice and immigrant reality—one that allows women to speak and critically underscores the gendered oppression and exploitation they suffer in El Salvador and the United States. Notably, these divergent yet dialogic responses concerning the gendered nature of Salvadoran migration and transnational community building are not entirely dissimilar from the conflicts giving way in postwar El Salvador. As I explored in Chapter 3, the Salvadoran postwar process of reconstruction has been characterized by efforts not only to undermine the agency women acquired through their involvement in the civil war and their integration in the national economy under neoliberalism, but also to restrict any further attempts by women's organizations to foster gender equality and secure political rights. To a certain extent, then, Bencastro's *Odyssey* and Hernández-Linares's poems exemplify the ways in which Salvadoran cultural processes and debates permeate the Salvadoran transnational community.

Beyond this, however, their works are testament to how international migration and the construction of immigrant subjectivities—especially those of women—and life in the United States are equally influencing these dynamics. These Salvadoran-American texts reveal tensions regarding women's roles and agency outside the confines of the nation. In so doing, they also speak to the constant redefinition of what it means to be or define oneself as Salvadoran in a broader transnational context. For Bencastro, this notion of transnational identity is rooted in the Salvadoran homeland and is in keeping with traditional discourses of nation building as well as a migratory experience that is male centered and patriarchal. For Hernández-Linares, the construction of Salvadoran transnational identity is also steeped in the past; however, women do not remain on the periphery, nor do they fail to question their subordination. Women move forward, toward a different future, one in which they can reclaim a space and an identity for themselves and their daughters that is not solely tied to home or the homeland, an intergenerational view that, similarly, foregrounds a conceptualization of Salvadoran transnational identity that includes second-generation Salvadoran-Americans.[13]

Chapter 5

Salvadoran-American Sleuthing in the U.S. South and Beyond

McPeek Villatoro's Romilia Chacón Mysteries Series

In the prologue to *Home Killings*, the first installment of the Romilia Chacón mystery series by Marcos McPeek Villatoro, Romilia, lead detective and protagonist, provides readers with a snapshot view of her complex subjectivity. Opening with the line "I'm twenty-eight, Latina, and a southerner," Romilia lays claim to her pan-ethnic and gendered identity as a Latina while also distinguishing her connection to a specific geographic area within the United States, the South (McPeek Villatoro vii). Further complicating this self-portrait is the fact that Romilia is of Central American descent, specifically Salvadoran, as well as a single mother, and as the series progresses she migrates westward and relocates to Los Angeles, prompting another redefinition of her identity. Understood within the broader context of detective fiction and even that of multiethnic mystery novels, this multifaceted characterization of Romilia by McPeek Villatoro offers a pioneering example of a Salvadoran-American female sleuth. However, read against the backdrop of recent demographic shifts in the U.S. South and Central American migratory flows, Romilia's portrayal also helps to disclose the multiple contours of Central American identity making and incorporation into the United States.

As such, in this last chapter I examine how Romilia's depiction and her crime solving in Marcos McPeek Villatoro's Romilia Chacón series—*Home Killings* (2001), *Minos* (2003), and *A Venom beneath the Skin* (2005)[1]—allow for a nuanced exploration of the complexities of

123

being Latina and a second-generation Salvadoran-American. Emphasizing the question of Romilia's identity affords an added critical dimension to the ongoing discussion in this book regarding Salvadoran women's experiences, for Romilia deepens our understanding of female agency but does so by underscoring the process of Salvadoran-American ethnic individuation. As a second-generation Latina of Salvadoran descent, Romilia negotiates her existence in the United States in diverse ways from those of newly arrived immigrants. In addition to seeing herself as part of a larger pan-ethnic group of Latinos, she struggles to define herself in relation to a history of civil war and migration that is unknown to her. Figuratively speaking, Romilia calls to mind the notion of a Salvadoran immigrant nation marked by its different generations and cultural roots that has become part of the multiethnic landscape of the United States. Somewhat distinct from the construct of "woman as nation" seen in other trans-Salvadoran narratives, Romilia's representation as such is also inherently linked to Central American history. Moreover, as much as Romilia's overall portrait, including its allegorical functions, underscores the emergence of new Salvadoran-based gendered subjectivities and ethnicity, it also gives way to a broader discussion of Central American-American identities. Critical to Romilia's depiction is her ensuing relationship with her adversary, Rafael Murillo, a Guatemalan-American, which signals her as part of a growing community of Central American-Americans whose identity politics are still, in many ways, "in process."

Making these novels all the more provocative is that, although Romilia's investigating leads her to California, where the third installment of the series takes place, the initial point of reference for her identity formation is the U.S. South, a geographic location that has traditionally been marked by a black and white racial divide and has only recently experienced a significant upsurge in Latino immigration and settlement. Thus, unlike the U.S. Salvadoran narratives that informed my discussion in the previous chapter, McPeek Villatoro's texts allow for a complementary yet divergent view of Salvadoran immigration and incorporation into the United States that falls outside the scope of urban locations such as Washington, D.C., and Los Angeles—well-known destinations and sites of migrant networks for Salvadorans and other Central Americans. It is on account of this unique vantage point that my analysis of Romilia within these novels will be largely premised and filtered through her construction as a Salvadoran-American and Latina with southern roots, even as I address the shifting nature of this identity in more ethnically diverse settings such as Los Angeles.

Central Americans in a New Latino South

Given its significance to McPeek Villatoro's narratives, a basic outline of the recent demographic shifts transforming the U.S. South is necessary. In what follows, I provide a brief summary of these changes before engaging in a more expansive debate regarding Central American identity politics—the theoretical base for understanding my analysis of Romilia's portrayal. With the exception of the Cuban-American community in Florida and the smaller populations of Mexican farm workers who emigrated to the U.S. South as a result of the Bracero Program (1942–1964), until recently, the Latino presence has been minimal in this region (Alabama, Arkansas, Florida, Georgia, Kentucky, Louisiana, Mississippi, North Carolina, South Carolina, Tennessee, and Virginia).[2] Following the data reported by the Pew Hispanic Center, the Latino populations in states throughout the region increased exponentially between 2000 and 2005.[3] Central Americans comprise a significant sector of these new groups, as recent studies such as Leon Fink's *The Maya of Morganton* (2003), which chronicles the work and communal experience of a Guatemalan immigrant indigenous community in a small town in North Carolina, attest. Statistical reports draw a similar picture, revealing that in 2005, Virginia's Central American–born population was 107,411, whereas in Georgia and North Carolina this group numbered well over 50,000 ("A Statistical Portrait of the Foreign Born" Table 9).

The change in Latino demographics in these southern states, and especially the presence of Central American communities, is the result of varying factors. The political unrest and economic instability that marked much of Latin America, and Central American countries in particular, throughout the 1970s and 1980s gave way to unprecedented waves of immigration to the United States. U.S. foreign policies as well as neoliberal economic and political reforms, including free trade and privatization policies such as the North American Free Trade Agreement (NAFTA) and the Central American Free Trade Agreement (CAFTA), have likewise contributed to an increase in international immigration from Latin America. Added to this political and financial restructuring are the effects of legislation such as the 1986 Immigration Reform and Control Act (IRCA), the 1997 Nicaraguan Adjustment and Central American Relief Act (NACARA), and the Temporary Protected Status program initiated in the early 1990s, which provided different avenues for legalizing a large number of immigrants, particularly Salvadorans and Guatemalans who had been denied asylum as political refugees and remained undocumented immigrants. Acquiring some form of legal status facilitated greater mobility among immigrants residing in the United States, allowing many of them to relocate in different regions such as the U.S. South, which, unlike major urban centers on the East and West Coasts, had been less impacted by the influx of immigrants, as Rubén Hernández-Leon and Victor Zuniga suggest.

Both the economic structure and social fiber of the U.S. South have been considerably altered by the influx of this diverse group of Latin American immigrants and U.S.-born Latinos. Economic opportunities for low-skilled workers in industries located primarily in rural sectors as well as affordable housing have attracted and fomented a new Latino labor force (Furuseth and Smith 9, 12). Still subject to extreme forms of exploitation, particularly given the undocumented status of many, this new labor force, according to Sandy Smith-Nonini, is a vital element of chemical, automobile, furniture, poultry, and meatpacking factories as well as more traditional agricultural industries and construction.[4] The socioeconomic incorporation of Latinos has likewise influenced the racial dynamic in the U.S. South, which has been historically divided along black and white lines.[5] Although this integration has given way to tensions among the diverse racial and ethnic groups and the rise of anti-immigrant sentiments, recent scholarship by Ellen Spears and Fran Ansley and Susan Williams has also emphasized the formation of coalitions and cultural exchanges. In this sense, the U.S. South has become a veritable site of transculturation, what Fernando Ortiz defines "as a process of transition from one culture to another" that does not merely imply the act of acculturation or the acquisition of another culture, but also that of deculturation, the "loss or uprooting of a previous culture" (102). Additionally, as Ortiz further emphasizes, transculturation "carries the idea of the consequent creation of new cultural phenomena, which could be called neoculturation" (102-03). Thus, Latin American immigrants and Latinos living in the U.S. South struggle to adapt to "American" culture at the expense of losing partial aspects of their own. Yet in the process they also forge and influence hybrid cultural formations and expressions, all giving way to a reconceptualization of this regional space, what R. Mohl terms a "New Latino South" or a "New Nuevo South."

McPeek Villatoro's Romilia Chacón series provides a novel look at this extensive process of racial and ethnic transformation in the U.S. South while also evincing the uniqueness of the Salvadoran, and by extension Central American, experience. Combining aspects of a more traditional female sleuth with those of the hard-boiled detective, Romilia is, on the one hand, an aggressive, no-nonsense cop who enjoys southern bourbon, is haunted by the murder of her sister, and is prone to violence.[6] On the other, she is a single mother who is constantly feeling guilty for not dedicating enough time to her son and her mother. Caught at the crossroads of multiple subject positions, Romilia is a figure who has to continuously renegotiate her identity on the basis of her gender, as she struggles to be a "good cop" and a "good mother," as well as her ethnicity. As the series progresses, she must also contend with her identity in light of her travels and relocation away from the U.S. South to Los Angeles, an urban setting with a more diverse and pronounced Latino population, including a substantial Salvadoran community.

Within this larger web of identity traits, perhaps the most central of all is Romilia's Salvadoran-American background. While identifying with the pan-ethnic label of "Latina," Romilia's representation in these texts is also explicitly defined by her Salvadoranness. Along with using the *voseo*, a common form in Spanish prevalent in many parts of Central America, when talking with her son or her mother, Romilia also references Salvadoran oral traditions, cultural symbols, and foods such as *pupusas*.[7] Complementing this depiction of Salvadoran-American identity is Romilia's nemesis, Rafael Murillo, a drug lord with ties to the Guatemalan military, whose Guatemalan-American background likewise marks his Central American roots. The entangled relationship between these two characters—detective and *bête noir*—not only serves as an important catalyst for Romilia's investigation into Central America's history of civil war and violence during the 1970s and 1980s but also is fundamental to Romilia's representation as an allegorical construct of El Salvador. More importantly, it allows for a wider conceptualization of Central American identities. It is for these reasons that any discussion emphasizing Romilia's Latina ethnicity and Salvadoranness cannot be necessarily divorced from broader issues of Central American identity and representation.

Arturo Arias calls attention to what he perceives as the "invisibility" of the Central American population within the United States. Arias ascribes the purposefully pleonastic label of "Central American-American" to this group and maintains that this identity is one that cannot be fully subsumed either within the label of "U.S. Latino" or "Latin American" given that "[t]he Guatemalan, Salvadoran, or even Central American experience as a whole is independent and irreducible to large unities that seek to discipline its singularity" (171). In fact, for Arias the redundancy of "Central American-American" and its "clumsiness" serves precisely to underscore how this identity resides "outside of th[e] se two signifiers from the very start" (171). Thus, drawing from Gustavo Pérez-Firmat's and Juan Flores's theories of hyphenated Latino identities and cultures, Arias contends that Central American-Americans remain on "the margins of those hyphenated others (Cuban-Americans, Mexican

Americans) [. . .] a population that has not yet earned the hyphen to mark its recognition, its level of assimilation and integration within the multi-cultural landscape of the United States" (171).

Arias acknowledges that the broader regional emphasis in the term "Central American-American," as opposed to individual national origins such as Salvadoran-American or Guatemalan-American, is problematic given its potential to obscure the historical and cultural particularities that characterize individual Central American countries and their peoples. Nevertheless, he contends that his insistence on this regional categorization serves as a means "[f]or opening the possibility" of recognition for this segment of the U.S. population, and, as he also clarifies, the "risk of reifying the Central American identity" is a necessary one "because the Latino identity is often constructed in areas of the United States like Los Angeles through the abjection and erasure of the Central American-American [. . .]" (172). We can further argue whether or not this regional affiliation is also an effect of the double marginalization of Central American-Americans raised by Arias. If on the whole Central Americans have not earned recognition or visibility, what can be expected for the separate national identities that comprise this group? Perhaps, then, to identify with "Central America" is a first step toward claiming more diverse subjectivities, as suggested in many ways by Romilia's emphasis on her Salvadoranness while also establishing a key connection to Rafael Murillo.

Arias continues his discussion by stating that the "erasure" of Central American-Americans is not only a consequence of a process of "Latino" identity formation, but is also rooted in specific historical conditions such as Central America's subordination to Mexico, beginning with the colonial period and extending into the present day. Not only are many Central Americans forced to adopt a Mexican identity as a strategy of survival in the United States, but, as Arias states, many of them also perceive themselves as less than Mexican, that is, belonging to an even more devalued and underrepresented community than that of Mexican immigrants. Central Americans are likewise marked by the stigma of their past, fleeing wars sponsored by the U.S. government that tainted them as "illegals" and "Communists" (178). Along with psychological traumas, these sociohistorical factors, which have conditioned the reception and social reality of Central American immigrants, have resulted in the "denial of their own beingness" and a "non-identity" that "negates the possibility for an identity politics" (183). Consequently, the inability to lay claim to the past makes the construction of an identity difficult for Central Americans, therefore also contributing to their erasure in a multicultural U.S. imaginary.

Romilia's Salvadoran-American identity and "sleuthing" in these detective novels allow for a critical exploration and rethinking of the claims made by Arias with regard to Central American "invisibility" in the United States. One may argue that the complex representation of Romilia's "Latina" subjectivity in these texts, which seems to privilege a U.S.-based pan-ethnic self-identification, exemplifies Arias's assertion concerning the eclipsing of Central Americans in the construction of a "Latino" identity. Yet McPeek Villatoro's inclusion of Central American characteristics tied to the U.S. South continuously works to undermine this potentially homogenizing representation of Romilia, for although Romilia identifies as a "Latina southerner," it is impossible to ignore her Salvadoranness, which comes through in her speech, food preferences, and cultural allusions. Within the context of a biracial U.S. South, Romilia's Salvadoran background sets her apart not only from Anglos and African-Americans but also from the predominantly Mexican and Mexican-American Latino groups in the area. As such, her Salvadoranness calls attention to a *Latinidad* or what Frances Aparicio defines as the "interlatino negotiations" and form of knowledge production that is taking shape at the margins of the margin. Notably, being Salvadoran also signals Romilia as different even in Los Angeles, where Romilia forms part of a more ethnically diverse community with an extensive Central American populace. Understood in reference to a conceptualization of Central American identities and peoples, her Salvadoran background also speaks to the heterogeneity that characterizes this region.

Aside from her Salvadoran heritage, Romilia's process of Latina identity formation is heavily influenced by her interactions with Rafael Murillo—another Central American-American—which lead her to "unearth" a Central American history that is unfamiliar to her, but just as pivotal for understanding her cultural and ethnic background. It is within this context that the figurative dimensions of Romilia's portrayal are most evident. In addition to representing a Salvadoran immigrant nation that has begun to establish roots in the United States, Romilia, together with Murillo, function as allegories for the Central American countries from which their families originate—El Salvador and Guatemala—and, as I posit later in this chapter, reenact the past of war and migration experienced by both of these nations.[8] Consequently, this revealing of history—by way of both Romilia's literal sleuthing and use as an allegorical referent for the nation—is suggestive of another key way in which McPeek Villatoro's texts contest a monolithic view of Latino identity. Moreover, if, as Arias suggests, another reason for the "nonidentity" of Central Americans in the United States is the denial of their past, then Romilia's investigation of the civil wars that ravaged

El Salvador and Guatemala also creates a space for a Central American-American identity politics that has not been possible.

Being "Latina" and a "southerner" in these narratives does not necessarily occlude Romilia's Salvadoran-American or Central American-American identity. To the contrary, McPeek Villatoro's multifaceted construction of Romilia works against this erasure, rendering Central Americans discernible while also begging the question: what does it mean to be a Latina, specifically Salvadoran-American, in a New Latino South and beyond? Thus, I argue that by showcasing the complexities of Romilia's Latina identity formation, a process that involves her performance of Salvadoranness and the "detection" of a hidden past of civil strife, violence, and trauma, McPeek Villatoro's detective series "makes visible" Central American-Americans. Because Romilia's portrayal and identity are likewise informed by discourses of gender, geography, and her developing relationship with Murillo, I further maintain that McPeek Villatoro's recognition of Central Americans by way of a "Latina southerner" and her investigation into the past complicates and, in the process, broadens Arias's conceptualization of Central American-American marginality and identity politics in the United States.

Romilia Chacón: Salvadoran, Southern, and a Sleuth

As critics such as Priscilla L. Walton have suggested, popular forms such as the detective genre have been scrutinized precisely because "such texts are not 'individualized' after the fashion of 'High Culture' literature" (258). Recent scholarship about detective fiction, especially focused on feminist and multiethnic works, has attempted to counter this limited understanding by calling attention to the ways in which this genre can also be used by authors to consciously underscore issues and tensions with regard to gender, ethnicity, and race.[9] In his analysis of Chicana/o detective novels, Ralph Rodriguez affirms that although "detective novels can be entertaining and delightful reads . . . they also answer questions about writers who produce them and the cultures that consume them" (2). Rodriguez further suggests that "[t]hese detective novels demonstrate the emergence of new discourses of identity, politics, and cultural citizenship" (2). It is in keeping with this same premise that I approach my analysis of the Romilia Chacón mystery series as a cogent site in which a new discourse of Salvadoran-American, and by extension Central American-American, identity is being produced and debated.[10]

Although I draw from examples in all three installments of the series, the first, *Home Killings*, serves as a key anchor for this exploration, because it is in this text that Romilia's Salvadoran and southern roots are most nuanced and in which she first comes in contact with Murillo and her family's unknown past of violent conflict—factors that will influence her and her detective work in the remaining two narratives. I first explore McPeek Villatoro's depiction of Romilia, focusing on her gendered representation primarily in reference to the ethnic and racial dynamic of the U.S. South and Romilia's performance of Salvadoranness. Included in this discussion is also an examination of Murillo's Guatemalan-American background as it relates to Romilia's portrayal but also Central American-American identity formation. Second, I address the text's engagement with Central America's history of war and migration and the ways in which Romilia's unveiling of this "hidden past" as well as her allegorical construction not only contribute to Romilia's sense of her Latino identity, but also have implications for the broader Central American population in the United States.

   Home Killings introduces readers to Romilia—the newest member and only Latina of the Homicide Unit of the Nashville police force. Set in the late 1990s, the novel follows Romilia's first assignment, an investigation into the murder of Diego Sáenz, a Latino journalist responsible for the bilingual supplement in the local newspaper and an important source of information for the Spanish-speaking community in the Nashville area. One of Romilia's lead suspects in the case is Rafael Murillo, an entrepreneurial businessman who secretly runs an international drug trafficking operation and about whom Sáenz was writing a story. Murillo's street name, Tekún Umán, a reference to a Guatemalan Indian who died fighting the conquistador of Central America, Pedro de Alvarado, links him to the Mayan populations of the region and their use of jade. More importantly, as Romilia discovers, Murillo is an ex-member of the *kaibiles*, one of the most feared death squads and military units in Guatemala during the latter part of the civil war, which encompassed the period from 1960 to 1996.

   Stuart Hall's theories of cultural identity provide a useful base for exploring Romilia's complex subjectivity and depiction in this and subsequent texts. Drawing from a notion of identity as a " 'production' that is never complete, always in process, and always constituted within, not outside representation" (392), Hall suggests that cultural identities should be understood as "the points of identification, the unstable points of identification or suture, which are made, within the discourses of history and culture. Not an essence but a *positioning*. Hence, there is always a politics of identity, a politics of position, which has no absolute guarantee in an unproblematic, transcendental 'law of origin' " (395). Among the more salient points raised by Hall's conceptualization is his emphasis on cultural identity as a "positioning" that is not only contingent upon varying historical and cultural discourses but is also an ongoing process encompassed within the act of representation. Romilia's multifaceted cultural identity can be understood in this light. It is a product being formed through the many intersections of culture, history, gender, and geographic location that characterize Romilia's world. As such, it is also an identity that is continuously evolving, privy to changes given the incorporation of or contact with new discourses and experiences. An example of this process is Romilia's ceaseless renegotiation of her identity in light of the "latinization" of the U.S. South, which conditions her own sense of what it means to be Latina/o and her performance of Salvadoranness.[11] In essence, with Romilia, McPeek Villatoro is showcasing a Salvadoran-American cultural identity "in process" that also speaks to the formation of Central American-American cultural identity and visibility.

Looking at this process of cultural identity formation requires, first, addressing what it means to be a Latina southerner, as Romilia claims; and second, working within the parameters of this pan-ethnic label in order to tease out the particularities of Romilia's Salvadoranness. Romilia was hired by the Nashville police force to bridge the cultural gap between them and the growing Latino population, or, as she phrases it, because the "small retinue of southern dicks had found their deductive reasoning and acumen stunted by their inability to speak Spanish" (McPeek Villatoro, *Home Killings* 16). Her hire is but one indicator of the growing Latino community in the area and the ways in which Latin American immigration has changed and influenced the region. While following a lead, Romilia visits a *taquería* [taco shop] in a poverty-stricken sector of Nashville. Blending restaurant with *bodega* [grocery store], the *taquería* is host to a "cornucopia of Latin foods" and Latino popular culture, including Gloria Estefan and Selena CDs as well as posters of our Lady of Guadalupe (32). According to the Mexican owner, Doña Marina, not only can she hardly keep up with the demand from her Latino clientele, but she even has begun to sell her products to "*gringos* and *negros*" (35). As with the need for Romilia's position on the police force, Doña Marina's *taquería* and its location in a predominantly Latino neighborhood highlights the burgeoning cultural interchange among Latinos, *gringos*, and *negros*.

However, this "latinization" of the U.S. South is also marked by deeper economic and political tensions that are revealed in the immigration backlash spurred by Romilia's investigation. Dining at a barbecue grill, Romilia overhears one of the locals, who, while commenting on "all them wetbacks coming into the area," is quick to associate immigrant workers with criminal activity, stating: "You're bound to have some nutcase in one of those trucks, saying he wants to pick tomatoes but what he really wants to do is to slit a few throats. That immigration needs to come in here and clean up" (182). This is a sentiment shared by both the white customer expressing it and the black man sitting next to him. A division is thus drawn between white and black southerners and the newer Latino settlers. To a certain extent, the segregation between whites and blacks that has traditionally defined the U.S. South is reconfigured in light of global economic and political developments to produce yet another binary also based on ethnic and racial differences as well as citizenship. Underlying this dynamic of "white and black against brown," as Romilia contends, is a discriminatory fear rooted in the influx of immigrant populations and their potential threat to "American" jobs and livelihoods, paralleling the economic and demographic changes the U.S. South had begun to undergo in the 1980s and 1990s. This problematic dynamic emphasizes the notion of "Americans" against Latino others and reinscribes a false understanding of all Latinos as foreign and homogenous.

For Romilia, these conflicts among Latinos, whites, and blacks are not easily navigated, given her status as a police officer. Despite revealing a heightened sense of the racism and sexism that permeate her unit, Romilia's critical stance is often undermined by her need to succumb to the exigencies of the institution. After discovering that one of Murillo's henchmen, Francisco Colibrí o *Pajarito* [Little Bird], is extorting money from undocumented immigrants in exchange for fake documents, Romilia and her partner, Jerry Wilson, who is a white Tennessean, decide to use the informants they captured in order to detain *Pajarito* and eventually reel in Murillo. The informants, both undocumented, agree to wear wires in exchange for being cleared from any possible connections to Murillo's drug trafficking. While preparing for the sting operation, Jerry hints at Romilia's physical inability to deal with both male informants and tells her that they will have to turn the men over to U.S. immigration. Romilia is quick to answer, "Look, I can't be bothered with their life stories, Jerry" (195). This calculated response is delivered within the context of a self-conscious power play between her and Jerry: "In his eyes, I suppose I was also cold-blooded, along with being sly. Perhaps my being Latina meant I had to think a certain way, specifically regarding undocumented foreigners. Right now all I wanted to think about was nailing Pajarito, and ultimately his boss" (195). Romilia's words reveal her need to prove herself to Jerry, solidifying her position as a cop over that of any possible ethnic allegiances, a preference that is also made clear by her ambivalence in critically addressing her ethnic-based hire.

Being a law enforcement agent may limit Romilia's behavior to a certain extent when it comes to her coworkers; however, it does not keep her from reflecting on her own sense of a Latina identity. In fact, Romilia's continuous negotiation between being a Latina police officer and working with a Latino population is a perpetual catalyst for this type of self-exploration. Following the capture of *Pajarito*, Romilia is unsettled by what she perceives as "every single eye [. . .] watching me, someone of familiar skin, doing something so very foreign to one of our own" (198). Although she is performing her duty by arresting *Pajarito*, Romilia is conscious of how this act could also be read as a betrayal of the Latino community with which she identifies. Even more egregious than a white cop is a Latina cop who betrays her own people. Romilia's contradictory feelings raise important questions about how her identity is constructed in reference to and as part of a broader and heterogeneous minority group. In this context, Romilia's Salvadoran-American identity is intrinsically linked to her own sense of being a Latina in the U.S. South. Romilia considers herself Latina even while enacting Salvadoranness through her *voseo* and cultural referents to differentiate herself from Mexican immigrants and Mexican-Americans. Thus, when she contemplates her sense of "loyalty," it is in reference to a diverse and wide-ranging Latino community.

According to Alejandro Portes and Rubén G. Rumbaut's work on second-generation immigrant children, the complex process of ethnic identification "begins with the application of a label to oneself in a cognitive process of self-categorization, involving not only a claim to membership in a group or category but also a contrast of one's group or category with other groups and categories" (151). Romilia's use of the pan-ethnic label "Latina" exemplifies this process; her self-identification stresses her need to be understood as a part of a larger Latino group as well as her intention to highlight the distinction of this group from that of others, particularly in the southern region in which she situates herself. This is notable in Romilia's incessant and at times contradictory subject positioning as a Latina southerner in a predominantly biracial U.S. South still marked by its Anglocentrism. Yet there is also another dimension to this process of ethnic individuation, and thus identity formation, given that Romilia's subjectivity is equally developed, in contrast to the dominant Latino groups in the area, immigrants and Mexican-Americans. It is in these "points of identification" but also differentiation that Romilia's Salvadoran heritage takes on new meaning. Moreover, it is through these intersections at the margins that Central American-Americans become visible.

One of the more salient ways in which McPeek Villatoro posits the distinctions among the varying Latino groups in the area is through the use of language. For Romilia, a defining characteristic of the Latinos she encounters is often their use of Mexican Spanish. This is evident in her interaction with the *taquería* owner, Doña Marina, who uses the word "chota," which according to Romilia is an unflattering Mexican term for "cop."[12] A similar instance occurs when Romilia attempts to access Diego Sáenz's computer files in the hope of finding a clue to help solve his murder. At her partner's suggestion that the password may be in Spanish given that Sáenz was Latino, Romilia tries the words "*mole, chilango,* and *momia*" because Sáenz was of "Mexican descent" (McPeek Villatoro, *Home Killings* 108). Implicit in Romilia's categorization of this Spanish as "Mexican" are the notions that other forms of Spanish exist, such as "Salvadoran" Spanish, and that not all Latinos are the same, contrary to the common perception by non-Latino groups in the area. Romilia's use of "Salvadoran" Spanish as well as her reference to other Salvadoran cultural markers serves to further highlight this point.

As a linguistic practice associated with the intimacy of the home, "Salvadoran" Spanish, characterized by the form of the *voseo*, draws attention to the familial bonds shared by Romilia, her mother, Eva, and her son, Sergio. Upon hearing Romilia say "dirty words" during one of their conversations, her mother is quick to admonish her: "*Cuidáte vos*" [Watch it] (66). Although the use of the *voseo* in this instance denotes the Chacón family's Central American background, the added inclusion of words used in El Salvador, such as *cipote* for boy and the allusion to *el zipitillo*, a popular figure of Salvadoran lore and oral tradition, likewise render this Spanish explicitly "Salvadoran." This distinctive use of language as a cultural marker, upheld by McPeek Villatoro's acknowledgement in *Home Killings* to his editor: "Special thanks to Nicolás Kanellos for his fine editing (and his allowance of Salvadoran Spanish throughout the text) [. . .]" (248), is the principle means through which Romilia marks and performs her Salvadoranness.

This way of performing Salvadoranness through language as well as the aforementioned cultural referents to folklore and food are consistent throughout the series. They are also, however, accompanied by and further underscored by nuanced allusions to El Salvador and what are perceived as Salvadoran cultural traits—especially according to Romilia's mother, Eva. Noteworthy examples are found in the second book, *Minos*, which focuses on Romilia's hunt for the serial killer who murdered her older sister, Catalina. Although in this text Romilia is forced to travel away from her comfort zone in Nashville, venturing out to the Midwest and California, her sense of Salvadoran identity and individuation remains grounded in the ethnic makeup of the U.S. South. Given the intimate nature of the plotline, this second mystery delves deeper into Romilia's psyche as well as her individual background, revealing not only her reasons for becoming a detective but also other personal aspects such as her deceased husband's identity. Similarly, in this sequel, Murillo's Guatemalan-American background takes more precedence.

Despite being mentioned only briefly, the description of Romilia's deceased husband, César, is pivotal given his characterization as an "*hombre cabal*," a "truly revolutionized" man like "Fidel," according to Romilia's mother, who "cooked *pupusas* and cleaned the kitchen" (McPeek Villatoro, *Minos* 116). While drawing an idealistic comparison between César and Fidel Castro—calling to mind El Salvador's own revolutionary history and movement—this portrait of César also draws attention to his Salvadoran heritage. As Romilia elaborates, "César's family was more Indio than ours was, coming from the northern mountains of El Salvador. César, although born north of Lake Ilopango, did not speak Nahuatl nor Pipil, not like his grandmother did" (116). Having been born in El Salvador, César constitutes for Romilia a direct link to her parent's country of origin and draws attention to the "Indio" or Indian ancestry of Salvadorans.[13] As such, César and Romilia's marriage to him signals another way in which Romilia establishes and broadens her Salvadoranness.

Like César, Romilia's mother, Eva, contributes to Romilia's sense of being Salvadoran. Eva's opinions betray some of the more general sentiments felt by first generations of Central Americans living in the United States—sentiments that newer generations like that of Romilia have inherited and, in many ways, internalized. On more than one occasion, Romilia alludes to her mother's anger at being mistaken for Mexican. When a local doctor examining Romilia asks her, "You're Mexican right?" her mother curtly responds, "Salvadoran" because, as Romilia explains, "She [Eva] hated it when people couldn't tell the difference" (12). The "rancor" that marks Eva's response is often counterbalanced by her pride in being Salvadoran. As Romilia states, "Mamá had a way of making sure I never forgot who we were, *guanacos*, Salvadoreños, people of the tiniest country in Central America, *la gente industrial* [industrious people], harder working than those neighboring Nicaraguans, more focused than the Panamanians" (McPeek Villatoro, *Minos* 85). Her mother's pride is based on what she sees as the distinguishable characteristics of Salvadorans by contrast with other Central American groups.

However, as the second portion of this quote reveals, this pride is also enacted in response to the perceived frictions that exist between Salvadorans and Mexicans, for, as Romilia continues:

> And don't get her started on the Mexicans. I once dated a
> young guy named Raul from Monterrey whose jawbone was

> like a sculpted rock but whose accent Mamá picked out in a
> second. She accused me of seeing Raul just to spite her, and
> of course she was right. . . . Of course, his family had fed
> him a headful about Central Americans as well. (85)

According to this account, the interrelations between Central Americans
and Mexican-Americans are laden with deeply rooted tensions and
prejudices. Romilia's acknowledgement that she dated Raul just to spite
her mother highlights Eva's dislike of Mexicans, but also how Romilia
has been molded by these sentiments, because she also feels the need
to stress her Salvadoranness. The fact that Raul's family "had fed him
a headful about Central Americans" hints to a similar experience on
his end. Although based on this example it is difficult to fully grasp
the origins of these beliefs and tensions, the historical factors outlined
by Arias that have led to the subordination of Central Americans to
other groups such as Mexicans come to mind. Additionally, one could
question if the mistaken assumption or stereotype that all Latinos are
Mexican—as the Anglo doctor illustrated—also adds to Romilia and her
mother's resentment.

Following Karen Christians's analysis of ethnic performances in
Latina/o fiction, Romilia's display of Salvadoranness problematizes "the
concept of cultural essence" (17). The fact that Romilia's Salvadoran-
American identity is set against that of Mexican-American identity in the
context of the U.S. South reveals her Salvadoranness to be a product
"in process," not an a priori essence that is devoid of historical, cultural,
or political influences. This notion of a Salvadoran identity "in process"
is all the more evident when we take into account how Romilia's
Salvadoranness is expressed and contemplated when she moves with her
family to Los Angeles. Although in this new setting Romilia still finds
she has to clarify that she is not Mexican, she no longer negotiates
her identity only in reference to this specific Latino group or a clearly
demarcated black and white binary. On the contrary, she finds herself
in a city "where Latinos have become the majority," where Spanglish is
the norm, and where *pupuserías* serving up El Salvador's national dish
are everywhere (McPeek Villatoro, *A Venom beneath the Skin* 6). Romilia
is also surrounded by relatives, namely her uncle Chepe, Eva's brother,
who as a caterer provides Romilia with an endless supply of *pupusas*.

Like the notion of Salvadoran identity formation or "*Salvadoreñidades*"
postulated by Ana Patricia Rodríguez in her essay "Departamento 15,"
Romilia's identity in this new setting is shaped and influenced in reference
to a Salvadoran "translocal" and "transnational" community—adding to
and prompting a reconceptualization of her self-definition as a Latina

southerner with Salvadoran roots. It is telling that despite performing and emphasizing her Salvadoranness throughout the other two books, it is not until the third book, *A Venom beneath the Skin*, set in California, that Romilia uses the notion of "Salvadoranness" in relation to herself. Before leaving the South, Romilia makes a final stop at her sister's grave site in Atlanta. While kneeling before her sister's grave, Romilia describes her intention to kiss the tombstone as an action inspired by "some forgotten Catholic tendency from childhood or my Salvadoranness" (13). Considered within the context of the strong Salvadoran presence that awaits her in Los Angeles, which will help her further claim her ethnicity, this statement at the beginning of *A Venom* marks how Romilia is once again redefining her identity. Ultimately, Romilia's performance and embracing of her Salvadoranness, be it in the U.S. South or Los Angeles, enacts the same critical functions—it debunks dominant stereotypes of Latinos, accentuating heterogeneity and the "very complexities of *Latinidad*" that, according to Alicia Arrizón, "may be the crucial distinguishing mark of Latino culture and identity in the Americas" (13). Just as important, it brings to the fore Central American-American identities.

Complicating this exploration of Central American visibility and identity politics is Romilia's interaction and relationship with her *bête noir*, Rafael Murillo. Unlike Romilia, Murillo's ties to the U.S. South are not the result of the international migration prompted by the civil wars in Central America. His parents met while attending Vanderbilt University. His Guatemalan father belonged to the coffee oligarchy, and his mother, a white woman from Chattanooga, Tennessee, came from a well-established southern family. Murillo is a "true Latino southerner," as he boasts to Romilia the first time he meets her (McPeek Villatoro, *Home Killings* 55). It is clear from Murillo's self-categorization as a "true" Latino southerner that his embracing of a pan-ethnic label is meant to mark him as "Latino" but also as "American." He is, after all, half white, which in the context of the U.S. South is of particular relevance, as it aligns him with an Anglo and empowered population. Still, like Romilia, Murillo has an understanding of a southern *Latinness* that also encompasses a Central American heritage and sets him apart from immigrants and Mexican-Americans.

Murillo identifies strongly with Guatemala's indigenous origins as well as its broader national identity—the latter being exemplified by his service in the Guatemalan armed forces. Inasmuch as these key attributes ground Murillo's characterization, they also provide a wider basis for viewing the Central American presence in the United States and conceptualizing a Central American-American identity that is not limited to Romilia's construction and representation. After eluding capture at the end of *Home Killings*, Murillo manages to escape to the northern jungles of Guatemala to the town of Poptún. Although somewhat physically distanced from the investigation Romilia is pursuing in *Minos*, Murillo's personal story and actions remain considerable factors. Murillo's connection to Guatemalan indigeneity,[14] including the significance of his nickname, "Tekún Umán," is clarified as Murillo immerses himself in the Guatemala of his youth and that of his father. One of Murillo's initial stops on his way to his hideout is a local marketplace where he runs into an old acquaintance, *doña* Celia, whose cousin works as an *oreja* [informant] for Murillo. They talk to each other in Q'eqchi, one of the twenty-two Mayan languages spoken in Guatemala, and as Murillo states, it is precisely for this reason that he visits Celia, "to remember" the language and, broadly speaking, his cultural roots (McPeek Villatoro, *Minos* 42).

Murillo's link to the Mayan populations of Guatemala—his ability to speak Q'eqchi and his nickname, a result of having been born on the feast day of the historical figure—is, in many ways, contradictory given his role as a *kaibil*, an active member of a military group and death squad implicated in the genocide of the indigenous population during the civil war in Guatemala. Still, it is this element of Murillo's multicultural background that helps to expand the discussion of Central American-American identity prompted by Romilia's process of ethnic individuation and performance of Salvadoranness. One could say that Murillo, like Romilia, enacts a form of Guatemalan indigeneity and, in so doing, highlights a component of Central American ethnicity and visibility in the United States that must also be considered—that of indigenous populations who neither speak Spanish nor are easily subsumed under the category of U.S. Latino.

Romilia is made to ponder this very notion when she visits Murillo's family home in Tennessee in an attempt to gather information about Murillo's whereabouts. Upon arriving at the plantation home with its manicured appearance and grandness, Romilia is greeted at the door by a young maid whom Romilia describes in the following manner: "She spoke Spanish, though it sounded simple, with grammatical mistakes a child would make (*Dicieron* for *dijeron*, or the common *haiga* for *haya*, similar to our *ain't*). But she was not a simpleton; Spanish, I could see, was her second language. She looked Aztec, or Mayan" (33). What is most revealing about this encounter is the fact that despite noting the maid's "Aztec or Mayan" features, Romilia's close examination of this woman's Spanish and physiology betrays how little she has actually contemplated the notion of Central American indigenous identities in the United States. Consequently, the inclusion of Murillo and the question of Central American indigenous subjectivities afford another critical intervention regarding Central American identity politics and representation.

Central American History and Allegory at the Margins

Although informed, to a large extent, by the ethnic and racial politics of the geographic locations Romilia inhabits, her subject position as a Salvadoran-American is also rooted in and contextualized by McPeek Villatoro's engagement with Central American history. Her inquiry into the past is, in essence, an inquest into her own Salvadoran identity and background—thus underlining how a particular historical discourse informs and forces her to redefine her Latina identity. To fully comprehend the meaning of "Latina," as it refers to Romilia, "requires an understanding of the ongoing historical and socio-political processes of immigration, annexation, and exile" that particularize Latino communities (Arrizón 5). In addition to an emphasis on "Salvadoran" Spanish, food, and cultural references, Romilia's family also has a distinct history of immigration that sets her apart from other groups. Moreover, given their differing Central American backgrounds and histories, Romilia and Murillo's charged antagonism also functions as an allegorical representation of the past. This multilayered focus on both El Salvador's and Guatemala's hidden pasts of struggle and migration provides insight into the Central American immigrant experience, enacting a vital "unveiling" that is inherently tied to the assertion of a Central American social and cultural presence in the United States and an identity politics. Coupled with Romilia's performance of Salvadoranness, this historical investigation foments Central American visibility.

As with Latin American models that rely on the convergence of "fact" and fiction in order to stress history as a central theme, in McPeek Villatoro's mysteries, Central America's legacy of civil war, including U.S. intervention and foreign policy, also becomes the subject of the investigation.[15] This subplot is one that is developed through the inclusion of specific historical facts pertaining to Central America and Romilia's ongoing relationship with Murillo. Having never been to El Salvador and knowing only that returning is impossible for her family, Romilia's knowledge of Central American history and her family's past is limited. Each of her assignments and what it ultimately reveals about Central America provide Romilia with another piece of a larger puzzle into her own subjectivity and ethnic identity. Unlike Romilia's cases, however, this broader investigation into the past does not have a clear-cut resolution, nor can it be traced back to the crimes of just one individual.

One of the more salient examples of how McPeek Villatoro interweaves Central American history into his detective narratives is the allusion to death squads that appears in *Home Killings*. Upon discovering Murillo's affiliation with the *kaibiles*, Romilia begins to suspect that Murillo may be responsible for Diego Sáenz's murder. On one occasion, after hearing Romilia question one of Murillo's henchmen regarding the word *kaibiles*, her mother is prompted to remember the events leading to the murder of Romilia's grandparents: ". . . It was the weekend of the *Kaibil/Atlacatl* 'graduation' or whatever they call it. . . . That's when it all happened . . ." (McPeek Villatoro, *Home Killings* 133). Eva's account brings into focus the traumatic experience she underwent in El Salvador. The silence and ellipses that mark her testimony exemplify the "loss of voice, . . . of knowledge, of awareness, of truth, of the capacity to feel . . . and to speak" that Shoshana Felman and Dori Laub contend traumatic experience creates in victims (231–32). The horrific acts perpetrated against civilians by the *kaibiles* and the *atlacatlas*, the Salvadoran equivalent of the Guatemalan military unit, have not only rendered Eva voiceless but have also resulted in her suppression of a Central American history with which she does not want to identify.

Given only her mother's "muttered scenes," Romilia must use her imagination to fill in the blanks: "As I had never met my grandparents, I could only imagine an old couple whom I had seen in pictures, now dead underneath rubble and fire and the pile of other bodies strewn over a once active town" (133). This exchange, whereby Romilia pieces together her mother's repressed memories, calls to mind the notion of transgenerational trauma posited by Nicolas Abraham and María Torok in *The Shell and the Kernel*. In sum, the psyche of the next generation locks away and contains the unspeakable experiences and secrets of the prior generation; the second generation thus becomes haunted by the trauma of the first. As will be seen, however, Romilia is not fated to voicelessness like her mother and countless other Central Americans. Through her uncovering of the past and related quest for justice, Romilia enacts a way of coming to terms with this familial history of trauma.

Following a leak to a local newspaper, Romilia's working theory of a possible death squad operating in Nashville becomes public knowledge. The article begins with the phrase " 'Death squads' is not a term we Nashvillians are accustomed to using" and emphasizes the existence of death squads in "countries like El Salvador or Colombia, where drug cartels and oligarchies use such terrorist groups to keep the population in check" (178). The almost exclusive focus on the death squads in the article underscores the problematic manner in which Central America's history of war and violence has been construed and continues to be represented by the media in the United States. Jean Franco's reflection on the "ethical vacuum in metropolitan societies" calls attention to the "tendency" of the metropolis "to regard the repressive regimes in Latin America [. . .] as purely local aberrations" ("Gender" 22). This is an apt description of how the newspaper account ideologically positions Nashville (and the United States) in contrast to El Salvador or Colombia and, by extension, Nashvillians in reference to Central American (and Latina/o) others. Although death squads and revolutionary struggle are not new occurrences for immigrants like Romilia's mother, they are for the majority of the Nashville public who are reading these accounts and have not been exposed to this history before. Moreover, any reference to the United States' role in helping to financially sustain the oligarchic governments in El Salvador and Guatemala that made use of death squads is noticeably absent from this report.[16] Only when the death squads threaten the general well-being of Nashvillians does this Central American social reality become credible. And even when it does, the "average citizen" can only conceive of it in a way that continues to privilege U.S. experience over that of the so-called Third World and affirms negative cultural stereotypes.

Implicit in such a myopic portrayal of Central American history are also the social and political mechanisms that have contributed to the systematic silencing of Central American immigrants. One of Romilia's immediate concerns following the publication of the article is the backlash against Central Americans that it would generate: "Shit, I thought. No Nashvillian was going to come out of this thinking highly of Central America or its people" (179). For Central American immigrants, this dynamic is linked, and can be traced to, the political context that marked the first waves of mass emigration, mostly from El Salvador and Guatemala, to the United States during the 1980s. Discriminating asylum policies premised on U.S. involvement in the region coupled with their undocumented status led many Salvadorans and Guatemalans to hide their personal histories of trauma, including from their children (Hamilton and Chinchilla 203). Their personal experiences of oppression and violence were not only rendered invalid but also "erased" from public view.

Given this erasure, Romilia's speculations regarding the past and her investigations of the death squads are all the more relevant. Her mother's testimonial calls into question the dominant version of Central American history constructed by the metropolis that is projected by the newspaper article. By "detecting" this history of Central American immigration, Romilia gives voice and precedence to the experiences of civil conflict and flight that have been silenced in Central America and the United States. In this sense, McPeek Villatoro's novel works in tandem with Arias's claim discussed earlier in this chapter regarding the denial of self experienced by immigrants due to the violent oppression carried out by Central American military regimes against their own peoples and the institutionalization of discriminatory immigration policies in the United States. However, beyond exemplifying Arias's assertions, the recuperation of this distinct history by Romilia also postulates an active response to these theories. The barring of this traumatic past, which adds to Romilia's knowledge of her family's legacy, emphasizes and foments a more informed understanding of her Central American-American identity.

The inclusion of themes such as that of the death squads is not the only means by which McPeek Villatoro engages with Central America's revolutionary history and social reality. Romilia's complex and evolving relationship with Murillo throughout the series is also a key avenue for both exploring this past as well as contemplating its present and possible future effects on newer generations. As previously mentioned, at the close of *Home Killings*, Murillo manages to escape. Before fleeing to Guatemala, however, he leaves Romilia one last parting gift, a love letter and an engagement ring, which she rejects. This significant turn of events—as Romilia and Murillo's seemingly frictional relationship also gives way to sexual attraction—is certainly a literary recourse meant to further the detective narrative by providing an open ending and the potential for future encounters. Yet it also signals the prolonging of a literal and metaphorical conversation initiated in this first book between Romilia and Murillo regarding Central American history, which reaches its fullest culmination in *A Venom*.

In this third book, Romilia is recruited by the Federal Bureau of Investigation to work in their Los Angeles branch after her successful capture of the serial killer, Minos. Like her second case, the mystery in *A Venom* is also characterized by personal motives, as one of the murders Romilia is investigating is that of her lover, Samuel "Chip" Pierce, a fellow special agent whom the FBI suspects was killed by Murillo. Pierce's death, however, is tied to a bigger case involving the search for the "Crack Killer," a vigilante believed to be responsible for the Olive Street bombing and the deaths of several drug dealers. He is also secretly hunting Murillo, who along with Romilia has migrated to the West Coast. Yet, unlike Romilia, Murillo resides covertly in Tijuana, on the other side of the U.S.-Mexican border, where he continues to manage his drug trafficking operation as well as keep an eye on Romilia.

The appearance of Murillo in this contact zone extends the exploration of the Central American migrant reality in these books beyond that of the U.S. South, shifting focus to the main point of entry for Central American immigrants.

Claiming to be protecting Romilia, Murillo orchestrates her kidnapping and delivery to his home in Tijuana. While establishing the foundation for a key shift in the plot—eventually Romilia will have to join forces with Murillo in order to save her family from the Crack Killer—this encounter in another "southern" space also gives way to one of the more revealing discussions between these two characters concerning Central American history. Discussing the possibility that a terrorist group may be involved in the bombings, Murillo posits the following query to Romilia: "[. . .] [W]hat's the difference between the terrorist of today and the guerrilla movement of your beloved El Salvador?" followed by another comment about her mother's "sympathy" toward the insurrectionist group (120). Romilia is quick to respond, stressing that there are no similarities between the two groups and then retaliating by reminding Murillo that he was a *kaibil* and "trained to bring down the guerrilla movement" in his own country (121) and therefore incapable of understanding her perspective.

Romilia and Murillo's charged debate is significant, as it showcases Romilia openly discussing with Murillo a history that had eluded her until he came into her life. What is more, this exchange provides Romilia with an unprecedented opportunity to directly confront Murillo regarding his own role in Central America's legacy of war. Yet, for all this, the conversation between these two is not a simple back and forth of accusations. Rather, it is a dialogue allowing for critical reflection, as suggested by Murillo's reply to Romilia's last observation about his occupation as a *kaibil*: "Unlike some of my . . . brothers in the force, I also had an education. I could still see who the guerrillas were, why they formed. They had a purpose . . . to fight for the rights of the poor" (121). With this last comment, Murillo offers a perspective that shows he understands the significance of his class position as well as the greater objectives set forth by the opposition. In many ways, Murillo exposes the fallacy of simple political binaries and draws attention to the "gray matters" that, more often than not, characterize armed national conflicts.

Beyond these literal exchanges, Romilia and Murillo's relationship also functions as a figurative reiteration of the civil wars that ravaged El Salvador and Guatemala. It is in this sense that Romilia can be understood as an allegory for the Salvadoran nation. Although Romilia is Salvadoran and Murillo is Guatemalan, both share, to varying degrees, a history of violence, strife, and displacement. In fact, it is these two

Central American populations that are often coupled together, given their similar political trajectories and problematic context of reception in the United States. As Romilia discovered through her mother, her family is a part of the civilian populations in Central America that were subjected to economic exploitation, violent repression, and familial disintegration at the hands of oligarchic governments and military forces. Murillo's class ties to the Guatemalan oligarchy and his militancy as a *kaibil*, by contrast, signal him as a part of and an active agent of those same oppressive government and military institutions. Although there is no reference to a "guerrilla" element, as a detective, Romilia acts as a similar countering force. As the revolutionary undertones associated with Romilia's husband and her mother's sympathies suggest, Romilia's family aligns itself with the revolutionary movement and its aims, recalling Gareth Williams's claim concerning the spectral existence of the "national and national-popular . . . within certain Salvadoran migrant realities" (196). In essence, then, Romilia and Murillo evoke the "two sides" of Central American civil war history: the popular and armed struggle of the people versus the oppression of the oligarchic state.

An added element of this particular figurative rendering of history is the issue of immigration. Romilia and Murillo, for example, are both products of the mass migration from Central America that took place as a consequence, in part, of the armed struggles. In this sense, their relationship raises the question of the past and how it bears upon the present—a dynamic that is at the heart of Central American-American visibility and identity formation. In this case, the Central American migrant reality is underscored in several unique ways, one of which is when Romilia, Murillo, and Murillo's assistant (Romilia's FBI partner, who has been secretly working for Murillo all along) must cross the U.S.-Mexican border clandestinely because of Murillo's status as a fugitive. When Romilia's family is taken hostage by the Crack Killer, Romilia is forced to work with Murillo, especially because the Crack Killer agrees to release Romilia's mother and son in exchange for Murillo—the person he has really been after all along. On their way to the drug trafficking tunnel they will be using as a means of crossing the border, Romilia makes a sarcastic remark about their having to travel as "*mojados*" [wetbacks], to which Murillo humorously replies, " 'Well, considering we're all U.S. citizens, I wouldn't say we're illegal immigrants' " (156). In its obvious and ironic reference to undocumented immigrants, this underground journey brings to mind the numerous surreptitious crossings made by Central Americans fleeing from political repression and economic strife.

Such are the experiences of a select few of the secondary characters in the text, Romilia's uncle Chepe and the Guatemalan men who agree to work for Murillo in Tijuana. As Romilia discloses, her uncle Chepe fled El Salvador in the mid-1970s "because he had acted in a *sociodrama* at the age of fifteen, with a group of street actors who liked to thumb their noses at all authorities, including, from time to time, the military" (11). After three of the actors were found dead with the words "*comunistas jodidos* (fucking communists) carved into their chests," Romilia's mother paid various coyotes to make sure Chepe, her only surviving brother, made it to the United States. Having first arrived in the U.S. South where his sister was already living, Chepe had then decided to migrate west to Los Angeles. Like Romilia's mother, Chepe also carries a past of violence difficult to recount, yet with his story, we are also made aware of the other part of that history—the saga of migrating "illegally." This particular account speaks to the additional traumas individuals like Chepe have experienced because of the precarious border crossings they have had to undertake.

Similarly, the inclusion of *chapines*—the nickname by which Guatemalans are known throughout the Central American region—living alongside the U.S.-Mexican border adds to this context by denoting how this phenomenon of mass emigration from Central America, initially spurred by the wars, persists today, albeit fuelled primarily by economic needs. While looking for men to hire to help with his drug schemes, Murillo locates a group of Guatemalan indigenous men of Q'aqci'quel origin in one of the barrios near the Tijuana desert. They welcome Murillo, but only after he speaks a few words to them in their native tongue, "words that sounded, after the long haul from Guatemala through Mexico, comforting" (73). In addition to noting the arduous trek these men have made through Mexico—the first of two borders they must cross to get to the United States—Murillo also observes that the men have traveled alone, leaving their wives behind, which, in essence, evokes a traditional model of migration unlike that of Romilia's family. Although it is never explicitly stated, according to the accounts given in these novels regarding Romilia's uncle Chepe, it is Romilia's mother, Eva, who makes the initial journey to the North. What is more, there is no real reference to Eva having been married or journeying with Romilia's father.

Viewed in relation to these accounts, Romilia and Murillo's crossing becomes all the more symbolic. As second-generation Central American-Americans and U.S. citizens, neither of them has had to undergo this defining experience that characterizes a large portion of the Central American community in the United States. In physically reenacting this "crossing," these two characters are once again calling to mind Central America's hidden history—this time, in what concerns migrant trajectories. As such, we can make a similar claim regarding the figurative dimensions of Romilia and Murillo's relationship as that made earlier concerning Central American civil war history. To a certain extent, Romilia and Murillo also function as allegories for El Salvador and Guatemala as Central American "migrant nations" whose incorporation into the United States has been mediated by the ethnically diverse and historic circumstances brought to light by both Romilia's investigation of and her involvement with Murillo.

The dynamic interface with history achieved by way of this relationship, both literally and allegorically, consequently facilitates Central American visibility. By the same token, it also expands the parameters of what we understand as this process of ethnic self-individuation and representation by raising two additional issues not necessarily broached in Arias's theorization: the role of justice (linked to the previous point I made regarding Romilia's ability to work through and give voice to the trauma of the past) and the possibility of conciliatory ties. As I have been arguing, Romilia and Murillo render a figurative portrait of Central America's opposing forces. Yet they do so in a new field of battle—the United States—in which their roles and their circumstances are slightly altered. The fact that Romilia is a law enforcement agent in many ways keeps her from being a disempowered victim. By contrast, Murillo is no longer part of the state military apparatus, nor is he above the law, as he had been in Guatemala as a *kaibil.* Although he lives comfortably in the United States, he is a wanted criminal and is continuously on the run. Throughout the series, Romilia's pursuit of Murillo is primarily spurred by this fact. As the "history" that binds them together unfolds, however, her quest to capture him allows for another interpretation—that of seeking justice, at least on a symbolic level, for the crimes against humanity Murillo perpetrated in Central America. What is more, it implies that this symbolic and literal pursuit of justice does not necessarily reside exclusively in the hands of Central American immigrants, but also with future U.S.-born generations, as is the case with Romilia.

Romilia raises this very point when she contemplates the correlations between her work as an FBI agent and her family's past:

Both my mother and my uncle had seen too much in their past, in our old country. They had seen back in El Salvador what I stand over every day; only they did not have the chance that I have: they could never try to make order of chaos. They had no tools of investigation; they had no access to a group or a company or a government that would help them figure out the who, and the why, of so many killings (42).

In emphasizing her skills and function as a detective, Romilia lays claim to the agency that she—unlike her family back in El Salvador—has, which enables her to capture criminals like Murillo. Most importantly, her job provides her with a way to figure out the "why" of certain criminal actions, to make sense of the "chaos" or trauma. Hence, beyond her ability to bring a war criminal like Murillo to justice, Romilia has the capacity to come to terms with, or as Dominick LaCapra contends, "work through" her family's trauma.[17] As such, obtaining justice in these narratives becomes a feat associated with working through trauma.

It is also a feat, however, complicated by sexual attraction and even love, for as Romilia and Murillo's relationship deepens and evolves, their feelings for each other are made clear—a development that alludes to another key aspect of Central American-American interrelations. Despite both being Central American-Americans and southerners, Romilia and Murillo have experienced the effects of the war in different ways, which has, in part, resulted in the oppositional positions they occupy. This is suggestive of the fact that, along with differing ethnic and racial makeups, Central American-Americans are also defined by disparate political and social views that were caused or further demarcated by the civil conflicts. Both victims of the repression like Romilia's family as well as those who took up arms with either the guerrilla or military forces migrated, and although their initial "crossing over" may render them all immigrants and/or minority others in the U.S. context, it does not suffice to completely ameliorate differences or to erase the oppressive acts perpetrated by some and suffered by others. Even so, the amorous feelings of these characters for each other and the ending of *A Venom* hint at the possibility and importance of establishing conciliatory ties among Central Americans.

Toward the close of the novel, Murillo is captured by the Crack Killer while attempting to help Romilia save her family. Although Romilia's mother and son are eventually freed, Romilia decides to stay in San Francisco, where the Crack Killer is hiding out and planning a final bombing of the Golden Gate Bridge, to try to save Murillo. Following a series of fast-paced events, including Romilia's rescue of Murillo, who has been tortured by the Crack Killer, the novel culminates with all three of them engaged in a struggle on the Golden Gate Bridge. Romilia and Murillo prevail, killing the Crack Killer—whose real name is Carl Spooner, a former DEA agent whom Murillo had mutilated in Guatemala a few years prior and who was thought dead. As he is still a fugitive wanted by the FBI, Murillo chooses to jump off the bridge to his almost certain death rather than turn himself in.

Interestingly, this final act of Murillo's is not narrated through Romilia's perspective but through a third-person point of view limited to Murillo. These final pages are meant to focus the reader's attention and sympathy toward Murillo and allow for a broader understanding of his thoughts, including Carl Spooner's assertion that Murillo was "poison" and Murillo's recognition that given his actions throughout his life, Spooner was right (229). Murillo remembers his military training in Guatemala, the first time he saw Romilia in a Nashville bookstore, and his longing for her. A reflexive account of Murillo's life before dying, these thoughts allude to some form of repentance or at least self-acknowledgement of his wrongdoings—a significant act given that, as Murillo plunges himself into the San Francisco Bay, he is also cleansing himself. Surviving the fall would, in essence, signal his "rebirth" as with a Christian rite of baptism.

This symbolic process of renewal is underscored by the novel's closing paragraph describing Murillo's descent into the water: "There is a cold blast, another current—yes. How it reminds him of other rivers, and the safety of their depths, and how he, while burying himself in the deepest, coldest current, felt most awake" (230). While suggesting, perhaps, that Murillo does not physically die, this ending also draws attention to some form of "redemption" for Murillo and the possibility of a second chance. As part of the underlying theme of reconciliation, Murillo achieving this significant turning point calls to mind the necessary validation and recognition of the past that is fundamental for Central American visibility but that is equally essential for any form of healing and unification among Central Americans. Of course, this recognition of the past also involves justice, as Romilia's role and presence indicate. Although both characters acknowledge, as Romilia states, that "[i]t would have never worked out" (228), the novel's ending certainly allows for other possibilities as they pertain to Romilia and Murillo and, more generally, to Central Americans.

Revealing More Than Just Clues

With Romilia Chacón, McPeek Villatoro delivers a compelling portrait of a tough and savvy female sleuth. The fact that she is of Salvadoran descent draws our attention to the ways in which Salvadoran women are affected by and influence national and transnational developments—in this case, the incorporation of Central American populations into the United States. Romilia's characterization as a Latina southerner articulates the existence of a complex subjectivity that is being forged from within multiple peripheries: as a Latina woman, as a second-generation Salvadoran whose Central American past has been obscured, and as a southerner. As such, her portrayal allows for an exploration of a specific process of Salvadoran-American identity formation and, by extension, that of Central American-American Latino identities. It is precisely Romilia's sleuthing of identity and history that brings the contours and complexities of this ethnic individuation to the fore.

Although in these narratives the most prominent means by which Romilia enacts her Salvadoranness is through her use of "Salvadoran" Spanish, the cultural referents to food and folklore, as well as the nuanced debates regarding Salvadoran identity transmitted by way of her mother, are also fundamental to this display. With all of its dimensions, Romilia's Salvadoranness not only sets her apart from other predominant Latino groups such as Mexican-Americans, but also, by the same token, contributes to the visibility of Central Americans in the United States. Because history is also integral to Romilia's self-definition, her detecting of Central America's hidden past of war and immigration is just as pivotal in these texts. Notably, it is not just the footprints and themed clues that Romilia follows but also her relationship with Rafael Murillo that lead her to this historical reality. Moreover, the allegorical dichotomy set up between Romilia and her *bête noir* gives way to a broader discussion of heterogeneity among differing Central American-American realities and identities.

Romilia and Murillo's ties undoubtedly link them to a past they cannot escape. Yet, as Central American-Americans living in the United States, they are also mediating this history from a different point in time and "homeland." They bridge the past and present through their literal conversations as well as their allegorical depictions. In doing so, their relationship engenders other questions regarding Central American identity politics and representation, critically adding to Arias's initial incursion into the topic. Among these is the quest for justice, the ability to make sense of past traumas, and the possibility of conciliatory ties. In both of these aims, Romilia and her portrayal are pivotal, for as a detective she holds a certain degree of legal and judicial power, not to mention that, as a woman, she also evinces an innovative form of female agency in the broader Central American-American community. Although cast in the traditional role of Murillo's object of desire, Romilia is nevertheless indicative of the potential for conciliatory ties among Central Americans affected differently by the war and its legacy.

As I have contended throughout this analysis, this dynamic and provocative rendering of Romilia opens the possibility for a Central

American-American politics of identity that, to recall Arias one last time, has not been feasible. How these politics are being negotiated and shaped is still "in process," as Romilia's own trajectory throughout the series suggests. As she moves outside the scope of Nashville and undertakes new cases, which eventually lead her to California, Romilia's Salvadoranness becomes infused by the presence of a more predominant Central American immigrant community in Los Angeles as well as new discourses regarding the current state of Central American immigration to the United States. Although she has been witness to new faces from Latin America in the U.S. South, it is not until Romilia migrates to Southern California and across the U.S.-Mexican border that this reality has an impact on her. Her ethnic individuation as a Salvadoran-American thus acquires another significant dimension related to undocumented migrants and border subjectivities that awaits exploration, perhaps, in a future installment. Suffice it to say, Romilia's sleuthing in the U.S. South and beyond reveals more than just clues. It complicates, but also initiates, new ways of thinking about Central American-American visibility, identity, and representation.

Conclusion

In March 2008, the *Los Angeles Times* published an article titled
"Grad Puts Central America on the Map." The story focused on the
accomplishments of Vanessa Guerrero, a young student of Salvadoran
descent who was the first individual in the United States to graduate
with a degree in Central American Studies. Guerrero's graduation was
an important milestone for the Central American Studies Program,
the first of its kind, established in 2000 at California State University,
Northridge, an institution that has one of the largest Central American
student populations in the country. According to the article, Guerrero
sought a degree in Central American Studies because she wanted to learn
more about her cultural origins and El Salvador's past, a history no one
spoke about at home. Guerrero was seeking answers to "why people
migrated" and how it was that she came to be "here" in the United
States, questions that are an important foundation for understanding her
Salvadoran-American identity. In addition to its significance for the Central
American Studies Program at CSUN, the article underscored that this
event was indicative of the ways in which the waves of Central American
migration initiated in the 1980s have transformed and are continuing
to transform various aspects of communal life in Southern California,
including higher education. Guerrero's achievement called attention to
the growing visibility of Central Americans as an ethnic minority and
collectivity within the multicultural "map" of the United States.

Vanessa Guerrero's trajectory and personal story are suggestive
of many of the same issues raised by this analysis and the underlying
motivations that have led me to explore the symbolic representations of
women in trans-Salvadoran narratives. Having been raised in Los Angeles
by two Salvadoran immigrant parents, like Guerrero, I too felt the need
to know why Salvadorans migrated, to better understand the factors
that led to the civil war, and how such a social reality contributed to
the formation of Salvadoran-American subjectivities. But I also wanted
to know what key roles women had played in all of these processes

and how it was that gender also shaped our understanding of why we are "here." The initial questions I posed in the introduction of the book regarding what insight can be gained by examining the literary representations of women with regard to female agency and participation in national and transnational endeavors, the construction of gendered identities, and lastly, the gender dynamics that mark the redefinition of Salvadoran national identity that has taken shape over the last three decades were a way of facilitating a discussion that would lead to the answers I sought. Such inquiries, however, also provided an avenue for thinking beyond my own personal interests so as to engage broader debates focused on immigration, transnationalism, women's rights, and Central American-American identity politics, all of which constitute either established or rising areas of interest not only in the academy but also in the world at large.

As I have argued, the representations of women elaborated in the trans-Salvadoran narratives I examine here give way to a gendered history that showcases how women and the nation have been transformed by the different national and transnational processes that characterize El Salvador's recent history, including civil war, postwar national reconstruction, international migration, and Salvadoran ethnic individuation and incorporation into the United States. The outbreak of the civil war in El Salvador led to a weakening and, in certain instances, a reconstitution of national and societal structures. Thus, previously marginalized and invisible sectors of the population, such as women from both rural and urban backgrounds, became key agents of change in public enterprises including popular activism and armed insurrection, both traditionally seen as male domains. Although in the postwar period the earlier fervor of the revolutionary project and its ideals has been all but extinguished, women continue to fight. They are now at the forefront of popular struggles for gender equality and citizenship rights for sexual minorities and children, who like themselves are considered secondary or expendable within the narrowly conceived notions of Salvadoran nationhood promoted by neoliberal governance and enterprise.[1] International migration has also resulted in alternate forms of Salvadoran female agency and roles. Women comprise a vital sector of the Salvadoran immigrant community in the United States, serving as economic mainstays for their families both in and outside El Salvador. They have been instrumental in the construction of a Salvadoran transnational community that newer generations of Salvadoran-American women such as Vanessa Guerrero are helping to further delineate.

The fact that in all of these texts women also function as either allegories for the nation or are posited as "republican mothers" makes discernible another parallel history, that of El Salvador as a national space. Like its women, El Salvador has undergone its own process of transformation. The massive migration occasioned by the war and that continues today—a historical occurrence whose impact can be likened to that of the civil war because of the degree to which it has altered El Salvador's economy, politics, and society—has resulted in the formation of a Salvadoran (trans)nation that brings together Salvadorans residing within and outside the country's geographic borders. Within this interstitial space, Salvadorans are redefining individual and communal identities on the basis of gender, sexuality, ethnicity, race, and citizenship. Similarly, they are proffering new notions of nationhood—some which recall the exclusionary models of the past and others that offer a more inclusive alternative, allowing for immigrants and second-generation Salvadoran-Americans to also consider themselves a part of the county they and/ or their parents were forced to leave.

Although this analysis has certainly shed light on many key issues, it has also fostered new queries and revealed areas of growing interest that are in need of further exploration. As is the case with Guerrero, the narratives by writers such as Leticia Hernández-Linares and Marcos McPeek Villatoro reveal a quest by second-generation authors to explore not only El Salvador's traumatic past of civil war and migration but also its culture, including its indigenous origins and folklore. In his or her own way, each of these authors recalls Argueta's testimonial novels about the *campesino* reality and its importance for understanding Salvadoran national identity. Ironically, the literary corpus of texts that has been produced in El Salvador's postwar period, at least in what pertains to fiction, does not evince the same level of interest in indigenous identities and representation. Although one can attribute this notable lack, in part, to the country's historical processes—those which I have mentioned previously, such as the 1932 *matanza*—it is telling that in a postwar era in which the notion of Salvadoran nationhood has been challenged in other respects, the indigenous presence continues to exist on the margins.

As with the topic of indigeneity, gay, lesbian, and transgendered realities also have yet to be fully examined in El Salvador's cultural production,[2] an absence that parallels the invisibility of these individuals within the broader Salvadoran (trans)nation. Although the peripheral existence of these subjects within the nation has begun to be challenged with the establishment of feminist and lesbian, gay, bisexual, and transgender (LGBT) movements in El Salvador and neighboring Central American countries such as Costa Rica, Guatemala, and Nicaragua, securing civil rights and justice for human rights violations against sexual minorities remains an uphill battle. Rampant sexism and discrimination are heavily entrenched within Salvadoran society and, to a certain extent, the immigrant communities that have been established abroad. Although I did not discuss this topic in great detail in this book, in my analysis of *Un día*, notably with regard to the state's construction of an empowered *campesino* populace as not only feminine but also sexually deviant, as well as my exploration of women's revolutionary *testimonios*, I called attention to the "anxiety" provoked by non-normative queer sexualities. This "anxiety" has yet to be acknowledged and addressed in the postwar period.

A final area of study, which is perhaps the best-known example of Salvadoran transnationalism to date, is the Mara Salvatrucha or MS-13. Having been labeled the "World's Most Dangerous Gang" by the popular media,[3] the Mara has been the subject of several sociological, anthropological, and political studies, including Elana Zilberg's groundbreaking *Space of Detention*. As Zilberg contends in her book, the Mara's existence and spread throughout the Americas, like the female-centered history I engage here, needs to be understood within the broader context of El Salvador's civil war, U.S. foreign policy and immigration, and the advent of neoliberalism. Despite the Mara's recognition as a topic of study within the social sciences and indeed its growing and problematic visibility in the U.S. popular imaginary, cultural-based analyses of the Mara's depiction in literature, film, and media are scarce, and those that raise questions with regard to gender and sexuality even more so. Such explorations bear important implications for comprehending notions of communal and national belonging and exclusion, as well as issues of cultural identity and politics tied to the Salvadoran (trans)nation.

The discernible presence of Salvadorans and the broader Central American community in the United States, of which the Mara is but one manifestation, will no doubt continue to play a key role in the future of the Salvadoran (trans)nation. Central Americans—Salvadorans being the majority—factor considerably in both the current as well as the projected increase of the Latino population in the United States. As discussed in Chapters 4 and 5, this new influx of immigrants and the incorporation of second-generation Central American-Americans into various parts of the United States are giving way to a new sense of identity politics. These "other Latinos," to borrow from José Luis Falconi and José Antonio Mazzotti's designation, are helping to broaden the scope of the U.S. Latino population. By the same token, cultural and interdisciplinary studies that center on Central American-Americans, such as this one, will complement and enrich Latino Studies focused primarily on Chicanos, Puerto Ricans, and Cubans, groups that have a more established history in the United States. Linked to María Josefa Saldaña-Portillo's observations regarding the need for a "transnational Latina/o studies," Central American-Americans showcase the emergence of Latino groups influenced by U.S. intervention and defined in reference to transnational migration and community building across multiple borders.

All of these issues will become all the more pressing as the Salvadoran (trans)nation continues to change. The election of the FMLN's presidential candidate, Mauricio Funes, in 2009 marked the end of an almost twenty-year reign by right-wing and conservative governments in El Salvador. It is yet too soon to tell how this new turn toward the left will impact El Salvador's future and that of its people.[4] Immigration debates in the United States and the tenuous prospects for reform will likewise be an important factor. Regardless of how these changes impact the Salvadoran (trans)nation, one thing is for certain: *salvadoreñas* will play a central role in all of them.

Notes

Notes to Introduction

1. Extensive studies exist on the causes, course, and outcomes of the Salvadoran civil war. Noteworthy studies include those by Montgomery, Lungo, Armstrong and Shenk, and Dunkerley.

2. With the exception of key figures such as Prudencia Ayala, a writer and activist who ran for president in 1930 and is discussed in greater detail in Chapter 4, and a partial suffragist movement that favored the rights of the elite, women remained relative outsiders to the male-dominated world of politics prior to the years leading up to and during the civil war.

3. Unlike in Mexico and other Southern Cone countries whose feminist movements can be traced to the mobilization of women during the 1970s, in El Salvador such a movement did not develop until the 1990s. As scholars such as Kampwirth and Shayne have recently argued, this new feminist consciousness is a result, in part, of women's participation in El Salvador's armed and popular struggles.

4. See Repak's, Menjívar's, Mahler's, and Zentgraf's studies on women in Central American migration to the United States.

5. Kearney has, similarly, contended and further clarifies that, unlike global processes, which are "largely decentered from specific national territories and take place in global space, transnational processes are anchored in and transcend one or more nation-states" (548).

6. On this last topic, see Kolodny's study *The Lay of the Land*.

7. Landolt's "El transnacionalismo político y el derecho al voto en el exterior" offers a preliminary look at the issue of voting rights for Salvadorans living in the United States.

8. In addition to the aforementioned studies by Kampwirth and Shayne, Stephen's discussion of the human rights organization Women for Dignity and Life (DIGNAS) is another fundamental reference on the political activism and mobilization of women in El Salvador's postwar period.

9. A growing number of U.S. Central American works have been produced recently in addition to the Salvadoran-American texts included here. Among these can be considered: Tanya María Barrientos *Family Resemblance* (2003);

Francisco Goldman's critically hailed novels *The Long Night of White Chickens* (1992), *The Ordinay Seaman* (1997), and *The Divine Husband* (2004); Rubén Martínez's *The Other Side* (1992); Roberto Quesada's *Big Banana* (1999) and *Never Through Miami* (2002); Silvio Sirias's *Bernardo and the Virgin* (2005); and Héctor Tobar's *The Tattooed Soldier* (1998).

Notes to Chapter 1

1. This attack was initiated on January 10, 1981, lasting a little more than a week. Although the FMLN did not succeed in completely defeating El Salvador's military, according to Dunkerly, the guerrilla offensive "had so severely shaken the regime that it is unlikely that it would have survived for long" had Washington not become involved and increased its military aid to the Salvadoran government (*The Long War* 177).

2. Gould and Lauria-Santiago's book, *To Rise in Darkness*, offers a detailed historical account of the events that led to the 1932 uprising and its aftermath.

3. Prior to the arrival of grassroots organizations and the outbreak of the civil war, women in rural settings had lived a sheltered and isolated life. *Campesina* women were not taught the necessary skills to survive alone with children without their husbands or another male. From an early age, they learned that farming the land was a male activity. Men were the productive ones and women were prohibited from working the land, thereby limiting their ability to survive and earn a living for themselves. The relegation of *campesinas* to the house was reinforced by their absence from the public space, a result of public laws and societal norms perpetuated by a repressive government as well as their own belief that the home was the space of "buenas mujeres" [good women]. As Vásquez notes, this collective understanding of what it meant to be a good woman was for the most part homogenous among *campesinas* from the prewar generation, who were subordinate to a credo of obedience and who were accustomed to suppressing their emotions, including their sense of rebellion in the face of injustice (*Las mujeres refugiadas* 39).

4. Argueta's earlier works, *El valle de las hamacas* (1970) and *Caperucita en la Zona Roja* (1977), were both highly political works that received significant critical acclaim, helping to establish Argueta's reputation as one of the left's more prominent committed authors. *El valle de las hamacas* was awarded first prize in the Certamen Cultural Centroamericano, sponsored by the Consejo Superior Universitario Centroamericano, while *Caperucita en la Zona_Roja* won the prestigious Casa de las Américas Prize in 1977. It was *Un día*, however, that garnered the most international recognition and commercial success. It received several favorable reviews in U.S. newspapers when it was first published and was nominated by the *Modern Library* as the fifth best Latin American novel of the twentieth century. As Lara Martínez notes, it has also become a staple of reading lists in literature, anthropology, history, and political science departments in various universities ("Festival de pájaros" 89).

5. Argueta's novel *Milagro de Paz*, which he published in 1994, two years after the signing of the Peace Accords, also features *campesinas* as central

protagonists. Given its thematic shift away from the civil conflict, it falls outside the scope of this specific analysis.

6. Michael B. Miller, for instance, argues that the centrality of women in Argueta's *Cuzcatlán* is directly related to his use of testimonio, in keeping with Maureen Shea's assertions that in Central America, the testimonio serves specifically as an avenue for women's voices. In their overview of Central American literature of the revolutionary period, John Beverley and Marc Zimmerman suggest a similar reading, attributing Argueta's woman-centered portrayal to the "feminization of the Central American literary system" that took place during the 1970s and 1980s on account of the proliferation of testimonial narratives and poetry that permitted more women's voices to be heard (Beverley and Zimmerman 193). Perhaps one of the few exceptions, which I engage in more detail in this chapter, is Linda Craft's book *Novels of Testimony and Resistance in Central America*, which provides one of the most thorough examinations of Argueta's work and affords a look at both the testimonial and allegorical aspects of his texts.

7. See Craft, Waters Hood, and Beverley and Zimmerman.

8. Examples of these include Dalton's *Miguel Mármol* (1972) and Carpio's *Secuestro y capucha en un país del "mundo libre"* (1979).

9. See endnote 1.

10. Astvaldsson makes a strong case for this argument, suggesting that an "intimate relationship" exists between Lucía's first-person voice and that of the third-person narrator. The first reason is that even though one could ascribe the third-person voice to Argueta, the author, Astvaldsson reveals that Argueta wrote the novel "as if he *was* Lucía" (italics in original 612). The second reason has to do with Astvaldsson's claim regarding the purpose of all of this information and why Lucía is privy to it: so as to make an informed decision about her uncle. As Astvaldsson states, "for Lucía to reach the decision she comes to in her uncle's case she has had to have access to all kinds of information that would normally be available to only an omniscient third-person narrator: hence, they are virtually indistinguishable" (613).

Notes to Chapter 2

1. Karin Lievens's testimonio *El quinto piso de la alegría: Tres años con la guerrilla* (1988), which relates Lievens's experiences as a Belgium woman turned *guerrillera* and her work as a literacy teacher for the FMLN, provides a nice counterpoint to the testimonios analyzed in this chapter.

2. See Beverley and Zimmerman's discussion concerning Guevara's influence on the guerrilla testimonios produced in Central America during the 1970s and 1980s (173). Two of the more well-known examples they cite are Omar Cabeza's *La montaña es algo más que una inmensa estepa verde* (1982), which won the Casa de las Américas prize that same year, and Mario Payera's *Los días de la selva* (1980).

3. See also Smith and Padula's historical account of women in revolutionary Cuba, *Sex and Revolution* (1996).

4. Many of these political groups also fostered and encouraged women-centered organizations in both urban and rural sites. Among the most active were the Union of Salvadoran Women for Liberation "Melida Anaya Montes" (UMS), the National Coordinating Committee of Salvadoran Women (CONAMUS), and the Institute for the Investigation, Empowerment and Development of Women (IMU). In spite of differing agendas, these groups formed a vital nucleus of support for the FMLN, helping to establish and inspire international networks and solidarity movements. They were also a key denunciatory element of human rights violations and an effective means of pressuring the Salvadoran government to find solutions to end the war.

5. In her recent article "The Crying Game" (2004), Lombardi takes issue with what she notes was a general tendency in much of the criticism generated in response to *I, Rigoberta Menchú: An Indian Woman in Guatemala* (1984) to "direct our attention toward women in Guatemala only to stray in more 'compelling' (theoretical) directions" (24). Centering her discussion on John Beverley's essay "The Real Thing," included in the edited volume by George Gugelberger bearing the same title (1996), and Doris Sommer's "Resisting the Heat: Menchú, Morrison, and Incompetent Readers" (1993), Lombardi undertakes a meticulous deconstruction of how these critics employ (to their own benefit) psychoanalytic theory, in particular that of Jacques Lacan and Julia Kristeva, in their examinations of Menchú's testimonio. As Lombardi contends, such theorizations do little to address the content of and issues raised by Menchu's testimony; rather, they provide a means for the literary left to dialogue among themselves and ultimately give way to their own "angst and ethical dilemmas" in a post-Marxist age (25). As a result, "actual women" are nowhere to be found in their criticism—a notion conveyed in Lombardi's somewhat sarcastic yet poignant question: "Whatever happened to the Indian women of Guatemala (or of Chiapas, for that matter)?" (25).

6. I am referring to the scholarship by Treacy, Rodríguez, Lorentzen, and Shaw. Of all of these studies, Treacy's is the only one that contemplates the *guerrillera's* use of violence and militancy as a potential threat. Treacy, however, does not develop her argument in reference to the *guerrillera's* masculinity.

7. Throughout El Salvador's history, especially in the twentieth century, women have been actively involved in popular manifestations. In 1921, female market vendors protested against their inhumane living conditions and the government repression during the Meléndez-Quiñones dynasty (Gargallo 59). The following year, several women were killed when they gathered in support of the presidential candidate Miguel Tomás Molina (Gargallo 59). Many *campesina* women were also part of the 1932 uprising. The distinction I am making here is the participation of women as armed militants, a form of agency exhibited during the civil conflict.

8. See endnote 2.

9. According to María Josefa Saldaña-Portillo, Rodríguez's theories of revolutionary subjectivity do expose and contemplate a similar notion of "revolutionary androgyny" in the narratives of Guevara and Payera. However, she does so in relation to the *guerrillero's* feminized masculinity, not that of

the *guerrillera* (*The Revolutionary* 79). As Saldaña-Portillo explains, "Rodríguez observes that while the mountains are repeatedly feminized in these revolutionary texts, they are nevertheless the scene where women are eliminated and men beget men, albeit feminized ones. The new man, in a way, is the new woman, better at representing her than his female counterpart is at being her" (*The Revolutionary* 79).

10. One of the few exceptions is Jacinta Escudos's *Apuntes de una historia de amor que no fue* (1987), a novel about an ill-fated love affair between two clandestine members of the guerrilla forces. It is the *guerrillera*'s erotic and unfulfilled desires that take precedence in this text, not her maternal yearnings.

11. Martínez discloses that she has a daughter in a 1996 interview that appears in the anthology *A Dream Compels Us*.

Notes to Chapter 3

1. In *The Pacification of Central America*, Dunkerley maintains that throughout its history, the Central American electoral process has been a questionable one because of not only fraudulent and exclusionary practices by ruling political parties but also the involvement of the United States. Changes to the electoral process, such as the ones initiated in El Salvador, signal a first step toward much-needed improvements.

2. See studies by Cardenal and Martí y Puig, Robinson, and Vilas.

3. Regarding the link between El Salvador's cultural renovation and national identity, see López's article "Reflexiones sobre la esfera pública en El Salvador de posguerra."

4. Among the best-known supplements and magazines is the cultural supplement "Tres Mil" belonging to the *Diario Co-Latino*, and the magazine *Tendencias*, an interdisciplinary cultural journal that serves as an open forum for the discussion of art, literature, and politics. The importance of new printing presses is evidenced by the fact that Clásicos Roxsil and the FMLN's Arcoiris are responsible for having published two of El Salvador's most popular novels in recent years, Walter Raudales's *Amor de Jade* (1996) and Horacio Castellanos Moya's *El asco* (1998).

5. Although some groups, such as DIGNAS and MAM, adopted a feminist stance, not all of the women working with organizations such as CO-MADRES share the same definition of feminism or identify themselves as feminists.

6. Castellanos Moya has authored more than ten novels, as well the collection of essays *Recuento de incertidumbres* (1993) on postwar Salvadoran literature. Many of his novels, particularly those mentioned above, have been recipients of literary prizes in and outside Central America and have garnered him international acclaim. *Insensatez* was recently translated into English as *Senselessness* in 2008.

7. Castellanos Moya's narrative use of an exclusive monologue is influenced by the work of the Austrian novelist and playwright Thomas Bernhard, whose novels often feature a "loner" narrator who speaks to a silent listener and who

criticizes key aspects of Austria's national and cultural identity. In the novels by Castellanos Moya mentioned above, many of the narrators engage in long-winded tirades against all things Salvadoran, or in the case of *Insensatez*, convey a cynical view of Central America's history of violence and human rights abuses. It also bears mentioning that Castellanos Moya is not the only Central American writer to use this narrative technique or some variation of it. Both Jacinta Escudos and the Guatemalan writer Rodrigo Rey Rosa have likewise employed a similar style in their works. In fact, in his short story "Ningún lugar sagrado," Rey Rosa notes that Castellanos Moya's novels are the model for his work.

8. See Hume's analysis of violence, gender, and patriarchy in the context of El Salvador's civil war.

9. Like Castellanos Moya, Escudos has also made a name for herself in the postwar years. She has authored several collections of short stories as well as three novels, including the critically acclaimed *A-B sudario* (2003), which won the prestigious Mario Monteforte Toledo Prize for a Central American Novel.

10. Regarding this notable absence or lack of direct engagement with the immediate past, Hernández stated at a conference on postwar literature held at the Universidad Centroamericana José Simeon Cañas (UCA) in April 2009 that it is due to the fact that she belongs to a new cohort of writers who grew up during the civil conflict, but for whom the war did not constitute a politically defining event, as was the case with previous generations of committed authors who emerged during the 1970s and 1980s, among whom can also be included Castellanos Moya and Escudos, who initiated their writing careers in the late 1980s. Castellanos Moya's first novel, *La diáspora*, which focused on the internal conflicts and politics among different factions of El Salvador's armed movement, was published in 1989. Jacinta Escudos had a series of poems published under the pseudonym Rocío América during the war, as well as her first novel, *Apuntes de una historia de amor que no fue*.

11. Mackenbach's introduction to the anthology, *Cicatrices* (2004), posits that a dominant trend in postwar Central American narratives is a focus on and the denouncement of "everyday forms of oppression" (18).

12. "Vaca" was featured in El Salvador's literary magazine *Cultura*, published by CONCULTURA. It is one of the few stories by Hernández that does not appear in any of her short story collections, including *Otras ciudades* (2001), *Mediodía de frontera* (2002) (rereleased under the title *De fronteras* by the Guatemalan publisher Piedra Santa in 2007), and *Olvida uno* (2006).

13. *Cadejos* are linked to *nahualismo* or the indigenous belief in *el nahual*, an animal spirit that accompanies and protects a human being throughout his or her life (Espino 40).

Notes to Chapter 4

1. In 2002, U.S.-based Salvadoran organizations dissatisfied with the connotations of the phrase "Hermano Lejano" launched an initiative to change

the monument's name. In response to this proposal, the Salvadoran government held a contest, via Internet, that invited Salvadorans from around the globe to choose a new name by voting online from a list of proposed alternatives. Possible choices included "Salvadoreños sin fronteras" [Salvadorans without Borders] and "Tierra de encuentro" [Meeting Ground], expressions that stressed transnational ties rather than national ones. The winning name was "Hermano bienvenido a casa" [Welcome Home Brother], officially inaugurated on November 13, 2002.

2. Social scientists Mahler and Pessar call attention to the male bias that predominates in migration studies and more recently in much of the new scholarship focused on transnational migration in their piece "Transnational Migration: Bringing Gender In." Notably, this trend also seems to extend into the fields of literature and cultural production. Kanellos's discussion of immigrant literature in *Hispanic Literature of the United States* provides a general overview not only of the written works that are included in this category of literature but also of the general themes that typify it. Although Kanellos does not explicitly address this issue, the dominant characteristics outlined, including the predominance of male authors and protagonists (especially in earlier works), the nationalistic overtones, and the gendered dichotomies consistently drawn between male migrants and "American women" point to an overtly male view of migration and immigrant life in the United States.

3. Here I am referring to Ayalá's novel *Arizona Dreaming* (2007) and Hernández's collection of short stories *Olvida uno* (2005), both published by smaller presses in El Salvador.

4. This novel by Castellanos Moya is particularly noteworthy given the negative and, in some cases, extreme responses it provoked from Salvadorans both in and outside the country. Because of the death threats the author received when *El asco* was first published in El Salvador, Castellanos Moya was forced to relocate outside the country. The reaction from the Salvadoran immigrant community in the United States was not as excessive. However, as evidenced by written responses such as Raúl García's *El vómito: Carta a H. C. Moya* (1999)—a highly critical text attacking Castellanos Moya and his work—it was similarly disapproving and antagonistic.

5. Many scholars have noted these earlier waves of Salvadoran migration to the United States. Menjívar briefly addresses immigration to San Francisco at the turn of the century in *Fragmented Ties*. Repak documents migration patterns to Washington, D.C., in the 1950s and 1960s. Zentgraf's more female-centered focus likewise remarks on the recruitment of Salvadoran women to work in garment industries and the private sector in Los Angeles during the 1960s and 1970s.

6. Baker-Cristales *Salvadoran Migration to Southern California* is one of the most extensive studies of Salvadoran transnationalism to date. Landolt, Autler, and Baires provide an added discussion of how Salvadoran migrants participate in transnational practices at the economic and political levels. Cadaval also provides an engaging examination of how Guatemalan and Salvadoran immigrants negotiate national and cultural identity within the context of the Latino Festival in Washington, D.C.

7. See Menjívar's *Fragmented Ties* and "The Intersection of Work and Gender," Mahler, "Engendering Transnational Migration," Zentgraf, and Repak.

8. A significant correlation could also be drawn between Calixto and the protagonist, Calisto, from the classic work *La Celestina* by Fernando de Rojas. Notably, in the opening scene of Bencastro's novel, Calixto witnesses one of his coworkers fall to his death while he is cleaning the windows of a high-rise building. De Rojas's text ends with a similar death, though it is that of the main character, Calisto, who falls from a ladder while attempting to reach his beloved, Melibea. One could read this as an interesting inversion of events, for in Bencastro's narrative, Calixto walks away from his potential death, so as to initiate his story as an undocumented immigrant worker rather than mark its end.

9. See Danner's fundamental study, *The Massacre at El Mozote*.

10. Concerning the use of language in spoken-word poetry as well as the founding and history of the Nuyorican Poets Cafe, consult Algarín's introduction to the anthology *Aloud*.

11. Atahualpa Yupanqui, a name that pays tribute to two Inca kings, was the stage name of Argentine folk singer Héctor Roberto Chavero Aramburo. Yupanqui's popularity grew in the 1950s and 1960s with the rise of the *Nueva Canción* movement in Latin America. This form of social protest music originated in South America but gained currency throughout other parts of the region such as Central America and the Caribbean. Further reading on this artistic movement includes Carrasco, Bolívar Cano, and the publication *Nueva Canción Latinoamericana*.

12. According to Rivas, the name Ciguanaba also derives from the Nahuatl language. The first part, "cigua," comes from the root "sihuat" for woman, and the second, "naba," from the root "nahuali" for sorcerer (52).

13. Bencastro's most recent novel, *Viaje a la tierra del abuelo* (2004), engages this issue more explicitly. The narrative tells the story of Sergio, a seventeen-year-old Salvadoran-American who makes the journey back to the homeland of his grandfather as a means of better understanding and negotiating his Latino Salvadoran identity.

Notes to Chapter 5

1. At the time that I wrote this chapter, the fourth installment in the series *Blood Daughters* (2011) had not yet been published.

2. Not all scholars working on the U.S. South agree on how to define its geographic parameters. In this analysis, I utilize the demarcation of the region established by Furuseth and Smith.

3. Tabulations for the growth of Latino populations from 2000 to 2005 in southern states are as follows: Alabama 40.3% (from 70,305 to 98,624), Arkansas 58.6% (from 82,155 to 130,328), Florida 30.9% (from 2,623,787 to 3,433,355), Georgia 47% (from 425,305 to 625,382), Kentucky 23% (from 53,002 to 48,795), Louisiana 18% (from 107,541 to 126,856), Mississippi 41.3% (from

34,543 to 48,795), North Carolina 48.2% (from 367,390 to 544,470), South Carolina 51.4% (from 90,263 to 136,616), Tennessee 51.3% (from 113,610 to 171,890), Virginia 36% (from 324,314 to 440,988) ("A Statistical Portrait of the Foreign Born" Table 10).

4. Southern-based meat- and poultry-processing plants with a high number of Latino immigrant employees include Tyson Foods, based in Arkansas; Sanderson Farms in Mississippi; and Smithfield Foods and Case Farms in North Carolina. Carpet manufacturers such as Mohawk Industries in Georgia as well as the High Point furniture factories in North Carolina also rely on a largely Latino labor force.

5. Cole and Parker's collection of essays provides a vital intervention with regard to the defining characteristic of the U.S. South as biracial, drawing attention to the historical presence of Latino communities such as those of Cubans and Mexicans. They also include areas of the Southwest such as California and Texas as a means of broadening their scope regarding the subject matter.

6. Among the most famous female sleuths are Agatha Christie's Miss Marple and Dorothy L. Sayer's Harriet Vane. This archetypal figure is representative of the "spinster" detective who because of her age and sex operates outside police conventions and is more interested in solving the crime at hand than investigating or tackling the issues that gave way to the crime in the first place (Irons xi-xii). An in-depth and broader understanding of this classic figure can be found in the studies by Craig and Cadogan, and Swanson and James.

By contrast, the hard-boiled detective or private eye, who achieves his apotheosis in the 1930s with the introduction of classic figures like Dashiel Hammet's Sam Spade and Raymond Chandler's Philip Marlowe, is characterized by his status as a loner as well as his questionable methods for restoring some sense of "order" and justice to the chaotic, urban landscape he inhabits. Stephen Knight provides a comprehensive overview of the incorporation and evolution of this iconic personage in crime fiction and film. Of note are the feminist rewritings of this character by such authors as P. D. James, Sara Paretsky, Marcia Muller, and Sue Grafton. As Irons explains, this "new woman detective" alters the tough-guy formula and provides "a viable alternative to the cynical loner of another age" (xv). Not only does she seek and find support by way of a community, but through her detecting she is also capable of shedding light on gendered relations of power (xv). For further reading on the intersections of feminism and the hard-boiled genre, see Klein and Reddy.

7. According to Butt and Benjamin, *voseo* is generally considered an informal form in which the use of *vos* is akin to that of *tú* (you familiar) (130). In addition to most of Central America, it is also used in parts of South America such as Uruguay, Paraguay, Colombia, Chile, Ecuador, and Venezuela, as well as in the southernmost regions of Mexico.

8. Throughout the series, Romilia is referred to by her first name. Her antagonist Rafael Murillo, however, is oftentimes referred to by only his last name. With few exceptions, in my analysis I maintain the same distinction with regard to these characters' names.

9. See Gosselin, Fischer-Hornung and Mueller, and Knight.

10. Notably, in the conclusion of his book *Brown Gumshoes*, Rodriguez provides a brief discussion of McPeek Villatoro's Romilia Chacón series, highlighting the ways in which his own discussion of Chicana/o detective fiction is applicable to other Latina/o narratives working within the same genre. Rodriguez is not the only one to make this connection or to suggest that there are key affinities between Chicano detective fiction and McPeek Villatoro's mystery series. In *Chicano Detective Fiction*, Baker Sotelo also makes it a point to include McPeek Villatoro's work and a brief historical synopsis of Central American immigration in her selected list for further reading.

11. With regard to this notion of the "latinization" of the U.S. South, it is difficult to ignore Pérez-Firmat's work on Cuban-Americans in Miami. However, although there are certainly some commonalities that can be highlighted between the process of assimilation of Cubans in Florida and that of other Latino groups in other southern states, there are some important differences. For one, the historical, social, and political factors that have led to the establishment of the Cuban-American community in Miami and allowed for its visibility and political representation are distinct from those of other Latin American groups such as Central American-Americans. Second, as Hewitt argues, Afro-Caribbeans, in particular Cubans, have been a part of the population in Tampa and other South Florida cities since the late 1800s. Although sharing many of the U.S. South's racial divides and legacies, the ethnic and racial diversity of South Florida cities like Miami sets them apart from other southern urban settings such as Nashville and Memphis, where immigration from Latin America and a substantial increase in the existing Latino populations are more recent phenomena.

12. The colloquial term *chota* has various meanings in different Latin American countries. According to the examples listed in the Dictionary of the *Real Academia Española*, in Cuba it is often used to refer to someone who is a jokester or who likes to mock people. In Puerto Rico it can be ascribed to someone who is a *flojo* (lazy person) or is incompetent. Another example is the use of "chota" for someone who is a squealer or an informer. Romilia's translation of "chota" is in keeping with its use in Mexico, which denotes "the police" or "cops."

13. Following the 1932 massacre or *matanza* in El Salvador, many indigenous communities stopped openly identifying with their indigenous heritage for fear of being labeled as Communists by the Salvadoran government. This resulted not only in the eclipsing of the indigenous aspects of Salvadoran identity but also in the development of predominant notions of Salvadoran identity linked to *mestizo* and rural or *campesino* subjectivities as opposed to more explicitly defined indigenous ones. Tilley offers a provocative and perhaps the most extensive exploration of this dynamic and its implication for Salvadoran ethnicity and nation in *Seeing Indians*.

14. Regarding the topic of Mayan ethnic identity, see Nelson's, Cabarrús Pellecer's, Hale's, and Montejo's studies.

15. Here I am referencing Simpson's discussion of Latin American detective fiction and the precedence that history takes in certain texts, especially those in

which the crime is not necessarily solved and is not the main impetus behind the investigation.

16. On this topic, see Jonas.

17. LaCapra defines this concept of "working through" as the process by which a person "com[es] to term with the trauma, including its details, and critically engage[s] the tendency to act out the past and even to recognize why it may be necessary and even in certain respects desirable or at least compelling" (144). It is this coming to terms with the trauma as opposed to merely the "acting out" of the trauma, understood as the tendency to repeat things compulsively and relive the past or be haunted by it, that, according to LaCapra, renders the individual a possible "ethical and political agent" (142, 144).

Notes to Conclusion

1. See Padilla, "Of *Diosas, Cochones*, and *Pluriempleadas*."

2. This is not to say that there has not been any work produced in this area in other countries. In 2009, a special volume of *Istmo: Revista virtual de estudios literarios y culturales centroamericanos* was launched with the focus of "Sexualidades en Centroamérica." Similarly, Costa Rica published its first anthology of gay and lesbian writing in 2009, *La gruta y el arcoíris*. To my knowledge, this is the only such anthology of its kind in the Central American region. It is telling, however, that both of these cultural works have only recently been produced and that they appeared several decades after the founding of gay rights movements in other Latin American countries.

3. "World's Most Dangerous Gang" was the title of the National Geographic's documentary special about MS-13, which first aired on television in 2005.

4. Funes's elimination of El Salvador's National Council of Culture (CONCULTURA), run by the Ministry of Education during the first year of his presidency, has raised several concerns. Having done away with one of the country's foremost institutions with regard to the promotion of cultural production instigated a wave of protests from Salvadoran artists and intellectuals in the country and in the United States, who see Funes's decision as one that undermines the importance of cultural production as a site for citizen participation and voice and one that does not take into account the key role culture has played in the country's process of national rehabilitation following the civil conflict.

Works Cited

Abrahams, Nicolas, and Maria Torok. *The Shell and the Kernel: Renewals of Psychoanalysis.* Ed. and trans. Nicholas T. Rand. Chicago: University of Chicago Press, 1994. Print.

A Dream Compels Us: Voices of Salvadoran Women. Ed. New American Press. Boston: South End Press, 1989. Print.

Alarcón, Norma. "Chicana Feminism: In the Tracks of the Native Woman." *Between Woman and Nation: Nationalisms, Transnational Feminisms, and the State.* Ed. Caren Kaplan, Norma Alarcón, and Minoo Moallem. Durham: Duke University Press, 1999. 63–71. Print.

Alegría, Claribel, and Darwin Flakoll. *No me agarran viva: la mujer salvadoreña en la lucha.* El Salvador: UCA Editores, 1998. 8th ed. Print.

———, ed. and trans. *On the Front Line: Guerrilla Poems of El Salvador.* Willimantic, CT: Curbstone Press, 1989. Print.

———. *They Won't Take Me Alive: Salvadorean Women in the Struggle for National Liberation.* Trans. Amanda Hopkinson. London: The Women's Press, 1987. Print.

Algarín, Miguel, ed. "The Sidewalk of High Art." Introduction. *Aloud: Voices from the Nuyorican Poets Cafe.* Ed. Miguel Algarín and Bob Holman. New York: Henry Holt and Company Inc., 1994. 3–8. Print.

Anderson, Benedict. *Imagined Communities.* London: Verso, 1991.

Anglesey, Zoë, ed. Introduction. *Listen Up! Spoken Word Poetry.* New York: The Ballantine Publishing Group, 1999. xv-xxvi. Print.

Ansley, Fran, and Susan Williams. "Southern Women and Southern Borders on the Move: Tennessee Workers Explore the New International Division of Labor." *Neither Separate Nor Equal: Women, Race, and Class in the South.* Ed. Barbara Ellen Smith. Philadelphia: Temple University Press, 1999. 207–44. Print.

Anzaldúa, Gloria. *Borderlands/La frontera: The New Mestiza.* San Francisco: Aunt Lute Books, 1987. Print.

Aparicio, Frances R. "Jennifer as Selena: Rethinking Latinidad in Media and Popular Culture." *Latino Studies* 1 (2003): 90–105. Print.

Appadurai, Arjun. *Modernity at Large: Cultural Dimensions of Globalization.* Minneapolis: University of Minnesota Press, 1996. Print.

Argueta, Manlio. *Caperucita en la zona roja*. Havana: Casa de las Américas, 1977. Print.

———. *Cuzcatlán donde bate la Mar del Sur*. Tegucigalpa, Honduras: Editorial Guaymuras, 1986. Print.

———. *Cuzcatlán: Where the Southern Sea Beats*. Trans. Clark Hansen. New York: Vintage Books, 1987.

———. *El valle de las hamacas*. San Salvador: UCA Editores, 1970. Print.

———. "La mujer en mis novelas." Paper presented at the "La mujer en la literatura latinoamericana conferencia." Centro de Estudios Brasilennos, San Salvador. 1996. n. pag. Web. 5 May 2005.

———. *Milagro de la Paz*. San Salvador: Istmo Editores, 1994. Print.

———. *Un día en la vida*. Costa Rica: EDUCA, 1994. 7th ed. Print.

———. *One Day of Life*. Trans. Bill Brow. New York: Vintage International, 1983. Print.

Arias, Arturo. "Central American-Americans: Invisibility, Power and Representation in the US Latino World." *Latino Studies* 1 (2003): 168–87. Print.

Armstrong, Robert, and Janet Shenk. *El Salvador, The Face of Revolution*. Boston: South End Press, 1982. Print.

Arrizón, Alicia. *Latina Performance: Traversing the Stage*. Bloomington: Indiana University Press, 1999. Print.

Arrué, Salvador Salazar. *Cuentos de barro*. San Salvador: Editorial "La Montaña," 1933. Print.

"A Statistical Portrait of the Foreign Born Population at Mid-Decade." Fact sheet. pewhispanic.org. Pew Hispanic Center. 29 Aug. 2006. Web. 2 July 2011.

Astvaldur, Astvaldsson. "Toward a New Humanism: Narrative Voice, Narrative Structure and Narrative Strategy in Manlio Argueta's *Cuzcatlán, donde bate la mar del sur*." *Bulletin of Hispanic Studies* LXXVII (2000): 603–615. Print.

Ayala, Berne. *Arizona Dreaming*. El Salvador: Letras Prohibidas, 2007. Print.

Baker-Cristales, Beth. *Salvadoran Migration to Southern California: Redefining El Hermano Lejano*. Gainesville: University of Florida Press, 2004. Print.

Baker Sotelo, Susan. *Chicano Detective Fiction: A Critical Study of Five Novelists*. North Carolina: MacFarland and Company, Inc., 2005. Print.

Barrientos, Tanya María. *Family Resemblance*. London: Penguin Books, 2003. Print.

Bencastro, Mario. *Odisea del norte*. Houston: Arte Público Press, 1999. Print.

———. *Odyssey to the North*. Trans. Susan Giersbach Rascón. Houston: Arte Público Press, 1998. Print.

———. *Viaje a la tierra del abuelo*. Houston: Arte Público Press, 2004. Print.

Beverley, John, and Marc Zimmerman. *Literature and Politics in the Central American Revolutions*. Austin: UT Press, 1990. Print.

———. "The Margin at the Center." *The Real Thing: Testimonial Discourse in Latin America*. Ed. Georg M. Gugelberger. Durham: Duke University Press, 1996. 23–41. Print.

Bayard de Volo, Lorraine. "Drafting Motherhood: Maternal Imagery and Organizations in the United States and Nicaragua." *The Women and War Reader*. Ed. Lois Ann Lorenzten and Jennifer Turpin. New York: New York University Press, 1998. 24–53. Print.

Bhabha, Homi K. *The Location of Culture*. London: Routledge, 1994. Print.

Bolívar Cano, John Franklin. *Entrevista a la nueva canción latinoamericana*. Medellín: Universidad de Antioquia, 1994. Print.

Broyles-González, Yolanda. "The Powers of Women's Words: Oral Tradition and Performance Art." *A Companion to Latino Studies*. Ed. Juan Flores and Renato Rosaldo. Oxford: Blackwell Publishing, 2007. 116–25. Print.

Butt, John, and Carmen Benjamin. *A New Reference Grammar of Modern Spanish*. 3rd ed. Chicago: McGraw-Hill, 2000. Print.

Cabarrús Pellecer, Carlos Rafael. *Lo maya, ¿una identidad con futuro?* Guatemala: CEDIM-FAFO, 1998. Print.

Cabezas, Omar. *La montaña es algo más que una inmensa estepa verde*. Havana: Casa de las Américas, 1982. Print.

Cadaval, Olivia. *Creating a Latino Identity in the Nation's Capital*. New York: Garland, 1998. Print.

Cardenal, Ana Sofia, and Salvador Martí y Puig. *América Central: las democracias inciertas*. Madrid: Editorial Tecnos, 1998. Print.

Carrasco, Eduardo. *La nueva canción en América Latina*. Santiago: CENECA, 1982. Print.

Castellanos Moya, Horacio. *Donde no estén ustedes*. Mexico, DF: Tusquets, 2003. Print.

———. *El arma en el hombre*. Barcelona: Tusquets, 2001. Print.

———. *El asco: Thomas Bernhard en San Salvador*. San Salvador: Editorial Arcoiris, 1997. Print.

———. *La diabla en el espejo*. Madrid: Ediciones Linteo, 2000. Print.

———. *Insensatez*. Mexico, DF.: Tusquets, 2004. Print.

———. *Recuento de incertidumbres: cultura y transición en El Salvador*. San Salvador: Ediciones Tendencias, 1993. Print.

———. *La diáspora*. San Salvador: UCA Editores, 1989. Print.

Cayetano Carpio, Salvador. *Secuestro y capucha en un país del "mundo libre."* Costa Rica: Editorial Universitaria Centroamericana, 1979. Print.

Christian, Karen. *Show and Tell: Identity as Performance in U.S. Latina/o Fiction*. Albuquerque: University of New Mexico Press, 1997. Print.

"Chota." *Diccionario de la Real Academia Española*. Real Academia Española 2 July 2009. Web. 2 July 2009.

Clifford, James. *Routes: Travel and Translation in the Late Twentieth Century*. Cambridge: Harvard University Press, 1997. Print.

Cole, Stephanie, and Alison M. Parker, eds. *Beyond Black and White: Race, Ethnicity, and Gender in the U.S. South and Southwest*. College Station: Texas A&M University Press, 2004. Print.

Cortez, Beatriz. "Estética del cinismo: la ficción centroamericana de posguerra." *Áncora: Supplemento Cultural de la Nación* 11 Mar. 2001. Web. 1 Jan. 2003.

———. *Estética del cinismo: Pasión y desencanto en la literatura centroamericana de posguerra*. Guatemala: F&G Editores, 2010. Print.

Craft, Linda J. "Mario Bencastro's Diaspora: Salvadorans and Transnational Identity." *MELUS* 30.1 (Spring 2005): 149–67. JSTOR. Web. 30 Jan. 2009.

————. *Novels of Testimony and Resistance from Central America*. Florida: University Press of Florida, 1997. Print.

Craig, Patricia, and Mary Cadogan. *The Lady Investigates: Women Detectives and Spies in Fiction*. London: Victor Gollancz Ltd, 1981. Print.

Crown, Kathleen. " 'Sonic Revolutionaries': Voice and Experiment in the Spoken Word Poetry of Tracie Morris." *We Who Love to Be Astonished: Experimental Women's Writing and Performance Poetics*. Ed. Laura Hinton and Cynthia Hogue. Tuscaloosa: The University of Alabama Press, 2002. 213–36. Print.

Cunningham, Lucía Guerra, ed. "Rite of Passage: Latin American Women Writers Today." Introduction. *Splintering Darkness: Latin American Women Writers in Search of Themselves*. Pittsburgh: Latin American Literary Review Press, 1990. 5–16. Print.

Dalton, Roque. *Miguel Mármol: los sucesos de 1932 en El Salvador*. San Salvador: UCA Editores, 1993. Print.

Danner, Mark. *The Massacre at El Mozote: A Parable of the Cold War*. New York: Vintage Books, 1994. Print.

"De Ahuachapán a Washington." Interview with Mario Bencastro. *La Opinion* 4 Oct. 2000. Web. 21 Feb. 2004.

De Rojas, Fernando. *La Celestina*. Barcelona, España: Ediciones B, 1990. Print.

Díaz, Nidia. *I Was Never Alone: A Prison Diary from El Salvador*. Trans. Deborah Shnookal. Melbourne: Ocean Press, 1992.

————. *Nunca estuve sola*. San Salvador: UCA Editores, 1998. 12th ed. Print.

Duncan, Nancy, ed. "Renegotiating Gender and Sexuality in Public and Privates Spaces." *Body Space*. London: Routledge, 1996. 127–45. Print.

Dunkerley, James. *The Pacification of Central America: Political Change in the Isthmus, 1987–1993*. London: Verso, 1994. Print.

————. *Power in the Isthmus: A Political History of Modern Central America*. New York: Verso, 1988. Print.

————. *The Long War: Dictatorship and Revolution in El Salvador*. London: Verso, 1985. Print.

Enloe, Cynthia. *Does Khaki Become You? The Militarization of Women's Lives*. London: Pluto Press Limited, 1983. Print.

Escudos, Jacinta. *A-B Sudario*. Madrid: Editorial Santillana, 2003. Print.

————. *Apuntes de una historia de amor que no fue*. San Salvador: UCA Editores, 1987. Print.

————. *Cuentos sucios*. San Salvador: Dirección de Publicaciones e Impresos, 1997. Print.

Espino, Miguel Ángel. *Mitología de Cuscatlán: como cantan allá*. San Salvador: Concultura, 1996. Print.

Fanon, Franz. *The Wretched of the Earth*. Trans. Richard Philcox. New York: Grove Press, 2004. Print.

Felman, Shoshana, and Dori Laub. *Testimony: Crises of Witnessing in Literature, Psychoanalysis, and History*. New York: Routledge, 1991.

Fink, Leon. *The Maya of Morganton: Work and Community in the Nuevo New South*. Chapel Hill: The University of North Carolina Press, 2003. Print.

Fischer-Hornung, Dorothea, and Monika Mueller, eds. *Sleuthing Ethnicity: The Detective in Multiethnic Crime Fiction.* Rutherford, NJ: Fairleigh Dickinson University Press; London: Associated University Presses, 2003. Print.

Flores, Juan. *From Bomba to Hip-Hop: Puerto Rican Culture and Latino Identity.* New York: Columbia University Press, 2000. Print.

Franco, Jean. "Gender, Death, and Resistance: Facing the Ethical Vacuum." *Critical Passions: Selected Essays.* Ed. Mary Louise Pratt and Kathleen Newman. Durham: Duke University Press, 1999. 18–38. Print.

———."Going Public: Reinhabiting the Private." Pratt and Newman. 48–65. Print.

———. "Killing Priests, Nuns, Women, Children." Pratt and Newman. 9–17. Print.

———. *Plotting Women: Gender and Representation in Mexico.* New York: Columbia University Press, 1989. Print.

Furuseth, Owen J., and Heather A. Smith. "From Winn-Dixie to Tiendas: The Remaking of the New South." *Latinos in the New South: Transformations of Place.* Ed. Owen J. Furuseth and Heather A. Smith. Hampshire, Eng.: Ashgate Publishing Company, 2006. 1–17. Print.

Gargallo, Francesca. "La relación entre participación política y conciencia feminista en las militantes salvadoreñas." *Cuadernos Americanos* 1.2 (1987): 58–76. Print.

García, María Cristina. *Seeking Refuge: Central American Migration to Mexico, the United States, and Canada.* Berkeley: University of California Press, 2006. Print.

García, Raúl. *El vómito: carta a H. C. Moya.* Los Angeles: Editorial Patria Perdida, Casa de la Cultura de El Salvador en Los Angeles, 1999. Print.

García Canclini, Néstor. *La globalización imaginada.* Buenos Aires: Paidós, 1999. Print.

Goldman, Francisco. *The Divine Husband: A Novel.* New York: Atlantic Monthly Press, 2004. Print.

———. *The Long Night of White Chickens.* New York: Atlantic Monthly Press, 1992. Print.

———. *The Ordinary Seaman.* New York: Atlantic Monthly Press, 1997. Print.

Gordan, Larry. "Grad Puts Central American on the Map." *Los Angeles Times Online* 9 Mar. 2008. Web. 29 Oct. 2008.

Gosselin, Adrienne Johnson, ed. *Multicultural Detective Fiction: Murder from the "Other" Side.* New York: Garland Publishing, Inc., 1999. Print.

Gould, Jeffery, and Aldo Ar. Lauria-Santiago. *To Rise in Darkness: Revolution, Repression, and Memory in El Salvador, 1920–1932.* Durham: Duke University Press, 2008. Print.

Guarnizo, Luis Eduardo, and Michael Peter Smith. "The Locations of Transnationalism." *Transnationalism from Below.* Ed. Michael Peter Smith and Luis Eduardo Guarnizo. New Brunswick, NJ: Transaction Publishers, 1998. 1–34. Print.

Gutiérrez, Gloria Aracely, comp. "El cadejo." *Tradición oral de El Salvador.* El Salvador: Concultura, 1993. 49. Print.

Halberstam, Judith. *Female Masculinity.* Durham: Duke University Press, 1998. Print.

Hale, Charles R. *Más que un indio/More Than an Indian: Racial Ambivalence and Neoliberal Multiculturalism in Guatemala.* Santa Fe: School of American Research Press, 2006. Print.

Hall, Stuart. "Cultural Identity and Diaspora." *Colonial Discourse and Postcolonial Theory: A Reader.* Ed. Patrick Williams and Laura Chrisman. New York: Columbia University Press, 1994. 392–403. Print.

Hamilton, Nora, and Norma Stoltz Chinchilla. *Seeking Community in a Global City: Guatemalans and Salvadorans in Los Angeles.* Philadelphia: Temple University Press, 2001. Print.

Herbert, Melissa S. *Camouflage Isn't Only for Combat: Gender, Sexuality, and Women in the Military.* New York: New York University Press, 1998. Print.

Hernández, Claudia. *De fronteras.* Guatemala: Piedra Santa, 2007. Print.

———. "Mediodía de frontera." *Mediodía de frontera.* San Salvador: Dirección de Publicaciones e Impresos, Consejo Nacional para la Cultura y el Arte, 2002. 113–16. Print.

———. *Olvida uno.* San Salvador: Índole Editores, 2005. Print.

———. *Otras ciudades.* El Salvador: Alkimia Libros, 2001. Print.

———. "Vaca." *Cultura* 84 (1999): 152–53. Print.

Hernández-Leon, Rubén, and Victor Zuniga. " 'Making Carpet by the Mile': The Emergence of a Mexican Immigrant Community in an Industrial Region of the U.S. Historic South." *Social Science Quarterly* 81 (2000): 49–67. Print.

Hernández-Linares, Leticia. *Razor Edges of My Tongue.* San Diego: Calaca Press, 2002. Print.

Hewitt, Nancy H. Introduction. *Beyond Black and White: Race, Ethnicity, and Gender in the U.S. South and Southwest.* Ed. Stephanie Cole and Alison M. Parker. College Station: Texas A&M University Press, 2004. xi–xxx. Print.

Huezo Mixco, Miguel. "La diabla en el espejo." 2002. Web. 31 Mar. 2003.

Hume, Mo. "The Myths of Violence: Gender, Conflict, and Community in El Salvador." *Latin American Perspectives* 35.5 (2008): 59–76. Print.

Instituto Universitario de Opinión Pública, Universidad Centroamericana José Simeón Cañas. "La violencia en El Salvador en los años noventa. Magnitud, costos y factores posibilitadores." Oct. 1998. 1–50. Web. 25 Sept. 2009.

Irons, Glenwood, ed. "Gender and Genre: The Woman Detective and the Diffusion of Generic Voices." Introduction. *Feminism in Women's Detective Fiction.* Toronto: University of Toronto Press, 1995. ix–xxiv. Print.

Jonas, Susanne. *The Battle for Guatemala: Rebels, Death Squads and U.S. Power.* Boulder: Westview Press, 1991. Print.

Kampwirth, Karen. *Feminism and the Legacy of Revolution: Nicaragua, El Salvador, Chiapas.* Athens: Ohio University Press, 2004. Print.

———. "Resisting the Feminist Threat: Antifeminist Politics in Post-Sandinista Nicaragua." *NWSA Journal* 18.2 (2006): 73–100. Project Muse. Web. 3 Mar. 2008.

Kanellos, Nicolás. "Hispanic Immigrant Literature." *Hispanic Literature of the United States: A Comprehensive Reference.* Westport: Greenwood Publishing Group, Inc., 2003. 24–31. Print.

Keane, John. *Violence and Democracy.* Cambridge: Cambridge University Press, 2004. Print.

Kearney, Michael. "The Local and the Global: The Anthropology of Globalization and Transnationalism." *Annual Review of Anthropology* 24 (1995): 547–65. Print.

Klein, Kathleen Gregory. *The Woman Detective: Gender and Genre.* 2nd ed. Urbana: University of Illinois Press, 1995. Print.

Knight, Stephen. *Crime Fiction 1800–2000: Detection, Death, Diversity.* New York: Palgrave Macmillan, 2004. Print.

Kolodny, Annette. *The Lay of the Land: Metaphor as Experience and History in American Life and Letters.* Chapel Hill: The University of North Carolina Press, 1975. Print.

LaCapra, Dominick. *Writing History, Writing Trauma.* Baltimore: John Hopkins University Press, 2001. Print.

La gruta y el arcoíris: antología de narrativa gay/lésbica costarricense. Comp. Alexander Obando. San José: Editorial Costa Rica, 2009. Print.

Landolt, Patricia. "El transnacionalismo político y el derecho al voto en el exterior: El Salvador y sus migrantes en Estados Unidos." *Votar en la distancia: la extensión de los derechos políticos a migrantes, experiencias comparadas.* Comp. Leticia Calderón Chelius. México: Instituto Mora, 2003. 301–23. Print.

Landolt, Patricia, Lilian Autler, and Sonia Baires. "From Hermano Lejano to Hermano Mayor: The Dialectics of Salvadoran Transnationalism." *Ethnic and Racial Studies* 22.2 (1999): 290–315. Print.

Lara-Martínez. "Festival de pájaros: por una poética de *Un día en la vida.*" *Antípodas: Journal of Hispanic and Galician Studies* 10 (1998): 89–101. Print.

———. *La tormenta entre las manos: Ensayos sobre literatura salvadoreña.* San Salvador: Dirección de Publicaciones e Impresos, 2001. Print.

———. "Mario Bencastro y la identidad salvadoreña-americana." *Ventana abierta* 6 (1999): 22–29. Print.

LeoGrande, William. *Our Own Backyard: The United States in Central America, 1977–1992.* Chapel Hill: The University of North Carolina Press, 1998. Print.

Lievens, Karin. *El quinto piso de la alegría. Tres años con la guerrilla.* N.p.: Ediciones Sistema Radio Venceremos, 1988. Print.

Lombardi, Marilyn May. "The Crying Game: Rigoberta Menchú and the Responsibilities of *Testimonio* Criticism." Maier and Dulfano. 21–45. Print.

López, Sylvia. "Reflexiones sobre la esfera literaria y la esfera pública en El Salvador de la posguerra." *Cultura* 85 (1999): 44–50. Print.

Lorentzen, Lois Ann. "Women's Prison Resistance: Testimonios from El Salvador." Lorentzen and Turpin. 192–202. Print.

Luciak, Ilja A. *After the Revolution: Gender and Democracy in El Salvador, Nicaragua, and Guatemala.* Baltimore: John Hopkins University Press, 2001. Print.

Lungo, Mario. *El Salvador in the Eighties: Counterinsurgency and Revolution.* Philadelphia: Temple University Press, 1996. Print.

Mackenbach, Werner, comp. Introduction. *Cicatrices: Un retrato del cuento centroamericano.* Nicaragua: Anama, Ediciones Centroamericanas, 2004. 13–20. Print.

Mahler, Sarah. "Engendering Transnational Migration: A Case Study of Salvadorans." *Gender and U.S. Immigration.* Ed. Pierrette Hondagneu-Sotelo. Berkeley: University of California Press, 1999. 287–313. Print.

Marín, Lynda. "Speaking Out Together: Testimonials of Latin American Women." *Latin American Perspectives* 18. 3 (1991): 51–68. Print.

Martínez, Ana Guadalupe. *Las cárceles clandestinas.* San Salvador: UCA Editores, 1999. 6th ed. Print.

Martínez, Zulma Nelly, and Manlio Argueta. "Manlio Argueta." Interview. *Hispamérica* 14.42 (1985) 41–54. JSTOR. Web. 15 Mar. 2010.

Martínez, Rubén. *Other Side: Fault Lines, Guerrilla Saints, and the True Heart of Rock 'n' Roll.* London: Verso, 1992. Print.

McClintock, Anne. " 'No Longer in a Future Heaven': Gender, Race and Nationalism." *Dangerous Liaisons: Gender, Nation, and Postcolonial Perspectives.* Ed. Anne McClintock, Aamir Mufti, and Ella Shohat. Minneapolis: University of Minnesota Press, 1997. 89–112. Print.

McPeek Villatoro, Marcos. *Blood Daughters.* Pasadena: Red Hen Press, 2011. Print

———. *Home Killings.* Houston: Arte Público Press, 2001. Print.

———. *Minos.* Boston: Kate's Mystery Books/Justin, Charles and Company Publishers, 2003. Print.

———. *A Venom beneath the Skin.* Boston: Kate's Mystery Books/Justin, Charles and Company Publishers, 2005. Print.

Menjívar, Cecilia. *Fragmented Ties: Salvadoran Immigrant Networks in America.* Berkeley: University of California Press, 2000. Print.

———. "The Intersection of Work and Gender: Central American Immigrant Women and Employment in California." *Gender and U.S. Immigration.* Ed. Pierrette Hondagneu-Sotelo. Berkeley: University of California Press, 1999. 101–28. Print.

Miller, Michael B. "*Cuzcatlán donde bate la mar del Sur* de Manlio Argueta: Homenaje a la raza." *Antípodas: Journal of Hispanic and Galician Studies* 10 (1998): 103–09. Print.

Miranda, Enrique. "Cambiarán el nombre del 'Hermano Lejano.' " *El diario de hoy* 6 Mar. 2002. Web. 21 Feb. 2004.

Mohanty, Chandra Talpade. "Under Western Eyes: Feminist Scholarship and Colonial Discourses." *Dangerous Liaisons: Gender, Nation, and Postcolonial Perspectives.* Ed. Anne McClintock, Aamir Mufti, and Ella Shohat. Minneapolis: University of Minnesota Press, 1997. 25–77. Print.

Mohl, R. "Globalization, Latinization, and the Nuevo New South." *Globalization and the American South.* Ed. J. Cobb and W. Stueck. Athens: The University of Georgia Press, 2005. 66–99. Print.

Montejo, Victor D. *Maya Intellectual Renaissance: Identity, Representation, and Leadership.* Austin: University of Texas Press, 2005. Print.

Montgomery, Tommie Sue. *Revolution in El Salvador: From Civil War to Civil Peace.* 2nd ed. Boulder: Westview Press, 1995. Print.

Nelson, Diane M. *A Finger in the Wound: Body Politics in Quincentennial Guatemala.* Berkeley: University of California Press, 1999. Print.

Nueva Canción Latinoamericana. Cuba, Ministerio de Cultura. Dirección de Artistas Aficionados. La Habana, Cuba: Editorial Orbe, 1980. Print.

O'Connell, Joanna. "Rereading Salvadoran testimonio after the Cease Fire." XXI LASA International Congress. Chicago. 1998. Web. Conference Paper.

Ortiz, Fernando. *Cuban Counterpoint, Tobacco, and Sugar.* Trans. Harriet de Onís. Durham: Duke University Press, 1995. Print.

Padilla, Yajaira M. "Of *Diosas, Cochones,* and *Pluriempleadas.* (En)gendering Central American Identities in Contemporary Short Stories by Women." *Letras Femeninas* 15.2 (2009): 91–112. Print.

———. "Setting *La diabla* Free: Women, Violence, and the Struggle for Political and Cultural Representation in El Salvador's Postwar Reality." *Latin American Perspectives* 35.5 (2008): 133–45.

———. "Sleuthing Central American Identity and History in the New Latino South: Marcos McPeek Villatoro's *Home Killings.*" *Latino Studies* 6 (2008): 376–97.

Payeras, Mario. *Los días de la selva.* Havana: Casa de las Américas, 1980. Print.

Pérez-Firmat, Gustavo. *Life on the Hyphen: The Cuban-American Way.* Austin: University of Texas Press, 1994. Print.

Pessar, Patricia R., and Sarah Mahler. "Transnational Migration: Bringing Gender In." *International Migration Review* 37.3 (Fall 2003): 812–46. Print.

Peterson, Anna L. *Martyrdom and the Politics of Religion: Progressive Catholicism in El Salvador's Civil War.* Albany: State University of New York Press, 1997. Print.

Portes, Alejandro, and Rubén G. Rumbaut. *Legacies: The Story of the Immigrant Second Generation.* Berkeley: University of California Press, 2001. Print.

Pratt, Mary Louise. "Tres incendios y dos mujeres extraviadas: el imaginario novelistic frente al nuevo contrato social." *Espacio urbano, comunicación y violencia en América Latina.* Ed. Mabel Moraña. Pittsburgh: Instituto Internacional de Literatura Iberoamericana. 91–106. Print.

———. "Women, Literature, and National Brotherhood." *Women, Culture, and Politics in Latin America.* Berkeley: University of California Press, 1990. 48–73. Print.

Programa de las Naciones Unidas para el desarollo. "Migraciones, cultural y ciudadanía en El Salvador." Cuadernos sobre desarrollo humano. No. 7. San Salvador, 2007. Print.

Puar, Jasbir K. *Terrorist Assemblages: Homonationalism in Queer Times.* Durham: Duke University Press, 2007. Print.

Quesada, Roberto. *Never through Miami.* Trans. Patricia J. Duncan. Houston: Arte Público Press, 2002. Print.

———. *The Big Banana.* Trans. Walter Krochmal. Houston: Arte Público Press, 1999. Print.

Quesada, Uriel, ed. "Sexualidades en Centroamérica." Edición especial. *Istmo* 19 (2009): n. pag. Web. 21 Sept 2009.

Randall, Margaret. "Reclaiming Voices: Notes on a New Female Practice in Journalism." *The Real Thing: Testimonial Discourse and Latin America*. Ed. Georg M. Gugelberger. Durham: Duke University Press, 1996. 58–69. Print.

Raudales, Walter. *Amor de jade*. El Salvador: Editorial Clásicos Roxsil, 1996. Print.

Reddy, Maureen T. *Sisters in Crime: Feminism and the Crime Novel*. New York: Continuum, 1988. Print.

Repak, Terry A. *Waiting on Washington: Central American Workers in the Nation's Capital*. Philadelphia: Temple University Press, 1995. Print.

Rey Rosa, Rodrigo. "Ningún lugar sagrado." *Ningún lugar sagrado: relatos*. Mexico, DF.: Planeta Mexicana, 1999. 65–92. Print.

Rivas, Pedro Geoffrey. *La lengua salvadoreña*. San Salvador: Ministerio de Cultura y Comunicación, 1987. Print.

Robinson, William. *Transnational Conflicts: Central America, Social Change, and Globalization*. London: Verso, 2003. Print.

Rodríguez, Ana Patricia. "Departamento 15": Cultural Narratives of Salvadoran Transnational Migration." *Latino Studies* 3 (2005): 19–41. Print.

———. "Second-Hand Identities: The Auto-ethnographic Performance of Quique Avilés and Leticia Hernández-Linares." *Istmo* 8 (2004): n. pag. Web. 5 May 2005.

Rodríguez, Ileana. *Women, Guerrillas and Love: Understanding War in Central America*. Minneapolis: University of Minnesota Press, 1996. Print.

Rodriguez, Ralph E. *Brown Gumshoes: Detective Fiction and the Search for Chicano Identity*. Austin: University of Texas Press, 2005. Print.

Román-Lagunas, Vicki. "Oppositional Discourse and the Notion of Feminism in Testimonial Narratives by Nidia Díaz and Ana Guadalupe Martínez." *Woman as Witness: Essays on Testimonial Literature by Latin American Women*. Ed. Linda S. Maier and Isabel Dulfano. New York: Peter Lang, 2004. 113–22. Print.

Saldaña-Portillo, María Josefa. "From the Borderlands to the Transnational? Critiquing Empire in the 21st Century." *A Companion to Latina/o Studies*. Ed. Juan Flores and Renato Rosaldo. Oxford: Blackwell Publishing, 502–12. Print.

———. *The Revolutionary Imagination in the Americas and the Age of Development*. Durham: Duke University Press, 2003.

Schirmer, Jennifer. *The Guatemalan Military Project: A Violence Called Democracy*. Philadelphia: University of Pennsylvania Press, 1998. Print.

Scott, Joan Wallach. *Gender and the Politics of History*. Rev. ed. New York: Columbia University Press, 1999. Print.

Shaw, Donald L. "Referentiality and Fabulation in Nidia Díaz's *Nunca estuve sola*." Maier and Dulfano. 100–11. Print.

Shayne, Julie D. *The Revolution Question: Feminisms in El Salvador, Chile, and Cuba*. New Brunswick: Rutgers University Press, 2004. Print.

Simpson, Amelia S. *Detective Fiction from Latin America*. Cranbury, NJ: Associated University Presses, 1990. Print.

Sirias, Silvio. *Bernardo and the Virgen*. Evanston: Northwestern University Press, 2005. Print.

Smith, Lois M., and Alfred Padula. *Sex and Revolution: Women in Socialist Cuba*. New York: Oxford University Press, 1996. Print.

Smith-Nonini, Sandy. "Federally Sponsored Mexican Migrants in the Transnational South." *The American South in a Global World*. Ed. James L. Peacock, Harry L. Watson, and Carrie R. Matthews. Chapel Hill: The University of North Carolina Press, 2005. 59–79. Print.

Sklodowska, Elzbieta. *Testimonio hispanoamericano: Historia, teoría, poética*. New York: Peter Lang, 1993. Print.

Sommers, Doris. *Foundational Fictions: The National Romances of Latin America*. Berkeley: University of California Press, 1991. Print.

———. " 'Not Just a Personal Story': Women's *Testimonios* and the Plural Self. *Life/Lines: Theorizing Women's Autobiography*. Ed. Belli Brodzki and Celeste Schenck. Ithaca: Cornell University Press, 1988. 107–30. Print.

Spears, Ellen. "Civil Rights, Immigration, and the Prospects for Social Justice Collaboration in Georgia." *Across Races and Nations: Building New Communities in the U.S. South*. Project Director Barbara Ellen Smith. Memphis: University of Memphis, Center for Research on Women, 2006. 65–75. Print.

Stephen, Lynn. *Women and Social Movements in Latin America: Power from Below*. Austin: University of Texas Press, 1997. Print.

Stoner, K. Lynn. "Militant Heroines and the Consecration of the Patriarchal State: The Glorification of Loyalty, Combat, and National Suicide in the Making of Cuban National Identity." *Cuban Studies* 34 (2003): 71–96. Project Muse. Web. 2 May 2010.

Swanson, Jean, and Dean James. *By a Woman's Hand: A Guide to Mystery Fiction by Women*. New York: Berkeley Books, 1994. Print.

Thompson, Marilyn. "Las organizaciones de mujeres en El Salvador." *Estudios Sociales Centroamericanos* 54 (1990): 119–35. Print.

Tilley, Virginia. *Seeing Indians: A Study of Race, Nation, and Power in El Salvador*. Albuquerque: University of New Mexico Press, 2005. Print.

Tobar, Héctor. *The Tattooed Soldier*. New York: Penguin Books, 2000. Print.

Torres-Rivas, Edelberto. "Epilogue: Notes on Terror, Violence, Fear and Democracy." *Societies of Fear: The Legacy of Civil War, Violence and Terror in Latin America*. Ed. Kees Koonings and Dirk Krujit. London: Zed Books, 1999. 285–300. Print.

———. *History and Society in Central America*. Austin: University of Texas Press, 1993. Print.

Treacy, Mary Jane. "Creation of the Woman Warrior: Claribel Alegría's *They Won't Take Me Alive*." *Claribel Alegría and Central American Literature: Critical Essays*. Ed. Sandra M. Boschetto-Sandoval and Marcia Phillips McGowan. Ohio: Center for International Studies, 1994. 75–96. Print.

Vásquez, Norma. *Las mujeres refugiadas y retornadas: las habilidades adquiridas en el exilio y su aplicación a los tiempos de paz*. Unidad de Análisis Documentación y Comunicaciones Las Dignas. S.A. de C.V.: Tipografía Offset, Laser, 2000. Print.

Vásquez, Norma, Cristina Ibánez, and Clara Murguialday. *Mujeres—montaña: vivencias de guerilleras y colaboradoras del FMLN.* Madrid: horas y HORAS, 1996. Print.

Vilas, Carlos M. *Between Earthquakes and Volcanoes: Market, State, and the Revolutions in Central America.* Trans. Ted Kuster. New York: Monthly Review Press, 1995. Print.

Walton, Priscilla L. "Bubblegum Metaphysics: Feminist Paradigms and Racial Interventions in Mainstream Hardboiled Women's Detective Fiction." *Multicultural Detective Fiction: Murder from the "Other" Side.* Ed. Adrienne Johnson Gosselin. New York: Garland Publishing, Inc., 1999. 257–79. Print.

Waters Hood, Edward. "Tragedia de la paz, *Milagro de la Paz.* Del testimonio al intimismo en las novelas de Manlio Argueta." *Antípodas: Journal of Hispanic and Galician Studies* 10 (1998): 119–27. Print.

William, Gareth. *The Other Side of the Popular: Neoliberalism and Subalternity in Latin America.* Durham: Duke University Press, 2002. Print.

Williams, Raymond. *Marxism and Literature.* Oxford: Oxford University Press, 1977. Print.

Winders, Jamie. "Placing Latino/as in the Music City: Latino Migration and Urban Transformation in Nashville Tennessee." *Latinos in the New South: Transformations of Place.* Ed. Owen J. Furuseth and Heather A. Smith. Hampshire, Eng.: Ashgate Publishing Company, 2006. 167–89. Print.

"World's Most Dangerous Gang." *National Geographics Explorer.* Host Lisa Ling. Narr. Salvatore Vecchio. National Geographics Channel. 12 Feb. 2006. Television.

Zentgraf, Kristine M. "Why Women Migrate: Salvadoran and Guatemalan Women in Los Angeles." *Latino LA: Transformations, Communities, and Activism.* Ed. Enrique C. Ochoa and Gilda L. Ochoa. Tucson: The University of Arizona Press, 2005. 63–82. Print.

Zilberg, Elana. *Space of Detention: The Making of a Transnational Gang Crisis between Los Angeles and San Salvador.* London: Duke University Press, 2011. Print.

Index

Abraham, Nicolas: *The Shell and the Kernel*, 141
A Dream Compels Us, 163 n. 11
A Venom beneath the Skin, 137–38, 143–49
Alarcón, Norma, 13, 113
Alegría, Claribel: *No me agarran viva* (They Won't Take Me Alive), 11, 43–69 passim; *On the Front Line* 63. *See also* Darwin Flakoll
Algarín, Miguel: *Aloud*, 166 n. 10
Alvergue, Reynaldo, 94
American Dream: in Bencastro's *Odyssey* 106; in Hernández-Linares's poetry, 114, 116–118, 120
Anderson, Benedict, 5
Anglesey, Zoë, 109, 112
Ansley, Fran, 126
Anzaldúa, Gloria, 88
Aparicio, Frances, 129
Appadurai, Arjun: *Modernity at Large*, 98
Argueta, Manlio, 15–22 passim, 41, 44, 45, 74, 155; *Caperucita en la Zona Roja*, 160 n. 4; *Cuzcatlán: Donde bate la Mar del Sur* (Cuzcatlán: Where the Southern Sea Beats), 10, 32–41; *El valle de las hamacas*, 160 n. 4; *Milagro de la Paz* 160 n. 5; *Un día en la vida* (One Day of Life), 10, 22–32, 160 n. 4

Arias, Arturo, 137, 143, 147, 150, 151; on Central American-American identity and invisibility, 127–130
Arrizón, Alicia, 138
Arrué, Salvador Salazar (Salarrué): *Cuentos de barro*, 20
Armstrong, Robert, 159 n. 1
Association of Salvadorans in Los Angeles (ASOSAL), 94
Astvaldsson, Astvaldur, 33, 161 n. 10
Autler, Lilian, 165 n. 6
Áviles, Quiqué, 94
Ayalá, Berne, 94; *Arizona Dreaming*, 165 n. 3
Ayala, Prudencia, 110–114, 121, 159 n. 2

Baires, Sonia, 165 n. 6
Baker-Cristales, Beth: *Salvadoran Migration to Southern California*, 165 n. 6
Baker Sotelo, Susan: *Chicano Detective Fiction*, 168 n. 10
Barrientos, Tanya María: *Family Resemblance*, 159 n. 9
Bayard de Volo, Lorraine, 45
Bencastro, Mario, 94–95, 98, 99, 114, 118, 121, 122, 166 n 8; *Odisea del Norte* (Odyssey to the North), 12, 99–108; *Viaje a la tierra del abuelo* 166 n. 13
Benjamin, Carmen, 167 n. 7

Beverley, John, 19, 20, 44, 161 n. 2, n. 6, n. 7, 162 n. 5
Bhabha, Homi, 7
Bolívar Cano, John Franklin, 166 n. 11
Bracero Program, 125
Broyles-González, Yolanda, 121
Butt, John, 167 n. 7

Cabarrús Pellecer, Carlos Rafael, 168 n. 14
Cabeza, Omar: *La montaña es algo más que una inmensa estepa verde*, 161 n. 2
Cadaval, Olivia, 165 n. 6
Cadogan, Mary, 167 n. 6
Cardenal, Ana Sofía, 163 n. 2
Carpio, Salvador Cayetano: *Secuestro y capucha en un país del "mundo libre*," 44, 161 n. 8
Carrasco, Eduardo, 166 n 11
Carter, Jimmy, 2
Castellanos Moya, Horacio, 74, 75, 85, 91–2, 94, 164 n. 9; *Baile con serpientes* 74; *Donde no estén ustedes*, 76; *El arma en el hombre*, 76; *El asco* 76, 94, 163 n. 4, 165 n. 4; *Insensatez*, 76, 163 n. 6, 164 n. 7; *La diabla en el espejo* (The She-Devil in the Mirror), 11, 76–81, 91; *La diáspora*, 164 n. 10; narrative style, 163 n. 7; *Recuento de incertidumbres*, 163 n. 6
Castro, Fidel, 136
Central America: as region, 3, 13, 146, 169 n.2; countries, 128, 129, 155; electoral process, 163 n. 1; military regimes, 143; *See also* El Salvador, Guatemala
Central American: and Latina/o identity, 129–130; as other, 142; background, 135, 140; community/-ies, 125, 146, 156; conciliatory ties, 148–150; descent, 8, 99, 123, 127, 138; ethnicity, 139; history, 99, 124, 129,

140–149, 156; first generation, 136; identity/-ies, 13, 72, 91, 123, 127, 128, 129; identity politics, 125, 138, 140, 150; immigrants, 99, 128, 142, 144, 147; immigration, 140, 151, 168 n. 10; indigenous identities and subjectivities, 139–140; in/visibility, 128–129, 138, 139, 140, 147, 149, 150, 153; in the U.S., 125–126, 127, 129, 131, 138, 140, 145, 149; literature, 13, 73, 159 n. 9; 161 n. 6; migration, 97, 123, 143–145, 147, 153, 159 n. 4; relations with Mexicans and Mexican-Americans, 128, 136–137; student population, 153; studies, 153; trauma, 13, 128, 130, 141, 142, 143, 146, 147, 148, 150, 155, 169 n.17; undocumented, 145; *See also* Central American-American, Salvadoran, Salvadoran-American
Central American-American: community, 150; ethnicities, 13; identity/-ies, 13, 124, 130, 131, 132, 138, 137, 143, 145, 150, 151; identity politics, 124, 130, 154; interrelations, 148; in/visibility, 127–128, 130, 132, 134, 145, 151; second-generations, 146, 156
Central American Free Trade Agreement (CAFTA), 125
Christians, Karen, 137
Ciguanaba, 110–114, 121, 166 n. 12
civil war (El Salvador): and migration, 7, 95, 96, 97, 117, 155; causes, 2, 159 n. 1; gendered dynamics, 13, 164 n.8; in Argueta's novels 17, 35, 41; impact on women, 10, 45; participation of women, 2–3, 45, 49, 122, 159 n. 2, 160 n. 3; re-imagining of nation, 5, 79; related to second generations, 7,

8, 153, 155; U.S. intervention, 2, 51, 56, 103–105
Clifford, James, 96
Cole, Stephanie, 167 n. 5
Consejo Nacional para la Cultura y el Arte (CONCULTURA), 72, 164 n. 12, 169 n. 4
Cortez, Beatriz, 72, 87
Craft, Linda J.: *Novels of Testimony and Resistance*, 21, 22, 161 n. 6 and n. 7; "Mario Bencastro's Diaspora," 106, 107
Craig, Patricia, 167 n. 6
Cuba, 45, 46, 161 n. 3, 168 n. 12
Cuban-American: as hyphenated other, 127; community in the U.S., 10, 125, 156–157, 167 n. 5, 168 n. 11
Cuentos sucios, 81
"culture of violence," 75
Cuzcatlán: Donde bate la Mar del Sur (Cuzcatlán: Where the Southern Sea Beats), 10; analysis of, 32–41

Dalton, Roque: *Miguel Mármol,* 161 n. 8
Danner, Mark: *The Massacre at El Mozote,* 166 n. 9
Del Carmen Letona, Mercedes, 53
De Rojas, Fernando: *La Celestina,* 166 n. 8
detective fiction: as popular form, 130; Chicana/o, 130, 168 n. 10; feminist, 130, 167 n. 6; hard-boiled, 167 n. 6; Latin American models of, 140, 168 n. 15; multiethnic, 130
Diario Co-Latino, 163 n. 4
diaspora, 96, 106
Díaz, Nidia: *Nunca estuve sola* (I Was Never Alone), 11, 43–69 passim
Duncan, Nancy, 76
Dunkerley, James, 159 n. 1; *The Pacification of Central America,* 163 n. 1

El Salvador: 1932 *matanza* (massacre), 16, 155, 160 n.2, 162 n. 7, 168 n. 13; *campesinos* (rural community), 15–42 passim, 49, 53, 74, 90, 100, 105, 106, 155, 156, 168 n. 13; civil war, 1, 2, 4, 13, 51, 71, 144, 154, 159 n. 1; colonization, 33, 34–35; decolonization, 36–37; democratization, 1, 71, 76; El Mozote massacre, 103, 166 n. 9; emigration, 2, 73, 95, 142 (*see also* immigration, migration); feminist movement 3, 73, 159 n. 3 (*see also* women); folklore, 90, 110, 111, 118, 121, 122, 135, 164 n. 13; indigenous elements, 8, 10, 13, 18, 19, 22, 27, 33, 34, 36, 90, 110, 136, 155, 164 n.3, 168 n. 13; LGBT movement, 155, 169 n. 2; national identity, 1, 7, 8, 9, 12, 72, 85, 90, 98, 100, 154, 155, 163 n. 3; national reconstruction, 1, 3, 7, 11, 71, 72, 76, 91, 154 (*see also* neoliberalism); oligarchy, 10, 15, 71, 78–79, 81, 105; postwar period, 3, 5, 8, 10, 11, 12, 71–92 passim, 95, 118, 122, 154, 155, 156, 159 n. 8; U.S. influence, 2, 23, 26, 86, 142, 163 n. 1; *See also* Salvadoran
Enloe, Cynthia, 46
Escudos, Jacinta, 74, 75, 85, 91–92, 163 n. 7; *A-B Sudario,* 164 n. 9; *Apuntes de una historia de amor* 163 n. 10, 164 n. 10; "La noche de los escritores asesinos" (The Night of the Murderous Writers), 11, 81–85, 91
ethnic: categorization of Latinos, 12; identities, 12; identification, 134; incorporation into U.S., 8, 123, 147, 149, 154; individuation, 12, 124, 134, 139, 147, 150, 151, 154; literatures, 10, 123, 130; performances, 137; tensions and

ethnic *(continued)*
   transformations in U.S. South,
   126, 133
ethnicity/-ies: 1, 8, 21, 130, 155;
   Central American, 139; Central
   American-American, 13; gendered
   1; indigenous, 13; Mayan, 168 n.
   14; Salvadoran, 124, 168 n. 13

Falconi, José Luis, 156
Farabundo Martí National Liberation
   Front (FMLN), 2; depiction in
   Argueta's *Cuzcatlán*, 18, 32, 35;
   demobilization, 71; election in
   2009, 157; first major offensive,
   32, 160 n. 1; integration of
   women into ranks, 46, 49, 56, 61;
   meeting in La Palma, 52; project
   of national liberation, 15, 47, 48,
   64, 70; women's organizations,
   162 n. 4; work with the rural
   sector, 15–16, 18, 35; vision of
   revolutionary nationhood, 42
Felman, Shoshana, 141
feminism: and the hard-boiled
   detective genre, 167 n. 6; Chicana,
   113; in El Salvador, 3, 54, 73,
   159 n. 3, 163 n. 5; in Guatemala;
   155; in Nicaragua, 3, 155; Latin
   American, 54
Fink, Leon: *The Maya of Morganton*,
   125
Fischer-Hornung, Dorothea, 167 n.
   9
Flakoll, Darwin: *No me agarran viva*
   (They Won't Take Me Alive), 11,
   43–68 passim; *On the Front Line*
   63
Flores, Juan, 127
Franco, Jean, 5, 17, 26, 48–49, 142
Funes, Mauricio, 157, 169 n. 4
Furuseth, Owen J., 166 n. 2

García, Raúl: *El vómito: Carta a H.
   C. Moya*, 165 n. 4
García Canclini, Nestor, 4

gender: 1, 48; changes of roles
   due to migration, 9, 97; equality
   and liberation, 2, 9, 12, 47, 49,
   52–55, 101, 122, 154; questioning
   under neoliberalism, 72, 80, 85,
   91; reaffirmation of traditional
   roles 3; restructuring of roles
   during war, 16, 17
gendered: binaries, 101, 108;
   discourses of nation, 5, 96;
   division of labor, 88, 106, 117,
   121; dynamics of civil war, 13,
   26–27; dynamics of migration,
   95, 98, 108, 122, 165 n. 2;
   dynamics of Salvadoran national
   identity, 1; ethnicity/-ies, 1,
   124; idealization of homeland,
   12; identity/-ies, 4, 123, 154;
   imaginings of nation, 5; immigrant
   reality, 117; inequality, 76; history,
   1, 154; hierarchies and divisions
   within revolutionary movement,
   48, 54, 62, 68; lens for viewing
   Salvadoran nation, 4, 22, 105;
   norms, 5, 101; oppression, 20,
   97, 114, 122; relations of power
   in detective fiction, 167 n. 6;
   resistance, 21, 30; revolutionary
   bridges, 46; subjectivities, 12, 124;
   symbolization of women, 18, 102;
   trans-, 155; transnational identity,
   99, 107; *See also* women
Goldman, Francisco: *The Divine
   Husband*, 159 n. 9; *The Long
   Night of White Chickens*, 159 n. 9;
   Ordinary Seaman, 159 n. 9
Gosselin, Adrienne Johnson, 167 n.
   9
Gould, Jeffery: *To Rise in Darkness*,
   160 n. 2
Guarnizo, Luis Eduardo, 96
Guatemala: as migrant nation, 147;
   civil war, 129, 130, 131, 139,
   140, 144, 169 n. 16; feminist
   movement, 155; indigenous
   immigrants in U.S., 125, 146;

indigenous elements, 138, 139; emigration, 142; language, 139; LGBT movement, 155; military, 131, 138, 141; national identity, 138; oligarchy, 138, 145; Rigoberta Menchú, 162 n. 5; political refugees from, 125; U.S. intervention, 142

Guatemalan-American, 13, 124, 127; origin, 128, 131, 136; trauma, 13

Guerra Cunningham, Lucía, 84

Guevara, Ernesto "Che," 44, 47, 55, 56, 61, 161 n. 2, 162 n. 9

Halberstam, Judith: *Female Masculinity*, 55–56

Hale, Charles R., 168 n. 14

Hall, Stuart, 8, 131

Herbert, Melissa S., 62

Hernández, Claudia, 74, 91, 94, 164 n. 10, 165 n.3; "Vaca" (Cow), 11, 85–87, 92, 164 n. 12; "Mediodía de frontera" (Midday Border), 11, 87–91, 92; *Olvida uno*, 164 n. 12, 165 n. 3; *Otras ciudades*, 164 n. 12

Hernández-Leon, Ruben, 126

Hernández-Linares, Leticia, 94–95, 98, 99, 121, 122, 155; *Razor Edges of My Tongue* 12, 108–121

Hewitt, Nancy H., 160 n. 11

Home Killings, 130–136, 139, 141–143

homosexuality, 62

Huezo Mixco, Miguel, 77

Hume, Mo, 164 n. 8

identity/-ies: Central American, 13, 72, 91, 123, 127, 128, 129; Central American-American, 13, 124, 130, 131, 132, 138, 137, 143, 145, 150, 151; cultural, 8, 9, 131–132; indigenous, 140, 155; Latina/o, 10, 123, 128, 129, 130, 131, 134, 140; oficial versions of, 8; Salvadoran (national), 1, 7, 8, 9, 12, 72, 85, 90, 98, 100, 154, 155, 163 n. 3; Salvadoran-American, 2, 7, 13, 127, 130; transnational, 96, 99, 102, 106, 108, 117, 188, 122

immigration, 70, 124, 154, 156, 157; and discriminatory asylum policies, 142; Central American, 125, 151, 168 n. 10; from Latin America, 10, 132, 168 n. 11; indigenous, 125, 139; in Romilia Chacón Mystery Series, 132–133, 140, 145, 150; Latino, 124; U.S. legislation, 125; related to Latina/o identity, 140; Salvadoran, 124, 165 n.5; undocumented, 7, 145; U.S. policy, 98, 103–104, 143; *See also* migration

Immigration Reform and Control Act (IRCA), 125

Irons, Glenwood, 167 n. 6

Istmo, 169 n. 2

James, Dean, 167 n. 6

Jonas, Susanne, 169 n. 16

Kampwirth, Karen, 3, 73, 159 n. 3 and 8

Kanellos, Nicolás, 135; *Hispanic Literature of the United States*, 165 n. 2

Kaplan, Caren, 13

Keane, John: *Violence and Democracy*, 89

Kearney, Michael, 159 n. 5

Klein, Kathleen Gregory, 167 n. 6

Knight, Steven, 167 n. 6 and n. 9

Kolodny, Annette: *The Lay of the Land*, 102, 159 n. 6

LaCapra, Dominick, 148, 169 n. 17

La diabla en el espejo (*The She-Devil in the Mirror*), 11, 91; analysis of, 76–81

La gruta y el arcoíris, 169 n. 2

La Momposina, Totó, 110

Landolt, Patricia, 96, 159 n. 7, 165 n. 6
"La noche de los escritores asesinos" (The Night of the Murderous Writers), 11; analysis of, 81–85, 91
Lara-Martínez, Rafael, 74, 99
Latino: and indigeneity, 139; changing demographics and presence in U.S. South, 123–151 passim, 166 n. 3, 167 n. 4 and n. 5, 168 n. 11; ethnic label, 12, 127; growing population in U.S., 156; identity, 127, 129–130, 138; imaginary, 13; literatures, 12; "other" groups, 156; popular culture, 132; reference to pan-ethnic group, 124; stereotypes, 137, 138; studies, 156
Las cárceles clandestinas de El Salvador (El Salvador's Clandestine Prisons), 11; analysis of, 43–69
Latinidad, 129, 138
latinization, 132, 168 n. 11
Laub, Dori, 141
Lauria-Santiago, Aldo: To Rise in Darkness, 160 n. 2
Liberation Theology, 16, 19, 24, 26, 47, 61, 78
Lieven, Karin: El quinto piso de la alegría: Tres años con la guerrilla, 161 n. 1
Lombardi, Marilyn May, 48; "The Crying Game," 162 n. 5
López, Sylvia, 163 n. 3
Lorentzen, Lois Ann, 162 n. 6
Lungo, Mario, 159 n. 1

Mackenbach, Werner: Cicatrices, 164 n. 11
Mahler, Sarah, 97, 159 n. 4, 165 n. 2, 166 n. 7
Mara Salvatrucha (MS-13), 156, 169 n. 3
Martí, Agustín Farabundo, 16
Martí y Puig, Salvador, 163 n. 2

Martínez, Ana Guadalupe: 163 n. 11; Las cárceles clandestinas de El Salvador (El Salvador's Clandestine Prisons), 11, 43–69 passim
Martínez, Rubén: The Other Side, 159 n. 9
Martínez, Zulema Nelly, 17
Maya: ethnic identity, 168 n. 14; languages, 139; myth of creation, 35 (see also Popol Vuh); population in North Carolina, 125
Mazzotti, José Antonio, 156
McPeek Villatoro, Marcos, 94; A Venom beneath the Skin 137–38, 143–49; Blood Daughters, 166 n. 1; Home Killings 130–136, 139, 141–143, Minos 135–7, 139–140; Romilia Chacón Mysteries Series, 12–13, 123–130, 150–151, 168 n. 10
Mélida Anaya Montes Women's Movement (MAM), 73, 163 n. 5
"Mediodía de frontera" (Midday Border), 11; analysis of, 87–91, 92
Mediodía de frontera, 87, 164 n. 12
Menjívar, Cecilia, 159 n. 4; Fragmented Ties, 165 n. 5, 166 n. 7
migration, 1, 6, 124; Central American history of, 131, 129, 140, 145, 153; gendered dynamics, 95, 122; in Salvadoran-American narratives, 98; in Odisea del Norte (Odyssey to the North), 99–108 passim; in Hernández-Linares's poetry, 102–121 passim; international, 3, 9, 13, 95, 96, 97, 122, 138, 154, 155; male vision of, 93–94, 98, 165 n. 4; related to Salvadoran transnational community building and identity, 94, 95–96, 121, 122; remittances as a result of, 7, 71, 93, 94, 95, 97, 99; Salvadoran, 3, 12, 94, 95, 165 n. 5 and n. 6; stories,

8; studies, 164 n. 2; traditional model of, 146; transnational, 129, 157, 165 n. 2, 166 n.7; women's involvement in, 1, 3–4, 7, 9, 12, 94, 95, 97, 99, 121
Miller, Michael B., 161 n. 6
Minos 135–7, 139–140
Moallem, Minoo, 13
Mohanty, Chandra Talpade, 7
Mohl, R., 126
Monseñor Romero Committee of Mothers and Relatives of the Political Prisoners, Disappeared, and Assassinated of El Salvador (CO-MADRES), 74, 163 n. 5
Montejo, Victor D., 168 n. 14
Montes, Mélida Anaya, 65
Montgomery, Tommie Sue, 16, 159 n. 1
Mueller, Monika, 167 n. 9

nation: *campesino* (allegorical), 10, 34, 37, 42, 47; Salvadoran, 4, 5, 9, 12, 18, 22, 76, 79, 80, 86, 100, 101; -hood, 8, 9, 19, 22, 42, 87, 155, migrant, 7; -state, 31, 57; trans-, 5, 7, 9, 155, 156, 157
National Association of Salvadoran Educators (ANDES), 65
National Resistance (RN), 46
Nationalist Republic Alliance Party (ARENA), 71
Nelson, Diane M., 168 n. 14
neoliberalism, 9, 72, 156; and women, 6, 122, 71–92 passim; as project of national reconstruction, 1, 11, 71–92 passim; critique of in literature, 71–92
Nicaragua: discourse of motherhood, 45; LBGT movement, 155; postwar feminism, 3, 155; Sandinista National Liberation Front (FSLN), 45, 46; refugees, 95; triumph of Revolution, 2

Nicaraguan Adjustment and Central American Relief Act (NACARA), 125
No me agarran viva (They Won't Take Me Alive), 11; analysis of, 43–69
North American Free Trade Agreement (NAFTA), 125
Nueva Canción, 110, 166 n. 11
Nunca estuve sola (I Was Never Alone), 11; analysis of, 43–69
Nuyorican Poets Cafe, 109, 166 n. 10

O'Connell, Joanna, 70
Odisea del Norte (Odyssey to the North), 12; analysis of, 99–108
Ortiz, Fernando, 126

Padilla, Yajaira, 169 n. 1
Parker, Alison M., 167 n. 5
Payera, Mario: *Los días de selva*, 55, 161 n. 2
Padula, Alfred: *Sex and Revolution*, 161 n. 3
Pérez-Firmat, Gustavo, 127, 168 n. 11
Pessar, Patricia R., 165 n. 2
Popol Vuh, 35
Popular Forces of Liberation (FPL), 46, 49, 52, 65
Popular Revolutionary Army (ERP), 46, 49, 50, 53, 58
Portes, Alejandro, 134
Puar, Jasbir K., 27
Pratt, Mary Louis, 80

Quesada, Roberto: *Big Banana*, 159 n. 9; *Never Through Miami*, 159 n. 9

Randall, Margaret, 21
Raudales, Walter: *Amor de jade*, 163 n. 4
Razor Edges of My Tongue, 12; analysis of, 108–121

Reagan, Ronald: administration, 59, 95

Real Academia Española, 168 n. 12

Reddy, Maureen T., 167 n. 6

Repak, Terrry A., 159 n. 4, 165 n. 5, 166 n. 7

republican motherhood, 4–7, 11–12, 47, 63, 70, 74, 81, 85, 91, 154; *See also* revolutionary maternity

revolutionary maternity, 63–69, 70

Revolutionary Party of Central American Workers (PRTC), 46

Rey Rosa, Rodrigo: "Ningún lugar sagrado," 164 n. 7

Rivas, Pedro Geoffrey, 166 n. 12

Rivera, Carolina, 94

Rivera, Marito, 118

Robinson, 163 n. 2

Rodríguez, Ana Patricia, 137

Rodríguez, Ileana: *Women, Guerrillas, and Love*, 6, 55, 162 n. 6, 162 n. 9

Rodriguez, Ralph, 130; *Brown Gumshoes*, 168 n. 10

Román-Lagunas, Vicky, 54, 64

Rumbaut, Rubén G., 134

Saldaña-Portillo, María Josefa, 156, 162 n. 9

Salvadoran: diaspora, 96, 106; identity/-ies, 1, 7, 8, 9, 12, 72, 85, 90, 98, 100, 154, 155, 163 n. 3; literature, 13, 19, 72, 74, 163 n. 6; im/migrants, 7, 8, 9, 93–95, 103, 118, 119, 165; immigration, 124, 165 n.5; migration, 3, 12, 94, 95, 165 n. 5 and n. 6; peoples 2, 3; *pupusas*, 107, 127, 136; refugees, 95, 125; Spanish, 135 (see also *voseo*); (trans)nation, 5, 7, 9, 155, 156, 157; transnational community, 9, 93–122 passim, 154; transnationalism 154, 165 n. 6; *See also* Salvadoran-American

Salvadoran-American: identity/-ies, 2, 7, 13, 127, 130; in the U.S.,

3, 134; second-generations, 7–9 passim, 12, 98, 109, 122; self-individuation, 8, 124; writers, 94

Salvadoran Communist Party (PCS), 46

Salvadoranness, 107; performance of, 13, 127–140 passim, 150–151

School of the Americas, 103

Shaw, Donald L., 162 n. 6

Shayne, Julie, 46, 73, 159 n. 3, 159 n. 8

Shea, Maureen, 161 n. 6

Shenk, Janet, 159 n. 1

Simpson, Amelia S., 168 n. 15

Sirias, Silvio: *Bernardo and the Virgin*, 159 n. 9

Sklodowska, Elzbieta, 21

Smith, Heather A., 166 n. 2

Smith, Lois M.: *Sex and Revolution*, 161 n. 3

Smith, Peter Michael, 96

Smith-Nonini, Sandy, 126

Sommer, Doris, 5, 20, 21, 162 n. 5

Spears, Ellen, 126

spoken-word poetry, 109

subjectivity/-ies: border, 151; campesino, 168 n. 13; female, 4, 11, 13, 74; female immigrant, 93–122 passim; revolutionary, 47, 48–55, 64; of Chicanas, 114; Latina, 129; Salvadoran-American, 123, 153

Swanson, Jean, 167 n. 6

Temporary Protected Status Program, 125

Tendencias, 163 n. 4

testimonio: by *guerrilleras* (female militants), 43–70 passim; by Latin American women, 20; definition of, 20; elements in Argueta's novels, 18, 19–22, 31; guerrilla model of, 44

Thompson, Marilyn, 2

Tilley, Virginia, 168 n. 13

Tobar, Héctor: *The Tattooed Soldier*, 159 n. 9

Torok, María: *The Shell and the Kernel*, 141
Torres-Rivas, Edelberto, 75
transculturation, 126
trans-Salvadoran; as concept, 4, 13; narratives, 5, 7, 8, 10, 12, 13, 124, 153, 154
transnationalism: and political rights, 159 n. 7; process of, 4, 159 n. 5; Salvadoran 154, 156, 165 n. 6
Treacy, Mary Jane, 63, 162 n. 6

Umán, Tekún, 139
Un día en la vida (One Day of Life), 10; analysis of, 22–32
United States: and the "American Dream," 117, 118; as destination for Salvadoran migration, 1, 3, 12, 94, 95, 97, 125, 165 n. 5; as emasculating territory, 102; as sight for justice, 147–148; assimilation to, 107; asylum policies, 95, 103, 105; border crossing to, 146; ethnic incorporation into, 8, 123, 147, 149, 154; foreign and economic policy in El Salvador, 2, 23, 26, 86, 142; Latino population in, 156; immigration policies, 143; multiethnic landscape of, 124; narrow ideals of nationality in, 8; related to Latino/a identities, 9, 12, 128; School of the Americas, 103; Southern region, 123–151 passim; subjugation of foreign economies to, 116

"Vaca" (Cow), 11, 164 n. 12; analysis of 85–87, 92
Vásquez, Norma, 3, 56, 160 n. 3
Vilas, Carlos, 78, 163 n. 2
Villalobos, Joaquin, 50
voseo, 127, 134, 135, 167 n. 7

Waters Hood, Edward, 161 n. 6
Wallach Scott, Joan, 73

Walton, Priscilla L., 130
Williams, Gareth, 145
Williams, Raymond, 8
Williams, Susan, 126
Women (Salvadoran): and neoliberalism, 6, 122, 71–92 passim; as allegory of *campesino* (rural) nation, 10, 18–19, 22, 34, 41–42; as allegory of El Salvador within Central American-American context, 124, 129, 144–145, 147; as allegory of "homeland" left behind, 12, 98, 100, 102; as allegory of postwar nation, 11–12, 74, 75, 80, 86, 91; as national allegories, 4–7, 10, 12, 108, 154; *campesinas* (rural women), 3, 10, 11, 15–42 passim, 49, 160 n. 3; feminism and feminist movement, 3, 54, 73–74, 159 n. 3, 163 n. 5; gender equality and liberation, 2, 9, 12, 47, 49, 52–55, 101, 122, 154; *guerrilleras* (female militants), 10–11, 43–70 passim, 161 n. 1, 162 n. 6; involvement in migration, 1, 3–4, 7, 9, 12, 94, 95, 97, 99, 121; link to nature, 5, 37; participation in civil war, 2–3, 10, 45, 49, 122, 159 n. 2, 160 n. 3; political representation, 9, 74; second-generation (Salvadoran-American), 7, 9, 12, 123–151 passim
Women for Dignity and Life (DIGNAS), 73, 163 n. 5

Yupanqui, Atahualpa, 110, 166 n. 11

Zentgraf, Kristine M., 159 n. 4, 165 n. 5, 166 n. 7
Zilberg, Elana: *Space of Detention*, 156
Zimmerman, Mark, 19, 44, 161 n. 2, n. 6, n. 7
Zuniga, Victor, 126